27756

E
842.9
.082

O'Toole
                The assassination tapes

THE ASSASSINATION TAPES

THE ASSASSIN

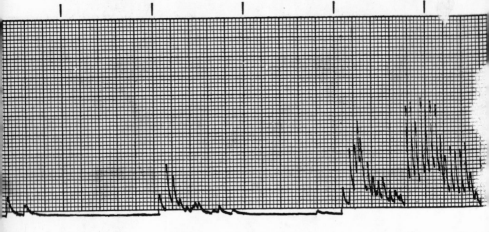

An electronic probe into the murder of

by George O'Toole

ATION TAPES

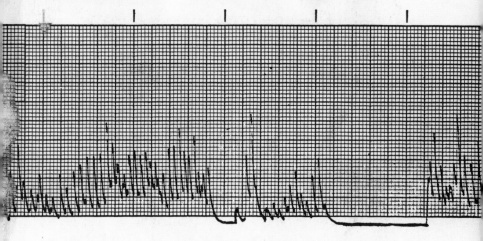

ohn F. Kennedy and the Dallas Coverup

Penthouse Press Ltd. New York

Library of Congress Catalog Card Number: 74–20157
ISBN 0-89110-000-8

Published by Penthouse Press Ltd.
909 Third Avenue, New York, N.Y. 10022

CONTENTS

For My Mother

INTRODUCTION

There is a certain Anglo-Saxon conceit that the really dirty and brutal kinds of political mischief happen only in the non-Protestant, non-English-speaking nations. *Coup d'état* is after all a French term, and it refers to a phenomenon we associate with Latin America, the Mediterranean and the Far East. We Americans seem to believe that political conspiracy requires the same soil and climate as bananas or palm trees.

Until very recently, we enjoyed the belief that our government was conducted, if not always by gentlemen, at least never by roughnecks. American political scandals always involved graft or some other white-collar crime—the continuation of commerce by other means. But then came Watergate.

The Watergate affair revealed a new and more muscular dimension to American political crime. The offenses included burglary, bugging, sabotage, and blackmail, with arson—the proposed fire-bombing of the Brookings Institution—planned, but never carried out. The White House Plumbers destroyed our cherished mythology. The men who broke into the Watergate were not looking for the Democrats' cashbox; they were out to steal the presidency.

When I began the work that culminated in this book, Watergate was merely "a third-rate burglary." A handful of overzealous and irresponsible men, on their own initiative, had broken into the Democratic National Committee headquarters. The White House was cleared of any involvement by what one senior Justice Department official described as "the most exhaustive FBI investigation since the assassination of President Kennedy."

The unraveling of the Watergate cover-up provided a strange counterpoint to my own investigation of the Kennedy assassination. As I crossed the country in search of witnesses to the Dallas drama of a decade ago, it seemed that every radio and television set carried the Senate Watergate hearings. I remembered that the Warren Commission's hearings were held *in camera:* no reporters, television cameras, or microphones were permitted. When the hearings were over, the commission published its Report, then promptly dissolved itself. There was no public dialogue, only public doubt. As the story of Watergate unfolded before a national television audience in the summer of 1973, I could only wish that we had demanded as much nine years before.

Why did Watergate receive a closer public accounting than the assassination of a president? I think the answer is that the decade separating the two events marked an end to public credulousness in America. The Gulf of Tonkin incident, the elusive "light at the end of the tunnel" in Vietnam, the My Lai massacre, the Kent State shootings—these and many other episodes of official deception made skeptics of us all. In the currently fashionable term, our consciousness was raised.

There is hope for us Americans because we do learn from history, and not all of us can be fooled all of the time. The tragic episodes of our recent history may bespeak a great sickness in our society, but their very revelation proves we have the strength to make ourselves well again. What other nation regularly cleans out the skeletons from its closets?

We have learned from Watergate that we cannot expect the government to dispense truth to us as though it were some kind of public dole. If there is government lying, we are as much to blame as the politicians and bureaucrats who invent the lies. We are a free people, and it is our responsibility as individuals to question official pronouncements. Truth must be earned through persistence and a willingness to think about the unthinkable.

Most Americans have never believed the official account of the assassination of President Kennedy, but public demands for the truth have quieted in recent years. There is, after all, no door on which to hammer; the investigation was the Warren Commission's responsibility, and there no longer is a Warren Commission. But on August

Introduction

9, 1974, one of the seven men who served on that commission became president of the United States. In his inaugural address, President Ford promised a new era of openness and candor. We can only hope that such openness and candor will extend retroactively to the assassination of President Kennedy and that our new president will order the investigation reopened.

It is my most fervent hope that this book will help to bring that about.

GEORGE O'TOOLE

Gaithersburg, Maryland
Winter 1974

1 ON DOUBTING THE REPORT

Man's most valuable trait is a judicious sense of what not to believe.
—Euripides: *Helen*

The assassination of Napoleon Bonaparte was a perfect crime: it went undiscovered for 140 years. There had been rumors and suspicions, of course. Napoleon himself wrote, just three weeks before his death, "My death is premature. I have been assassinated by the English oligarchy." But the official autopsy report stated that Napoleon died from natural causes, and there the matter rested for nearly a century and a half.

In 1961 two Swedish researchers decided to investigate the death of Napoleon through the use of one of the newest weapons in the arsenal of forensic science, a technique known as neutron activation analysis. They obtained some strands of hair taken from the head of the exiled French emperor immediately after his death. With the help of a scientist at the University of Glasgow, the Swedes placed the hairs in a nuclear reactor at Britain's Harwell atomic research laboratory and subjected them to a beam of neutrons. After twenty-four hours the specimens were sent to Glasgow for analysis.

The irradiated hairs yielded up their secret. They contained over ten times the normal amount of arsenic. Additional samples of Napoleon's hair were obtained, and the experiment was repeated. This time the hair was cut into segments, each corresponding to two weeks' growth. The distribution of arsenic in the segments showed that the exile of St. Helena had received regular doses of the poison during the last year of his life. The Swedish and Scots researchers were convinced: Napoleon Bonaparte had been slowly poisoned to death by his jailers.[1]

There is, of course, no doubt that the death of President John F.

Kennedy in Dallas was an assassination; yet, like the death of Napoleon, the event has been obscured by questions and doubts. During the eleven years since the assassination, the facts have been sifted again and again, first by the Warren Commission, then by a host of independent investigators. Few of the latter have been able to agree with the official conclusions of the commission, but none has offered a satisfactory account of what really happened on that November afternoon in Dallas. With the passage of time, the details of the controversy dim in our minds, leaving a dull residue of doubt and a despair of ever learning the truth. And yet we might hope that, as with the assassination of Napoleon Bonaparte, new scientific discoveries may someday shed some light on the murder of John Kennedy. It was just this hope that I began to cherish when I first heard of a remarkable device called the psychological stress evaluator.

There is no simple way of stating accurately in lay terms what the psychological stress evaluator (or PSE) is or what it does. But if the precision of scientific language can be abandoned for a moment, it can be said that the PSE is a new type of lie detector that works through the medium of the voice. Because it can detect deception in the voice, it can be used without the subject's cooperation or even his knowledge. Because it works quite well over the telephone, it does not even require the subject's presence. And because it works from tape recordings, it can be used to probe the past. It is the first lie detector that can be used on a dead man.

Sound recording technology is almost a century old (Edison invented the phonograph in 1877), and an enormous amount of history is stored away in the sound archives of the world. There are scores of mysteries from the past hundred years which could be cleared up once and for all if the related interviews, public pronouncements, and press conferences could be retrieved from the archives and subjected to the scrutiny of the PSE. But none of these mysteries can compare in terms of sinister murkiness, frustrating paradox, or sheer historical impact to the question of what really happened in Dealey Plaza at 12:30 P.M., central standard time, November 22, 1963.

At the outset, the assassination of President Kennedy seemed an ideal case for investigation with the PSE. The media covered the event as they had never covered anything before. Statements had been made before television cameras or tape recorders by nearly all of the actors in the drama: eyewitnesses, policemen, medical examiners, members of the Warren Commission, even Oswald and Ruby. Somewhere, in some television network vault, were the tapes and sound tracks, and on them were the tiny, inaudible variations in voice frequency which could settle once and for all the question, "Did Oswald, acting alone, shoot and kill John F. Kennedy?"

And yet, despite my own skepticism about the Warren Report and a compelling desire to learn the truth, it was with great misgivings that I contemplated a project which could lead me to add my name to the list of those writers and researchers who have investigated the Kennedy assassination and found the official account wanting. While relatively few people seem actually to believe the Warren Report, those who have published their doubts (the "scavengers," as they have been called)[2] have acquired a public aura of opportunism and eccentricity.

In 1967 Gallup and Harris public opinion polls revealed that approximately two-thirds of the American people did not believe that the Kennedy assassination was the work of only one man.[3] In that same year New Orleans District Attorney Jim Garrison announced that he had uncovered the assassination conspiracy and brought an indictment against Clay Shaw, a New Orleans businessman. Many of us believed that the truth was finally going to come out. But two years later, after a courtroom debacle that cost Garrison his credibility, Shaw was exonerated.

From the beginning, the press and other news media had been skeptical of Garrison, and this skepticism grew into hostility as time passed. Garrison claimed that his case had been sabotaged by the same government conspirators he said were responsible for the assassination; the media implied that he had never had a case, that he was a fraud. For whatever reason, Garrison was unable to make good on his earlier promises to prove that he had uncovered the truth about the assassination. The public was disappointed and outraged.

Rather than clearing up the case, the Garrison investigation made matters worse. A new layer of doubt was added to the mystery, but the elements added by Garrison seemed even more bizarre than those served up by the Warren Commission. The subject began to take on a flavor of hoax and paranoia. Garrison's investigation represented a focus of all the questions raised by the patient research and analysis of people like Mark Lane, Josiah Thompson, Edward Jay Epstein, Harold Weisberg, and Sylvia Meagher. But now all this seemed no more credible nor convincing than the Warren Report itself. The whole New Orleans business seemed to stand as evidence that we would never know the truth.

For many of us, the assassination of President Kennedy was the most painful thing that ever happened beyond the ambit of our own private lives. Because it was such a strangely personal tragedy, the inadequacies of the Warren Commission's official investigation provoked not only doubt, but anger. But the thought that our doubting and our mourning had been exploited by eccentrics and opportunists was almost too much to bear. Outraged, we rejected both commission and critics and took refuge in our cynicism.

Therefore, the prospect of writing yet another chapter in this unpleasant story was less than appealing, especially since it involved the use of something as outrageous as a voice lie detector. If opening old wounds didn't provoke hostility, then using something as intrinsically guileful as the PSE seemed sure to do so. There is, after all, a certain effrontery in criticizing an official government body, and to propose to use a mechanical device to examine the truthfulness of policemen, medical examiners, or the former chief justice of the Supreme Court may seem to many to be the height of arrogance. I could easily become the most egregious of the "scavengers."

But if there is anything that will dispel the taint of disrepute attached to such an undertaking, it is the roster of distinguished Americans and others who have challenged the Warren Report during the ten years since its publication. Far from crooks or cranks, the skeptics include some of the most eminent figures from every walk of public life.

Two former assistants to President Kennedy, Richard Goodwin and Arthur Schlesinger, have publicly called for a new probe into the assassination.[4] Goodwin's proposal that a new panel of qualified investigators review the work of the Warren Commission to determine whether the case should be reopened was seconded by the conservative newspaper columnist, William F. Buckley, Jr.[5]

Congressional doubters have been even more outspoken and emphatic. Sen. Strom Thurmond rejected the findings of the Warren Commission and attributed the assassination to a Communist conspiracy.[6] Sen. Russell Long of Louisiana (whose father had been the victim of an assassin) stated that he "always suspected that there was someone else involved" in the Kennedy assassination, noting that "whoever fired that second shot was a better shot than Oswald and he was using a better weapon."[7] In 1967 the late Sen. Thomas Dodd of Connecticut urged that the Warren Commission reopen its inquiry.[8] Former Sen. George Murphy of California also went on record as doubting the Warren Report and stated that he suspected the assassination was the work of a conspiracy.[9]

In the House, Reps. Ogden Reid, John Wydler, and the late William Ryan, all of New York, called for a congressional investigation into the assassination.[10] Rep. Theodore Kupferman of New York tried to establish a joint congressional committee to determine whether Congress should reopen the case.[11]

The late French president, Charles de Gaulle, was quoted as saying the assassination was the work of the police and that Oswald had been framed.[12] The distinguished Oxford historian, Hugh Trevor-Roper, described the Warren Report as a "smoke screen."[13] The late Richard Cardinal Cushing of Boston, an intimate of the Kennedy family, said in a 1967 news conference, "I never believed the assassination of President Kennedy was the work of one man," and "I don't think the Warren Report is complete. There are portions of it I think should be followed."[14] The late Episcopal Bishop James A. Pike also stated his belief in a conspiracy.[15]

The Vatican newspaper, *L'Osservatore della Domenica*, expressed doubt about the Warren Report in 1967,[16] and *Life* and *The Saturday Evening Post* have both called for a reopening of the case.[17] In 1966 Tom Wicker wrote in his *New York Times* column that the Warren Commission had failed to present "an ironclad and unarguable case that Lee Oswald, alone and without rational motive, was the assassin."[18] More recently, Dan Rather, a television newsman who conducted an investigation into the assassination for CBS and who had defended the Warren Report, was moved by some of the Watergate revelations to wonder publicly whether the Warren Commission's investigation should have been completely closed.[19]

Of course, this long (and incomplete) list of distinguished doubters doesn't, in itself, disprove the validity of the Warren Report: eminence does not necessarily mean expertise. But it does serve to demonstrate that skepticism about the official account of the assassination is not limited to muckraking journalists.*

There were a few people, however, who were very well-informed about the assassination and who harbor some doubts about the conclusions of the Warren Commission. One of these is Mr. Jesse Curry, who was chief of the Dallas Police Department at the time of the assassination. In 1969 Curry, then retired from the police department, said, "We don't have any proof that Oswald fired the rifle. No

*Former President Richard M. Nixon may recently have joined this company of skeptics. In a press conference held on August 22, 1973, Mr. Nixon turned to the subject of wiretaps, noting that Robert Kennedy, when attorney general in 1963, had authorized over 250 wiretaps. "But if he'd had ten more, and as a result of wiretaps, had been able to discover the Oswald plan, it would have been worth it," he said. A few minutes later, one of the reporters asked Mr. Nixon if he had meant that wiretaps might have prevented the assassination.

"No, what I said," Mr. Nixon replied, "let me correct you, sir. I want to be sure that the assumption is correct. I said, 'If ten more wire taps could have found the conspiracy—if it was a conspiracy—or the individual, then it would have been worth it!' As far as I'm concerned, I'm no more of an expert on that assassination than anybody else, but my point is that wiretaps in the national security area were very high in the Kennedy administration for very good reasons."

Obviously, in order to discover "the Oswald plan" through a wiretap, it would have to have been discussed in a telephone conversation, and that would necessarily mean the assassination was the result of a conspiracy. Mr. Nixon's comments seemed to indicate very clearly that he thinks it a distinct possibility that there was a conspiracy and, implicitly, that the Warren Commission may have been wrong. In fairness, however, it should be noted that these remarks were made during the heat of a press conference on the subject of Watergate while Mr. Nixon was trying to defend some of his own actions on grounds of national security. But it is interesting that Mr. Nixon did not see fit to issue a subsequent statement reaffirming his faith in the Warren Report.

one has been able to put him in that building with a gun in his hand."[20] In his book, *JFK Assassination File*, Curry wrote:

> The physical evidence and eye witness accounts do not clearly indicate what took place on the sixth floor of the Texas School Book Depository at the time John F. Kennedy was assassinated. Speculative magazine and newspaper stories led the public to believe that numerous eye witnesses positively identified Lee Harvey Oswald as the sniper in the sixth floor window. The testimony of the people who watched the motorcade was much more confusing than either the press or the Warren Commission seemed to indicate.[21]

Curry went on to raise several problems with the Warren Commission's version of events. He noted that the eyewitness who claimed to have seen Oswald shoot the president and upon whose testimony the commission relied heavily, had been unable to pick Oswald out of a police lineup and had changed his story several times prior to testifying before the commission.[22] Curry also pointed out, "A paraffin test taken of the right side of Oswald's face did not reveal any nitrates from having fired a rifle, thus offering no proof that Oswald had recently fired a rifle."[23*]

When I interviewed Mr. Curry in May 1973 he told me, "There are still doubts in the minds of a lot of people that I talk to that this [the Warren Commission's version] was the exact way it happened." He added that there was some evidence that a gunman fired at the president from the grassy knoll adjoining Dealey Plaza. "I don't have a strong feeling that there was someone there," he said, "but, on the other hand, it wouldn't surprise me at some time, at some point in history, that more proof will show that there was somebody up there."[24]

While the former Dallas police chief may have had doubts about

*The Warren Commission stated that the paraffin test "is completely unreliable in determining either whether a person has recently fired a weapon or whether he has not." It did not explain why, in view of this, the test is used by the Dallas police and other police departments throughout the country.

the Warren Report, there were two very well-informed individuals who flatly rejected the commission's finding that there was no conspiracy. One of these men was the late Sen. Richard Russell of Georgia, and his opinion carries considerable weight for one very simple reason: Senator Russell was one of the seven members of the Warren Commission.

In January 1970 Russell said, "I never believed that he [Oswald] did it [the assassination] without any consultation or any encouragement whatsoever. Too many things . . . caused me to doubt that he planned it all by himself."[25] In an earlier interview, Russell said that he had tried to have his dissenting view included in the Warren Report but, "Warren was determined he was going to have a unanimous report. I said it wouldn't be any trouble just to put a little asterisk up here [in the text] and then down at the bottom of the page saying: 'Senator Russell dissents to this finding as follows,' but Warren wouldn't hear of it. He finally took that part and rewrote it himself."[26]

But the most damaging rejection of the Warren Report came from the man who brought the Warren Commission into existence and for whom the Warren Report was written, President Lyndon B. Johnson. During a 1970 television interview with Walter Cronkite of CBS, Johnson made some statements which he later asked to have deleted "on grounds of national security" before the interview was broadcast.[27] A "CBS source" was reported to have said that in the deleted statements Mr. Johnson had expressed doubt and dissatisfaction with the Warren Commission's "single assassin" theory.[28] In the July 1973 *Atlantic Monthly*, Leo Janos, a journalist and former member of Johnson's staff, reported that he had interviewed Johnson in 1971:

> During coffee, the talk turned to President Kennedy, and Johnson expressed his belief that the assassination in Dallas had been part of a conspiracy. "I never believed that Oswald acted alone, although I can accept that he pulled the trigger." Johnson said that when he had taken office he found that "we had been operating a damned Murder Inc. in the Caribbean." A year or so before Kennedy's death a CIA-backed assassination team had been picked

up in Havana. Johnson speculated that Dallas had been a retaliation for this thwarted attempt, although he couldn't prove it.[29]

The executive order that created the Warren Commission charged that panel with the responsibility "to ascertain, evaluate and report upon the facts relating to the assassination of the late President John F. Kennedy . . . and to report to me [President Lyndon B. Johnson] its findings and conclusions."[30] Clearly the commission was judged to have failed by the president who issued that order, by one of the seven commission members, and by two-thirds of the American people. There is no certitude at all about what happened in Dallas. The case cannot be said to have been closed.

If the psychological stress evaluator or any other development of forensic science can remove some of the doubt, then it must be brought to bear on the mystery. For this reason, I went forward with my plan to investigate the assassination of President Kennedy through the use of the PSE. For nearly a year I collected tape recordings from television networks, from the Kennedy Library and other archives, and from private sources. I traveled to Dallas, and, in the guise of a magazine journalist writing a commemorative piece on the assassination, I taped interviews with some of the principal participants in the events of November 22, 1963. I processed the assassination tapes with the PSE and had my conclusions checked by some of the foremost experts in this new lie-detection technique. In some instances I was able to obtain documentation and other collateral evidence supporting my conclusions. The truth has slowly emerged.

Man has never devised an absolutely infallible machine, and the psychological stress evaluator is no exception. But, when properly used, the PSE is very reliable. In probing for deception in any one person, there is always some margin of error, but in using the PSE as I did to examine the statements of dozens of persons who had some direct knowledge of the Kennedy assassination, there is little chance that the instrument will be consistently wrong. The picture of events drawn by the PSE is coherent; there are no internal contradictions. It is consistent with the established facts of the case, including those facts the commission developed but ignored in its final conclusions. And it has been partially confirmed; in some of the instances where the PSE found deception, I can prove that the speaker was not telling the truth.

So now I must add my own name to the list of "scavengers." If eccentrics and opportunists have chosen to attack the Warren Report, that fact can add not a scintilla of credibility to the document. Beyond the omissions, the inadequacies, perhaps the outright deceptions that have been found in the work of the commission during the last ten years, there is now the evidence of one of the most powerful new instruments of forensic science. I believe that it has demonstrated, beyond any reasonable doubt, that every major conclusion of the Warren Report is wrong. But more than that, the PSE has finally penetrated the mystery of Dallas and uncovered a large part of the truth.

President Kennedy was killed by a conspiracy. The man who paid with his life for that crime in the basement of the Dallas City Hall was innocent. The murderers went free and are still at large. It is a bitter story, but I believe it to be true, and so I must tell it. Justice beckons.

2 PROBLEMS WITH THE REPORT

> "I ca'n't believe *that!*" said Alice.
>
> "Ca'n't you?" the Queen said in a pitying tone.
> "Try again: draw a long breath, and shut your eyes."
>
> Alice laughed. "There's no use trying," she said:
> "one *ca'n't* believe impossible things."
>
> "I daresay you haven't had much practice," said
> the Queen. "When I was your age, I always did it for
> half-an-hour a day. Why, sometimes I've believed as
> many as six impossible things before breakfast."
> —Lewis Carroll: *Through the Looking-Glass*

On the evening of February 22, 1861, President-elect Abraham Lincoln quietly left Harrisburg, Pennsylvania, in the company of an armed guard. The telegraph lines had been cut so that no word of his departure could be sent ahead. In Philadelphia Lincoln boarded the last car of a New York to Washington train, accompanied by a railroad detective named Allan Pinkerton who had arranged for Lincoln to travel under a pseudonym. At six o'clock the following morning Lincoln arrived secretly and safely in Washington.

These were elaborate security measures in pre-Civil War America, and they were taken because a New York police superintendent had uncovered a plot to assassinate President-elect Lincoln. The superintendent's men had learned that the attempt would be made as Lincoln passed through Baltimore on his way to his first inauguration. As Lincoln and Pinkerton traveled through the Maryland night, they did not know that an extra precaution had been taken to protect the president-elect's life: the police official who had uncovered the plot and warned Lincoln was riding, heavily armed, in the same car.

The name of this New York police superintendent who thwarted the first attempt on the life of Abraham Lincoln was John Kennedy.[1]

This is but one of a seemingly endless chain of coincidences binding the assassinations of Presidents Lincoln and Kennedy. Both men were shot in the back of the head, in the presence of their wives, on a Friday, shortly after referring to the possibility of assassination. Neither man ever regained consciousness. Kennedy had a secretary named Lincoln, and Lincoln had a secretary named Kennedy. Lincoln was elected in 1860, Kennedy in 1960, both after famous debates. Both men lost a child while president. Each was succeeded by a former senator and southern Democrat named Johnson. It is as if some vast tornado in time had mockingly driven together these two American tragedies.

While the coincidences between the Lincoln and Kennedy assassinations can have no deeper meaning, except perhaps that the laws of probability were suspended in favor of some strange example of Jungian synchronicity, there are other unlikely juxtapositions of events surrounding the Dallas shooting, and these have given rise to dark suspicions. The story of George de Mohrenschildt is a case in point.

De Mohrenschildt lived in Dallas until a few months before the assassination, and he was a friend of Lee Harvey Oswald. De Mohrenschildt was born in Russia in 1911, was educated in Europe, and emigrated to the United States in 1938. He became a petroleum engineer and was living in the Dallas-Ft. Worth area when Oswald moved there on his return from the Soviet Union with his Russian-born wife, Marina. The Oswalds struck up friendships in the local Russian émigré community and in this way met de Mohrenschildt, whom Lee Harvey Oswald came to think of as his closest friend.[2]

In 1960 de Mohrenschildt and his wife took an eight-month hiking tour from the United States–Mexican border to Panama and were in Guatamala when the CIA launched its abortive Bay of Pigs invasion of Cuba from bases in that country. The Warren Report states that de Mohrenschildt later presented films and a detailed report of the trip "to the U.S. Government."[3] This probably means the CIA.

The Warren Commission concluded that there was no evidence to link de Mohrenschildt to the assassination, yet some conspiracy theorists interpret Oswald's friendship with a man who seems to have some association with the CIA as evidence that the intelligence agency was behind the assassination. However, there is a much less tenuous link between Oswald and Soviet intelligence; Marina Oswald's uncle, who may have been instrumental in obtaining permission for the Oswalds to leave Russia in 1962, was a colonel in the Soviet MVD.[4]

Such coincidences may seem implausible or suspicious, but consider this: Shortly after George de Mohrenschildt emigrated to the United States, he made the acquaintance of a family named Bouvier and their small daughter, Jacqueline.[5] A quarter of a century before he befriended the accused presidential assassin, de Mohrenschildt met John F. Kennedy's future wife and in-laws! That such circumstances are coincidental is almost beyond belief, but how else, in sanity, can they be explained?

The problem with this kind of linkage is that it leads nowhere and everywhere. The Kennedy assassination abounds with suspicious coincidences, and, obviously, not all of them can, in fact, be sinister because they imply mutually contradictory explanations of what happened. Either the CIA *or* the KGB could be guilty, but not both. The unexpected discovery that two people knew each other or were distantly related or were in the same unlikely place at the same time is interesting and should not be discounted out of hand, but unless some means is available to distinguish between chance and malicious design, it does not move us closer to the truth. The world may be a smaller and less random place than we imagine.

However, some independent researchers who have examined the work of the Warren Commission have raised serious questions about its conclusions which are much more substantial than mere suspicious coincidence. The Kennedy assassination may have defied the laws of probability, but the commission asks us to believe that it also defied the laws of physics and logic. The real problem with the Warren Report is not that it failed to explain some suspicious coincidences, but that it failed to explain its own evidence about what happened in Dallas.

On the evening of Sunday, September 27, 1964, the Warren Commission released its report to the American public. The 888-page document, printed and bound in hard cover by the U.S. Government Printing Office, began with a list of the commission's conclu-

sions and recommendations. Chief among these were the findings
that President Kennedy and Governor Connally were shot by Lee
Harvey Oswald from a window in the southeast corner of the Texas
School Book Depository, that Oswald had fired three shots from a
vintage Italian bolt-action rifle he owned and had with him at the
time of the assassination, that 45 minutes later Oswald shot and killed
Dallas police officer J. D. Tippit, that Oswald acted alone and there
was no evidence that the assassination was the work of a conspiracy,
and that Jack Ruby, the Dallas nightclub owner who killed Oswald,
also acted alone. The Report slapped the wrists of the Secret Service,
the FBI, and the news media and offered several policy recommendations for the improvement of presidential security.

More than anything else, the Report conveyed the impression of
thoroughness. It was indexed, contained sixty-three pages of foot-
notes in small-point type, included the biographies of the commission
members, the commission counsel, and the commission staff and
such interesting items as the fact that Thomas Jefferson walked
unguarded from his boarding house to the Capitol to take his inaugural oath,[6] that a 1923 school report on the eleven-year-old Jack Ruby
said that he was quick-tempered and disobedient[7] but that the commission had established that, as of March 1964, the nightclub owner
loved dogs.[8] Several other editions of the document were brought out
by private publishers, including the *New York Times*. The *Times*
may have seen in the Report a reflection of its own promotional
slogan: You don't have to read it all, but it's nice to know it's all there.

If any doubt remained that the Warren Commission's investigation had been exhaustive, it was dispelled two months later on
November 24 when the commission published more than ten million
words of exhibits and testimony in twenty-six separate volumes. Less
than twenty-four hours later, after setting what must have been the
world's speedreading record, the *Times* announced that the twenty-
six supplementary volumes demonstrated that the commission had
done a "monumental and meticulous" job.[9] Shortly thereafter, the
Times published a one-volume abridgement of the commission hearings entitled *The Witnesses*.[10] Those portions of the testimony and
evidence excerpted and edited by the *Times* staff confirmed the
major conclusions of the Warren Commission. However, a few inde-

pendent researchers took the time and trouble to read the full text and found that nearly everything else in the twenty-six volumes pointed in the opposite direction.

One of the most exhaustive analyses was done by a remarkable woman named Sylvia Meagher, who devoted a year to studying and indexing the twenty-six volumes. In 1966 she published a work entitled *Subject Index to the Warren Report and Hearings and Exhibits*[11] and the following year, *Accessories After the Fact,*[12] a detailed critique of the Warren Report.

"There is much mention of the 26 volumes of the Hearings and Exhibits," wrote Meagher, in her foreword to *Accessories,* "but little familiarity with their contents, organization, or character."[13] But Meagher was thoroughly familiar with these things, and she relentlessly pursued every inconsistency, contradiction, and apparent evasion she found in the published documents of the Warren Commission. She did not concern herself with Thomas Jefferson's security precautions or Jack Ruby's childhood but focused on the questions of who killed the president, how solid was the case against Oswald, and how thorough and objective was the work of the commission. Meagher concluded that the Warren Report contained:

> 1) statements of fact which are inaccurate and untrue, in the light of the official Exhibits and objective verification; 2) statements for which the citations fail to provide authentication; 3) misrepresentation of testimony; 4) omission of references to testimony inimical to findings in the Report; 5) suppression of findings favorable to Oswald; 6) incomplete investigation of suspicious circumstances which remain unexplained; 7) misleading statements resulting from inadequate attention to the contents of the Exhibits; 8) failure to obtain testimony from crucial witnesses; and 9) assertions which are diametrically opposite to the logical inferences to be drawn from the relevant testimony or evidence.[14]

If Meagher's charges sound excessive, one need only open *Accessories After the Fact* at random, select any of the questions she raised, and look up the corresponding testimony and evidence in the twenty-six volumes. It will be seen that if Meagher was guilty of anything, it was understatement. For example, in her analysis of the shooting of Officer Tippit, she makes passing reference to the testimony of Dallas policeman Harry Olsen, who gave the commission a very unsatisfactory account of how he happened to be a few blocks from the scene of the shooting at the time it took place. Meagher notes that Olsen was a casual friend of Jack Ruby and a boyfriend of one his strippers, that he claimed to have been standing in for another cop that day in the off-duty job of guarding an estate in the Oak Cliff area of Dallas* and that he couldn't remember the name of the owner, the exact location of the estate, or the identity of the policeman for whom he was substituting.[15]

On reading the transcript of Olsen's testimony before the commission, one discovers a number of interesting details Meagher didn't mention in her book, though she must certainly have been aware of them. First, Olsen said that his girlfriend, Mrs. Kay Coleman, visited him while he was guarding this lost estate of the unnamed owner on behalf of the forgotten policeman.[16] The commission heard the testimony of Mrs. Coleman, who became Mrs. Olsen a few weeks after the assassination, and asked her about her acquaintance with her boss, Jack Ruby, but it never thought to inquire if she remembered the location of the missing estate.[17]

Second, Olsen testified that he had known Jack Ruby for three years, had visited Ruby's nightclub about once a week during that period, and had met with Ruby for two or three hours on the night of November 22.[18] Finally, Olsen said that he had left the Dallas police force and moved to California about a month after the assassination after having been asked to resign by Police Chief Jesse Curry. Arlen Specter, a commission Counsel who examined Olsen, asked

---

*Oak Cliff is a high-density, lower-middle-class residential section of Dallas. It was the location of Oswald's furnished room and the scene of the Tippit killing. Olsen claimed to have been guarding an estate "on 8th Street . . . in the Oak Cliff area . . . approximately two blocks off of Stemmons (Freeway)." (Hearings, Vol. 14, p. 629.) This writer visited the location in May 1973 and found nothing that could be characterized as an "estate" there or anywhere else in Oak Cliff. Most of the one-and two-family, middle-income homes in the area have been standing for more than ten years. Local inquiries failed to turn up any recollections of an "estate" on 8th Street in 1963.

him why Curry requested the resignation. Olsen replied that there were several reasons but that he could only remember one of them: he had used up his sick leave.[19] Specter didn't press him on this, and the commission never asked Curry if he might remember why he asked this officer to resign.[20]

Meagher noted in her book Olsen's connection with Ruby and one of his strippers and the policeman's failure to account adequately for his presence near the scene of the Tippit shooting, but she omits mention of Olsen's long meeting with Ruby after the assassination, his inability to remember most of the reasons he was asked to leave the police force a short time later, and the commission's lack of curiosity about these matters. Why did she leave these things out? The obvious answer is space. Meagher's 477-page book identifies hundreds of major flaws and deficiencies in the Warren Report; if she had also included the kind of relatively minor problem noted here, she would have had to write many books. Perhaps as many as twenty-six.

Accesories After the Fact never achieved the same wide distribution as the *Warren Report* (1,100,000 copies of The *New York Times*-Bantam Books paperback edition of the Report were printed within a week of its release by the commission),[21] and The *New York Times Book Review* found the Meagher book to be "a bore."[22] However, all independent students of the Kennedy assassination know Meagher's work well, and we are all in her debt.

Obviously, it is impractical to present all the questions Meagher and the other critics have raised about the Warren Report, but some of the major problems must be reviewed here because they form the background against which I undertook my PSE-aided investigation. Foremost among these problems are the defects in the commission's conclusion that all of the assassination shots were fired from one gun, the rifle the commission says belonged to Lee Harvey Oswald.

The Dallas police reported that, about fifty minutes after the assassination, they found a rifle hidden behind some boxes on the sixth floor of the Texas School Book Depository.[23] The earliest radio and television reports of this discovery during the afternoon of November 22 described the weapon as a British 303.[24] Later, Deputy Constable Seymour Weitzman, one of the two officers who said they found the rifle, reported that the weapon was a 7.65 Mauser.[25] Dallas District Attorney Henry Wade told the press the same thing, although it is not clear whether he was merely repeating Weitzman's report.[26] The day after the assassination, Weitzman signed an affidavit which said, "This rifle was a 7.65 Mauser bolt action equipped with a 4/18 scope, a thick leather brownish-black sling on it."[27]

The other officer who discovered the hidden weapon was Deputy Sheriff Eugene Boone. Boone submitted a report to his superior on November 22 which read, ". . . I saw the rifle, that appeared to be a 7.65 Mauser. . . ."[28] He later told the commission that he thought the rifle was a 7.65 Mauser.[29]

The rifle that was turned over to the FBI by the Dallas police was, of course, not a Mauser. It was a 6.5 Mannlicher-Carcano, with the words "made in Italy" and "cal. 6.5" stamped into the barrel.[30] This, however, was not made public until the day after the assassination, presumably after Weitzman and Boone had signed their statements. The discrepancy has prompted speculation that the Mannlicher-Carcano was substituted for a Mauser after the discovery or that *two* rifles were found in the book depository. The commission's handling of these questions was not very reassuring, as Meagher pointed out.[31]

The two policemen testified that they did not handle the rifle because the crime lab unit had not arrived to dust for fingerprints and so did not discover their apparent mistake. This is entirely plausible, since the rifles in question are similar in appearance. Still, Weitzman's description of the rifle in his sworn affidavit seems quite specific. And, as Weitzman told the commission, he was "fairly familiar [with rifles] because I was in the sporting goods business awhile."[32]

But assuming that the Mannlicher-Carcano was the rifle found in the book depository, did this weapon belong to Lee Harvey Oswald? The Warren Commission concluded that it did. Oswald's wife identified the weapon as her husband's.[33] The FBI discovered that the Mannlicher-Carcano had been purchased by mail from Klein's Sporting Goods Company in Chicago and shipped on March 20, 1963, to someone named A. Hidell at P.O. Box 2915, Dallas, Texas. The post-office box was said to have been rented by a Lee H. Oswald from October 9, 1962, until May 14, 1963, and identification in the name of Alex Hidell was reported by the Dallas police to have been in Oswald's possession when they arrested him.*[34]

The rifle was turned over to the the the FBI by the Dallas police on the night of the assassination, and when it arrived in Washington, fingerprint experts examined the rifle and found nothing that could be used to identify anyone who had handled the weapon.[35] Seven days later, however, the FBI lab received a fingerprint "lift" (a sheet of adhesive material used to lift fingerprint powder impressions from objects for a permanent record) from Lt. J. C. Day of the Dallas police, who said it had been taken from the underside of the Mannlicher-Carcano's barrel at a point which would have been covered by the stock when the rifle was assembled for use. The FBI lab confirmed that the lift had been made from the barrel and identified the print as Oswald's.[36]

Other evidence linking the rifle to Oswald consisted of some cotton fibers found in a crevice between the wooden and metal parts of the gun and a pair of photographs of Oswald holding a rifle. The FBI lab said that the fibers had come either from the shirt Oswald was wearing when he was arrested or from "another identical shirt."[37] The FBI also said that the rifle shown in the photographs, which Marina Oswald said she had taken earlier in 1963, appeared to be the Mannlicher-Carcano in question, but that "positive identification to the exclusion of all other rifles of the same general configuration" could not be made.[38]

The words "another identical shirt" are probably an overstatement, since the FBI lab couldn't have meant that the fibers had to come from a shirt of the same collar size and sleeve length as Oswald's, and the phrase "same general configuration" sounds like an inflated way of saying that the rifle in the photograph had a bolt action and a telescopic sight. The word "configuration" definitely did not include the sling by which the rifle is held in the picture, because the FBI experts testified that the sling was not the same as the one on the Mannlicher-Carcano they were given.[39] Few critics of the Report have questioned that the rifle in the photographs is the

*Whether or not Oswald used the Hidell alias, there is considerable doubt in this writer's mind that he was carrying such identification on the afternoon of November 22. The question is discussed in Chapter 9.

Mannlicher-Carcano, but many have doubted that the person holding it is Lee Harvey Oswald.

The first person to challenge the authenticity of the photographs
is reported to have been Oswald himself. According to the Dallas
police, Oswald was confronted with the pictures while in custody and
claimed that they had been fabricated by superimposing his face over
a photo of someone else holding a rifle.[40] Meagher and others have
analyzed the photographs and questioned descrepancies between the
fall of shadows across Oswald's face and the angles of other shadows
in the picture, concluding that the face may have come from another
photograph.[41] Also, using Oswald's known height as a reference and
measuring the relative length of the rifle in the photograph, Meagher
found that if the person in the picture is Oswald, the weapon may
have been longer than the Mannlicher-Carcano.[42] Others have questioned that the face in the photographs is, in fact, that of Lee Harvey
Oswald.[43] However, an FBI photographic expert testified that both
pictures were probably authentic.[44] The most substantial evidence
that the Mannlicher-Carcano rifle found in the book depository belonged to Oswald came from the testimony of handwriting experts
of the FBI and Treasury Department, who testified "unequivocally"
that the printing on the order coupon clipped from a gun magazine
and sent to Klein's Sporting Goods, and the handwriting on the
envelope and postal money order used to buy the gun were done by
Oswald. The experts also verified that the handwriting on the application for the post-office box to which the rifle was sent was that of
Oswald.[45] It should be pointed out, however, that handwriting identification is largely a subjective procedure and does not have the same
certainty as, for example, fingerprints. Among those unimpressed by
the testimony of handwriting experts are, no doubt, the executives
of McGraw-Hill and *Life* Magazine, who retained some of the
world's most respected handwriting experts and were told that Clifford Irving's forgeries were the authentic writing of Howard Hughes.
(See Chapter 3.)

There are a great many more unanswered questions in the chain
of evidence the commission used to link Oswald to the Mannlicher-
Carcano,[46] but I am inclined to believe that the rifle probably did
belong to him. If the weapon weren't Oswald's, then someone went

to a great deal of trouble to manufacture evidence linking him to the gun. And assuming someone did take this trouble, it's hard to imagine why he selected a $12.78 piece of junk.* If a rifle were planted on Oswald, it should have been one capable of being used in the assassination. And if the commission's evidence establishes anything beyond a shadow of a doubt, it is that the Mannlicher-Carcano rifle found in the book depository could not have been used to fire all the shots that struck in the presidential limousine and is unlikely to have fired any of them.

The commission's evidence that the rifle turned over to the FBI by the Dallas police was, in fact, the assassination weapon consists of three parts: shell casings found in the book depository, bullet fragments found in the presidential limousine, and a bullet found on the floor of Parkland Memorial Hospital. Shortly after their arrival at Parkland Hospital, President Kennedy was rushed into the emergency room where doctors tried against hope to save his life, and Governor Connally, also wounded in the shooting, was transferred by stretcher to an elevator and taken to an operating room for surgery. A few minutes later, a hospital employee removed a stretcher—perhaps the one that had borne Connally—from the elevator and placed it next to another stretcher against a corridor wall. Minutes later, he says, he bumped against one of the stretchers and a bullet dropped onto the floor.[47] The bullet was slightly flattened but otherwise in perfect condition. The FBI found that the bullet had been fired from the Mannlicher-Carcano.

Three rifle shell casings were reportedly found by the Dallas police near the southeast corner window on the sixth floor of the book depository about forty minutes after the assassination.[48] The FBI lab linked the shells to the Mannlicher-Carcano.

That night, two Secret Service agents searched the presidential limousine in Washington, where it had been taken by plane during

*Klein's price for the basic rifle was $12.78, and with the scope it was $19.95. Postage and handling charges were $1.50, bringing the total price of the rifle the commission says was used to kill the president to $21.45. (*Report of the President's Commission on the Assassination of President John F. Kennedy*, p. 119.)

the afternoon. They found two bullet fragments in the front seat. The FBI lab said that they were parts of a bullet or bullets fired from the Mannlicher-Carcano.[49] The shells, the bullet, and the bullet fragments would leave little doubt that the Mannlicher-Carcano was the assassination gun were it not for the fact that the shooting was recorded for history on motion-picture film by a home-movie buff named Abraham Zapruder.

There were at least twenty-two photographers in Dealey Plaza that day as the presidential motorcade turned left in front of the Texas School Book Depository and started down the gentle incline of Elm Street. Some were professionals, most were amateurs. There were at least nine motion picture cameras, but the best record of the sudden sequence of events is the eight-millimeter color film taken by Zapruder, a local businessman. Zapruder positioned himself on top of a concrete pedestal on a slope overlooking Dealey Plaza. As the motorcade came into view across the plaza on Houston Street, he began filming.[50]

The lead car turned onto Elm, followed by the motorcycle escort and the presidential limousine. Zapruder began to pan slowly to the right to keep the president's car in view. For a brief instant the car was obscured by a highway sign, and the crack of a rifle rang across Dealey Plaza. As the limousine moved back into view, the president's hands were rising toward his throat and Governor Connally in the jump seat ahead had turned part-way around toward the president. An instant later there was a second report, and Connally clutched his chest. Both men slumped to their left. Zapruder turned to keep the limousine in view as it came abreast of him. As he watched in horror through the camera viewfinder, a final shot struck the president in the head and seemed to drive him backward into the arms of his wife. Shocked and stunned, Zapruder followed the limousine with his camera as it sped out of view through the underpass at the bottom of the plaza.

Zapruder's camera and the 22-second strip of film proved invaluable to the commission in reconstructing the sequence and timing of events during the shooting. The FBI determined that the camera operated at a rate of 18.3 frames per second and numbered each of the frames, beginning with the one in which the motorcade first came into view.[51] Thus it was possible to measure the time intervals between the events recorded on the film.

When the president becomes visible as the limousine emerges from behind the highway sign in frame 225, it is apparent that he has been hit the first time and is reacting to the wound. The actual impact, then, had to occur before this point, while Kennedy is obscured from view by the sign. The presence of an oak tree in the field of fire makes it extremely unlikely that the bullet struck before frame 210, since a sniper in the window apparently used by the assassin would not have been able to see the back seat of the limousine until then. Therefore, the commission concluded that Kennedy was first hit sometime between frames 210 and 225.[52]

The commission investigators tested the Mannlicher-Carcano and determined that the rifle could not be fired twice in less than 2.3 seconds[53] or 42 frames in terms of the Zapruder film. Consequently, the second shot could not have struck Governor Connally until frame 252 at the earliest. However, Connally can clearly be seen reacting to the shot at frame 236. Connally examined the film and told the commission that he was hit sometime between frames 231 and 234.[54] The commission realized that, based on the photographic evidence, and the tests of the rifle, it was not possible that Connally had been hit by a second shot from the Mannlicher-Carcano. But rather than doubt that this weapon was the one and only assassination gun, the commission concluded that Connally must have been hit by the first bullet, that the bullet passed through the president and then struck the governor, all at some moment between frames 210 and 215. Thus was born the famous "single bullet theory."

The first of the many problems encountered by the commission in trying to prove the single bullet theory was Governor Connally. If he and Kennedy had been struck by the same bullet, the impacts would have occurred almost simultaneously. But Connally shows no reaction until frame 236, well over a second after Kennedy was hit. The bullet that struck Connally entered his back, emerged from his chest, shattered his wrist, and entered his thigh. The commission said that the governor had experienced a delayed reaction.[55] Whether or not this explanation is plausible, Connally's own recollection of events rules it out.

In an interview with CBS News broadcast in September 1964, Connally said that he heard a shot, turned back to look over his right shoulder—the direction from which he thought the sound had come —saw nothing unusual, faced forward again, began to turn to look over his left shoulder, "and that's when I felt the impact of the bullet that hit me. . . . I felt as if somebody had just hit me in the back a sharp blow with a doubled-up fist." Connally added, "I understand there's some question in the minds of the experts about whether or not we could both have been hit by the same bullet, and that was the first bullet. I just don't happen to believe that."[56]

The Zapruder film is completely consistent with Connally's recollection. As the limousine emerges from behind the sign in frames 223–225, Kennedy is clutching at his throat and Connally is half turned to his right. By frame 230, Connally is facing forward again (by his account, preparing to turn and look over his left shoulder). By frame 236, Connally is reacting to a shot.

The surgeons who operated on Connally in Parkland Hospital studied the Zapruder film and told the commission that the governor was shot after frame 231.[57] Mrs. Connally testified that she remembered turning and seeing the president clutching his throat and then seeing her husband shot. The Connallys reiterated their account for *Life* Magazine three years after the assassination:

"They talk about the 'one bullet or two-bullet theory,'" he continued, "but as far as I'm concerned, there is no 'theory.' There is my absolute knowledge, and Nellie's too, that one bullet caused the President's first wound, and that an entirely separate shot struck me."

"No one will ever convince me otherwise," added Mrs. Connally.

"It's a certainty," said the governor, "I'll never change my mind."[58]

Thus, the precise chronology of events established by Zapruder's camera shows the woundings of Kennedy and Connally too seperate in time to have been done by one bullet and too close together to have been accomplished by two successive shots from the Mannlicher-Carcano. The commission's hypothesis that Connally experienced a delayed reaction is contradicted by Connally, his wife, and the doctors. Yet this is not the only problem encountered by the single bullet theory.

According to the commission's reconstruction of events, a lone assassin fired three shots: the first shot passed through the president, emerged from his throat, then struck Connally; the second shot went wild and did not strike in the limousine; the third shot hit Kennedy, causing the massive head wound that killed him.[59] Which of these three bullets, then, was found on the floor of Parkland Hospital?

The commission concluded that the Parkland bullet—dubbed exhibit 399—was the first shot, the one believed to have hit both Kennedy and Connally.[60] The second shot was ruled out, since there was no conceivable way it could have gotten from wherever it landed in Dealey Plaza to a hospital corridor several miles away. The autopsy x-rays showed too many metal fragments in the president's head for the nearly intact exhibit 399 to have been the third shot. And the bullet was found in a place where it could have fallen from Connally's stretcher but not from Kennedy's. In fact, although the Report does not point this out, if exhibit 399 was not the cause of Connally's wounds, then it would almost certainly have to have been planted.

But the nearly perfect condition of exhibit 399 makes it almost impossible to believe that it was responsible for Connally's wounds. According to the commission's theory, the bullet passed through the president's body without striking bone; but when it hit Connally, it broke his fifth rib, emerged just below his right nipple, passed through the bones of his wrist and shattered them, and then penetrated about a centimeter into his thigh. The commission tried to replicate this by firing the same kind of ammunition from a Mannlicher-Carcano into the wrist of a cadaver from a distance of seventy yards. Unlike exhibit 399, the test bullet was severely flattened by the impact against the bones of the wrist.[61] Two of the commission's ballistics experts and two of its medical experts said that the bullet that hit Connally should have been smashed by the impact.[62] And two of the surgeons who operated on Governor Connally testified that they seriously doubted the governor's wounds could have been caused by the nearly intact bullet, exhibit 399.[63]

Thus, in order to believe that all of the assassination shots came from the Mannlicher-Carcano, we must believe along with the commission that Governor Connally experienced a delayed reaction; that his recollection of hearing a shot, turning around, turning back, and then being struck, is in error; that Mrs. Connally's account of the sequence of events is also wrong; that the commission's own medical and ballistics experts are wrong; that the surgeons who operated on Connally are wrong; and that the assassination bullet was able to survive intact after breaking several bones, even though the commission could not duplicate the feat. While any one of these assumptions (except, perhaps, the last one) may be plausible, it is very difficult to accept them all. And there are yet more problems with the single bullet theory and the conclusion that the Mannlicher-Carcano was the assassination weapon.

The commission had trouble explaining how a rifle bullet, fired from the angle and elevation of the "Oswald window" could pass through Kennedy's body and hit someone sitting directly in front of him. If the shot had struck a bone in the president's body, it might have ricocheted to the right and hit Connally, but the autopsy report states that this was not the case.[64] The commission investigators reconstructed the scene of the shooting using a Secret Service car and measuring the deflection angles with surveyor's equipment, but they concluded:

> The alignment of the points of entry was only indicative and not conclusive that one bullet hit both men. The exact positions of the men could not be re-created; thus, the angle could only be approximated . . . if the President or the Governor had been sitting in a different lateral position, the conclusion might have varied. Or if the Governor had not turned exactly the way calculated, the alignment would have been destroyed.[65]

Thus, the commission doesn't really ask us to believe that a rifle bullet made a right turn in mid-air, but it does ask us to add yet another assumption—that the president and the governor were sitting in just the right positions—to the growing list of unlikely things which must be believed to preserve the single bullet theory.

The commission seemed to have anticipated public disbelief of the single bullet theory when it stated early in the Report, ". . . it is not necessary to any essential findings of the Commission to determine just which shot hit Governor Connally. . . ."[66] But, having had so much trouble living with the theory, the commission declined to explain how it could live without it. In fact, without postulating the single bullet theory, the Commission would have had serious problems with other evidence, apart from the difficulty posed by the Zapruder film. For example, if Kennedy was struck by two bullets and Connally was struck by a third, then additional shots must have caused the bullet mark found on a curbstone at the shooting scene and the bullet fragment that wounded a bystander. Yet only three Manlicher-Carcano shells were found in the book depository. While the commission attempted to dismiss these questions in the Report,[67] the actual testimony and evidence regarding them in the twenty-six volumes raises even more doubts about the official conclusions.[68]

But whether the president and Governor Connally were struck by the same or different bullets, there is much reason to doubt that any of the assassination shots were fired from the Mannlicher-Carcano rifle said to have been found in the book depository. The rifle may have resembled better-quality weapons in its physical appearance, but an experienced marksman who tried to fire the Mannlicher-Carcano would know the difference immediately.

An FBI expert told the commission that the rifle was "a cheap old weapon."[69] An Army weapons expert who tested the rifle for the commission testified that an unusual amount of effort was required to work the bolt and that pulling the trigger was a "two-stage operation."[70] The latter comment was explained to mean that increasing rather than steady pressure was needed to pull the trigger all the way back to the firing point; the trigger had to be jerked, rather than squeezed, and this made accurate shooting difficult.[71]

The commission also heard rifle experts testify that the telescopic sight could easily be knocked out of adjustment and that this would make accurate shooting with the gun unlikely, [72] that shims had to be inserted to elevate and move the sight before the commission's three marksmen could fire the rifle accurately,[73] and that, even using stationary targets, expert marksmen were unable to equal Oswald's alleged accuracy.[74] This testimony was not included in the Report but relegated to the twenty-six supplementary volumes, along with evidence that the rifle's firing pin was worn and rusty[75] and testimony that the rifle in question had been part of a shipment of defective weapons[76] and that such rifles could be "purchased for $3.00 each in lots of 25."[77] However, the Report does admit that the commission's marksmen had not practiced with the rifle before the tests because they feared that pulling the trigger might break the firing pin.[78] And it also admits that the telescopic scope was defective but claims that the defect actually improved the rifle's accuracy.[79] The Report quotes the testimony of an FBI expert that "one would not have to be an expert marksman to have accomplished the assassination with the weapon."[80] Strictly speaking, this is true; one would have to be a magician.

While there are even more problems with the commission's conclusions about the weapon and the shots, one is forced to ask how long a chain of improbabilities must be before it becomes impossibility. The Warren Commission cannot address such questions because it dissolved itself shortly after publishing its report. The FBI considers the case closed and refers inquiries about it to the National Archives. The National Archives is not an investigative agency and cannot argue the merits of the commission's findings, although it will make the evidence it was given available to independent researchers except for those many items that the FBI, the Secret Service, the Department of Defense, and the CIA say must be kept locked up. But there is one institution that has not closed the book on the Kennedy assassination, a private organization known as the Committee to Investigate Assassinations.

The committee is a loosely organized group of independent investigators who continue to probe the assassinations of John and Robert Kennedy and Martin Luther King, the attempted murder of George Wallace, and other acts of political violence that have altered our recent history. The committee was founded and is directed by Bernard Fensterwald, a prominent Washington, D.C. lawyer.

Fensterwald's face became familiar to millions of television viewers in May 1973 as he sat next to his client, James McCord, one of the first witnesses to appear before the Senate Watergate Committee. Fensterwald, a quiet man who speaks in the soft accents of his native

Tennessee, is an alumnus of Harvard Law School and a veteran of the navy and the State Department. During the 1950s, he was speech writer and foreign-policy adviser (he holds a degree in international law) to Sen. Estes Kefauver. Later he served as chief counsel for Sen. Edward Long's investigation into government wiretapping and electronic surveillance.

Because of his legal training and background, Fensterwald was interested in the debate over the Warren Report from the moment it began in 1964. In 1967 his interest was heightened by reports of Jim Garrison's New Orleans investigation, and he undertook a careful study of the Warren Report and the twenty-six supplementary volumes. He soon realized that there were serious problems with the official conclusions of the commission. Fensterwald began to fear that the government's failure to solve the mystery of the assassination of a president might result in other political killings. In the nightmare months of April and June 1968, his fears became reality.

Late in 1968 Fensterwald traveled to Los Angeles, Dallas, New Orleans, Miami, and Memphis. While on this trip, he contacted many of the independent researchers who doubted or rejected the official truths offered to explain the Dallas, Memphis, and Los Angeles murders. He realized that the work of these people would be much more effective if there were some means of pooling their results, a kind of clearinghouse for research into the assassinations. The result was the committee.

The committee's board of directors includes, among others, two well-known investigative journalists, Fred Cook and Paris Flammonde, radio personality John Henry Faulk, former air force intelligence officer Fletcher Prouty, ex-FBI agent William Turner, philosophy professor Richard Popkin, and computer expert Richard Sprague. All have done some private investigation into one or more of the assassinations, but Sprague's work is typical of the most painstaking work of the committee: he traveled around the country for years, tracking down over five hundred still photographs and motion pictures taken in Dealey Plaza on November 22, 1963, immediately before, during, and after the assassination.[81]

The one member of the board who devotes all of his time to investigation and research into the assassinations is the committee's research director, Robert Smith. Smith, a lean, intense chain smoker in his mid-forties, may be the committee's most relentless skeptic, but his skepticism is double edged, directed equally at both the official assassination accounts and the conspiracy theories of the critics. In his role as the committee's chief of research, Smith receives letters, phone calls, and visits, day and night, from people who feel they have found some fragment of the truth about the assassinations. Patiently, he tries to follow up on every one of them. Most lead nowhere, and some are downright insane. Smith, perhaps more than anyone else, is in a position to know that many of the attacks on the Warren Report are groundless. "There are enough genuine mysteries about this thing," he says, "without having to make them up."

One of the genuine mysteries discovered by Smith and Fensterwald in the course of their own investigations is the case of the man who impersonated Oswald in Mexico several weeks before the assassination. The two researchers obtained some recently declassified CIA documents from the National Archives early in 1973. The papers revealed that a confidential CIA source reported that a man claiming to be Oswald visited the Soviet embassy in Mexico City in early October 1963. But the CIA agent's description of this "Oswald" in no way fits the real Lee Harvey Oswald.

Smith's careful reading of the CIA documents revealed the existence of several photographs of the mystery man, apparently taken by CIA surveillance cameras hidden near the Soviet and Cuban embassies. Fensterwald sued the government for release of the photos under the Freedom of Information Act, and the government released them at the eleventh hour, just before the case was to go to trial.

The man in the pictures is in his mid-thirites with a muscular build and doesn't bear the slightest resemblance to Lee Harvey Oswald. The CIA told Fensterwald that it did not know the identity of the mystery man and cannot explain the reason for the masquerade.

The possibility that one or more persons impersonated Oswald in the weeks before the assassination plagued the Warren Commission and has fascinated the critics. It began with the testimony of Mrs. Sylvia Odio, a Cuban émigré living in Dallas, who told the commission she had been visited on September 26 or 27, 1963, by three men, two of whom claimed to be anti-Castro Cubans. The third was an American named "Leon Oswald." Mrs. Odio said the three men mentioned in passing, "President Kennedy should have been killed by the Cubans." Both Mrs. Odio and her sister, on seeing pictures of Lee Harvey Oswald, identified him as the "Leon Oswald" who had visited them.[82]

But the commission established that Oswald was in Mexico at the time, that he entered that country on September 26 and returned to the United States on October 3, meanwhile visiting the Cuban and Soviet embassies. Therefore, the commission concluded, Oswald could not have been one of the men who visited Mrs. Odio. Whether he was or not, the fact that someone, either in Dallas or in Mexico City, may have been impersonating Oswald eight weeks before the assassination has stimulated the curiosity of independent researchers (but apparently not that of the commission members).

In his quest for more of the government's information about the assassination, Smith has come to know the people at National Archives and found them friendly and, within the limits of the restrictions imposed by other agencies, cooperative. One of the items of interest Smith has been allowed to examine at the archives is the bullet which the Dallas police say they dug out of the wall of Gen. Edwin Walker's home on April 10, 1963. General Walker retired from the army in 1961 after a controversy arose over his right-wing political indoctrination of the troops under his command in Europe. He continued his political activities in Dallas after leaving the military. On the evening of April 10, he reported that someone fired at him through a window of his home and nearly killed him. The commission concluded that the gunman was Lee Harvey Oswald. It based its conclusion on several things: photographs of Walker's home and vicinity reportedly found by the Dallas police among Oswald's effects and linked to Oswald's camera by FBI photographic experts; testimony of Marina Oswald and Oswald's mysterious friend, George de Mohrenschildt, who was living in Dallas at the time of the Walker shooting; more unequivocal identification by FBI handwriting experts of Oswald as the writer of a note Marina Oswald says she found that evening;* and the ballistics analysis of the bullet the Dallas

*The note did not actually say that the writer was going to kill Walker, but it implied that he was going to do something dire (". . . If I am alive and taken prisoner, the city jail is located at the end of the bridge through which we always passed on going to the city. . . .").

police say they dug out of General Walker's wall.[83] The bullet was "severely mutilated," according to the Report, but appeared to have been fired from the Mannlicher-Carcano rifle, although positive identification was not possible.[84]

Smith brought his camera to the National Archives and made several close-up photographs of the Walker bullet. Later he took the pictures to Dallas and sought out the policeman who had removed the bullet from General Walker's wall. The officer could not identify the bullet in the photos as the bullet he found, because he did not see his initials, which he remembered scratching into the metal surface (a standard police practice for identifying evidence found at the scene of a crime). Smith had photographed the entire surface of the bullet, but none of the pictures showed any initials. The policeman told Smith he specifically recalled inscribing his initials in the steel jacket of the bullet. This was especially interesting to Smith: the bullet he saw in the National Archives had a copper jacket.

The bullet had been kept by the Dallas police until requested by the commission investigators (presumably after other evidence seemed to link Oswald to the Walker shooting). In the months between the Walker shooting and the Kennedy assassination, the bullet could have been accidentally switched with evidence from some other crime under investigation by the Dallas police. But this writer is inclined to believe that if the bullet in the National Archives were not severely mutilated, it would match perfectly with the rifling marks of the Mannlicher-Carcano and that somewhere in the wall of a Dallas basement or garage, there is an eleven-year-old bullet hole.

As the committee's research director, Smith is interested in all of the assassinations, not only the killing of President Kennedy. But there are so many more different mysteries, so much more published and unpublished documentation, and so many more people involved, that the Dallas tragedy occupies the largest part of Robert Smith's time. He has developed an encyclopedic knowledge of the assassination of President Kennedy and can field questions regarding the most obscure minutiae of the case without referring to the committee's files or library. Because of his scientific background (he has a degree in chemical engineering from Carnegie Tech), he is particularly interested in the physical evidence of the Kennedy assassination and especially in the work of Dr. Cyril Wecht, with whom he has collaborated.

Dr. Wecht is the coroner of Allegheny County, Pennsylvania (including Pittsburgh), director of Duquesne University's Institute of Forensic Science, past president of the American Academy of Forensic Sciences and the American College of Legal Medicine, and is widely regarded as one of America's leading forensic pathologists. For years Wecht has been raising disturbing questions about the autopsy performed on President Kennedy. In 1972, after persistent requests, he finally succeeded in getting a look at some of the autopsy photographs and related evidence. In collaboration with Smith, Wecht presented his conclusions in *The Forensic Science Gazette:*

> The Warren Commission's "single-bullet theory" is untenable, and the Commission's conclusion that there was only one assassin cannot be reconciled with available evidence. Medical and photographic data, including measurement of wound angles and calculations of bullet trajectories, strongly suggest that there were two rifles used. The indicated locations are in the same building concluded by the Warren Commission to be the site of a lone assassin, but at points further west in this building and on two different floors."[85]

In other words, Wecht's findings indicate that there was more than one assassin and that none of the shots was fired from the "Oswald window." Why Dr. Wecht's professional opinion differs so greatly from the official autopsy findings touches on one of the most curious aspects of the official investigation of the Kennedy assassination, the autopsy conducted at Bethesda Naval Hospital on the night of November 22.

Within minutes after the shooting Kennedy had been rushed to the emergency room at Parkland Memorial Hospital, where Dr. Malcolm Perry tried to save his life. The physician could see that the president had suffered a massive head wound and a smaller wound in the throat. Perry performed a tracheotomy, cutting through the throat wound in an attempt to open a breathing passage. Afterwards, when hope for the president had been abandoned, Perry met with the press and declared that the wound in the front of the president's neck had been an entry wound.

After some dispute with the Dallas authorities, who correctly claimed that investigation of the crime was their responsibility and that the president's body should remain in Dallas for an autopsy—the Secret Service transferred the body to Air Force One for the trip back to Washington. Approximately eight hours after the shooting, an autopsy was performed at Bethesda Naval Hospital.

The first curious thing about the autopsy was the selection of the surgeons who performed it: Comdr. James J. Humes, senior pathologist and director of laboratories at Bethesda Naval Hospital, Comdr. J. Thornton Boswell, chief of pathology at Bethesda, and Lt. Col. Pierre A. Finck, chief of the Wound Ballistics Pathology Branch of the Armed Forces Institute of Pathology. Despite their impressive titles and valid credentials for the kinds of work they normally do, none of the three had much experience in dealing with gunshot cases. Humes told the commission:

> My type of practice, which fortunately has been in peacetime endeavor to a great extent, has been more extensive in the field of natural disease than violence. However, on several occasions in various places where I have been employed, I have had to deal with violent death, accidents, suicides, and so forth.[86]

Humes did not elaborate as to whether the "suicides and so forth" ever included any gunshot wounds, but his experience with forensic pathology was apparently limited to a single course he took in that subject at the Armed Forces Institute of Pathology.[87] Humes supervised the autopsy, assisted initally only by Boswell, who also lacked any special qualifications to conduct an autopsy in a murder case.[88] After they began, they were joined by Lieutenant Colonel Finck, who, unlike Humes and Boswell, was a member of the American Academy of Forensic Sciences. Finck was not a fellow of the academy, but a provisional member, commensurate with his limited background in forensic pathology; his experience with autopsies of gunshot deaths was mainly confined to reviewing files, pictures, and records of autopsies conducted by other surgeons.[89]

In the autopsy report signed by Humes, Boswell, and Finck, two gunshot wounds are described as the cause of death. The one in the right rear portion of the head caused extensive brain damage; the other "entered the right superior posterior thorax above the scapula" —in other words, above the right shoulder near the base of the neck —"and traversed the soft tissues of the supra-scapular and supra-clavicular portions of the base of the right side of the neck . . . damaged the trachea and made its exit through the anterior surface of the neck"[90] In other words, the bullet passed through the president's neck and exited below his Adam's apple, presumably causing the hole the Dallas doctor described as an entry wound. The commission concluded that the neck wound was caused by exhibit 399, the nearly intact bullet found in Parkland Hospital, the miraculous single bullet.

However, the autopsy report presented to the commission was not the original version. Humes testified that there had been an earlier draft which he later revised. What became of the earlier version? Humes burned it in his fireplace on Sunday morning, November 24.[91] How did it differ from the final, official version? The answer may be inferred from the report of two FBI agents who were present during the autopsy:

> During the latter stages of this autopsy, Dr. Humes located an opening which appeared to be a bullet hole which was *below the shoulders* and two inches to the right of the middle line of the spinal column.
>
> This opening was probed by Dr. Humes with the finger, at which time it was determined that the trajectory of the missile entering at this point had entered at a *downward position of 45 to 60 degrees.* Further probing determined that the distance travelled by this missile was a short distance inasmuch as *the end of the opening could be felt with the finger.*
>
> . . . Dr. Humes stated that the pattern was clear that the one bullet had entered the President's back and *worked its way out of the body during external cardiac massage.*[92] (Emphasis added.)

Thus, the FBI report suggests that the draft of the autopsy report Dr. Humes destroyed may have differed from the final version in three important points regarding the wound in the president's back:

1) it was below the shoulders, not in the base of the neck, 2) the bullet entered at a steep downward angle which could not line up with the "exit wound" in the throat, and 3) the bullet did not traverse the president's body, but only penetrated a short distance.

Dr. Humes's own testimony before the commission makes it clear that he did not even know of the wound in the president's throat during the autopsy. It had been obscured by the tracheotomy performed in Dallas, and Humes only learned of it during a long-distance telephone conversation the next day with Dr. Perry, who had performed the emergency surgery.[93]

Obviously, the bullet that struck the president's back could not have caused his throat wound if it did not pass through his body. Nor could it have done so if it entered at a steep downward angle, unless it struck bone and turned upward. And if the entrance wound were below the shoulders, how could the "Oswald window," above and behind the president, be lined up with an exit wound under his Adam's apple? And what does all this do to the single bullet theory, which requires the bullet after leaving the president's body to strike Governor Connally?

The absence of satisfactory official answers to these questions has led to more skepticism about the Warren Report. Many critics have charged that the throat wound was caused by the entry of a bullet, as Dr. Perry in Dallas believed, and have found this theory consistent with much additional evidence that some of the shots came from the grassy knoll ahead and to the right of the limousine. The FBI report also seems to present yet another major problem for the single bullet theory. And the fact that the autopsy surgeons changed their conclusions the day after the autopsy and destroyed the earlier version of their report suggests to many that they were ordered to reverse their findings to comply with the official account of the shooting.

Dr. Cyril Wecht's investigation of the medical evidence has set some of these suspicions to rest while exacerbating other doubts. On August 23 and 24, 1972, Wecht was permitted to examine the autopsy photographs, x-rays, and other materials. Dr. Wecht reports: "The x-rays and photographic materials give every indication of being authentic . . . and the facial features, *where they can be seen,** are

*Emphasis added by this author in order to highlight a point not further

consistent with the examining author's recollections of the President."[94]

Regarding the location of the wound in the president's back, Wecht says that it is 5.7 centimeters (about 2 1/4 inches) "below the lowest crease in the neck." An unpublished diagram prepared by Wecht and Smith further clarifies this location: it is just about where the final version of the autopsy report has it, not below the shoulders as reported by the FBI agents.

Wecht found no support for the "grassy knoll theory." "The available evidence, assuming it to be valid, gives no support to theories which postulate gunmen to the front or right-front of the Presidential car," Wecht and Smith report.

Of the wound in the throat Wecht says, "lack of sharp focus in the photographs showing the tracheotomy prevented the author from identifying and locating the alleged exit wound of the bullet." He further states that he was unable to corroborate earlier reports of the location of the exit wound through his own observations, but assuming the location given—nine centimeters below the lowest crease in the neck—and the position of the president shown in photographs of the assassination, Wecht concludes that the angle of passage of the bullet precludes its having been fired from the sixth-floor window of the book depository identified by the commission as the position of the lone assassin.

Wecht also notes that the x-rays of the president's upper back and chest and of Governor Connally's chest reveal metallic fragments unreported by the Warren Commission or the official autopsy report, and he raises the question of whether the nearly intact exhibit 399 could have been the source of all this metal. Exhibit 399 was found to weigh about 2.5 grains less than a completely intact bullet of the same type, and one fragment from Governor Connally's wrist alone weighed 0.5 grains.

The Wecht-Smith analysis of the evidence made available to Dr.

---

addressed by Wecht and Smith in their report. However, Dr. Wecht's reputation as a medical detective is formidable. If, as implied in the report, he were satisfied that all of the autopsy photographs he was shown were, in fact, pictures of the body of President Kennedy, then I reserve no doubts about the matter.

Wecht in the National Archives is lengthy and detailed and concludes that the assassination was the work of at least two gunmen firing from the Texas School Book Depository but that no one fired from the commission's "Oswald window." But the other questions raised by Wecht and Smith are based not on medical evidence, but on the absence of some medical evidence and the circumstances surrounding the autopsy.

Wecht and Smith report that an unidentified army general claimed to have been in overall charge of the autopsy, that orders were given not to dissect the president's back-throat wound, and that a roll of film taken during the autopsy was seized from a medical corpsman by a Secret Service agent, who then deliberately destroyed it. But their most macabre and suspicious discovery concerns medical evidence which is missing from the National Archives.

Government reports confirm that the president's brain was removed during the autopsy and preserved for further study,* that sections of brain and other tissue were prepared for microscopic analysis, and that photographs of the brain and the interior of the chest cavity were also made. All of these items were reportedly turned over to the National Archives by Adm. George Burkley, President Kennedy's personal physician, but the archives has no record of them. The brain and other essential medical evidence are missing, and the government offers no accounting for them.

Certainly emotions, propriety, and questions of taste must be acknowledged as possible explanation for some of the suspicious conduct of those persons and organizations involved in the autopsy and having custody of the medical evidence. The Secret Service agent who confiscated and destroyed photographs of the murdered president may have seen them only as an ultimate indignity to the leader he and his fellows had failed to protect. Surely the autopsy pictures must not be published, if only out of respect for the feelings of those close to John Kennedy.** Even

*A standard autopsy procedure where the brain must be examined. Examination of a brain for bullet paths, fragments, and so forth can only be done after it has been stored for a period in a preservative solution.

**Unfortunately, such sensitivity does not extend to the family of Lee Harvey Oswald; a gruesome photograph of Oswald's body, taken after the

public discussion of these matters is repugnant. But such consid-
erations should not be used to keep qualified, independent medical investigators such as Dr. Wecht from getting at the truth.
The government owes a debt of candor to the people, and it has
not discharged it. As Dr. Wecht wrote:

> As the person trained in criminological procedures delves more
> deeply into the case, the more certain he becomes that the truth
> about the Kennedy assassination is not the "official truth" con-
> tained in the Warren *Report.* Truth was not the aim of the
> Commission, nor was truth the end product of its labors. We will
> know the real truth about the assassination only when impartial
> and scientific investigation replaces governmental promulgation
> and official obfuscation.[95]

In reviewing some of the problems that have been raised with the
Warren Report, I cannot claim to have summarized adequately the
thorough, painstaking work of Wecht and Smith, Meagher, Josiah
Thompson, Edward Jay Epstein, Harold Weisberg, Mark Lane, or
the others who have refused to accept anything less than the truth
about the Kennedy assassination. Nor, in fairness, can I claim to have
represented fully the Warren Commission's case in support of its
conclusions.

The serious student of the Kennedy assassination must begin with
the Warren Report, then read the critics, meanwhile keeping the
twenty-six volumes of testimony and evidence within reach. Only a
few of us have the time and opportunity to do so, and, in the long
run, this works in favor of the official account. The medical, ballistic,
and photographic points in the controversy are difficult for the layman to follow, and memory of them blurs rapidly with the passage
of time. Finally, most of us are left with nothing but the recollection
that a handful of individuals disagreed with the investigative resources of the federal government and a panel of demonstrably hon-

---

autopsy surgeons had sewed it back together, was released by the Dallas
police and published in national tabloids. Perhaps this was a reversion to the
medieval practice of displaying the mutilated bodies of felons in a prominent
position near the city gates.

orable men. Official history tends to survive.

But anyone with enough doubt and energy to pursue the mystery of Dallas will find, at the very least, that a staggering number of questions remain unanswered. He will find that this brief review presents only some of those questions, none of them fully. He will find, in other words, that this summary of the problems with the Report is only the tip of an iceberg.

3 THE TECHNOLOGY OF TRUTH

All sin is a kind of lying.
—St. Augustine: *Against Lying*

The idea of using a machine to catch someone in a lie is one of the most repulsive ever conceived in our technological society. It is also among the most fascinating. In our world information is power, and the machines that process information—from printing press to computer—have become the instruments of power. The most potent of these is the device that can separate truth from falsehood.

Lie detection is a curious craft that lurks on the fringes of scientific respectability. Senator Ervin called it twentieth-century witchcraft, but lie detection played a prominent role in the unfolding Watergate drama, as it does in nearly every important case in which one person disputes another's testimony. There are over twelve hundred practitioners of the craft in the United States, and they conduct more than two hundred thousand examinations annually.[1] Police departments routinely give narcotics informers polygraph tests before acting on their tips. Rape victims are often asked to submit to a test to support their accusations. Retail chain stores have turned to the polygraph in the face of rising employee pilferage, and several departments of the federal government, including the Central Intelligence Agency and the National Security Agency, require all prospective employees to undergo a polygraph examination. Yet twelve states* have passed laws prohibiting the lie-detector test as a condition of employment.[2] Lie detection is clearly one of the most controversial and least-understood issues in America.

In the popular imagination, the polygraph is a kind of litmus for liars that gives a clear and unequivocal signal if someone takes liber-

*Alaska, California, Connecticut, Delaware, Hawaii, Maryland, Massachusetts, New Jersey, Oregon, Pennsylvania, Rhode Island, and Washington.

ties with the truth. In fact, this is completely wrong. Lie detection is a subtle and complex psychological game played by the interrogator and the suspect. The polygraph and its successor, the psychological stress evaluator, are highly sensitive instruments necessary to the game. They are, in effect, the board on which the game is played. But the essence of lie detection is the game, not the board.

Lie detection is basic to my investigation of the assassination of President Kennedy. The psychological stress evaluator, because of its unique features, permitted me to play the game with new rules. It enabled me to play the game with "opponents" remote from me by thousands of miles and ten years. But it also let me play at close hand, covertly, sitting down with some of the major characters of the Dallas drama, with only a journalist's tape recorder separating us. The game as I played it bore little resemblance to chess. It was more like hunting.

The PSE led to discoveries, probabilities, and conclusions. Sometimes when the PSE indicated that a person was lying, the things he said were manifestly implausible and could be called into question without the aid of the instrument. In other cases I was later able to prove that, whether or not the person was intentionally lying as the PSE indicated, what he said was not true. But for the reader to comprehend fully all the results of my investigation, he should understand the lie-detection game in general and the PSE in particular.

One of the most puzzling and disturbing incidents uncovered by the PSE is a mysterious polygraph examination given by the Dallas police in the middle of the night of November 22, 1963. The full meaning of what took place in that interrogation room can only be understood by contrasting normal polygraph practice with what amounts to a very strange deviation from established lie-detection procedures.

So, to provide the reader with the background to evaluate critically my results and draw his own conclusions, I offer here a short course in the technology of truth—the art, craft and science of lie detection.

Nearly every society known to recorded history has used some means of settling matters of disputed truth. The Old Testament recounts the familiar story of King Solomon and the two women who both claimed to be the mother of the same infant. As we know,

Solomon settled the matter by proposing to cut the child in two and award half to each claimant and was able to identify the real mother by her reaction to this suggestion. Solomon's technique had two things in common with nearly every other lie detection procedure subsequently devised: it depended on close observation of the subject, and it involved a bit of trickery.

The effectiveness of any lie-detection technique is enhanced by the subject's belief that the technique will work. There is an apocryphal account of a primitive tribe that kept a mule in a darkened hut to function as the community lie detector. Whenever a crime was committed, the elders lined up the tribe members and sent them into the hut one at a time. Each person was told to go into the hut and pull the mule's tail. The guilty party, they were told, would be kicked by the mule. However, the mule's tail had been smeared with soot, and the tribal elders got their man by watching for someone to emerge from the hut with clean hands.

Obviously this system had two defects: a guilty person who didn't believe in it could pass undetected, and the innocent person who put his trust in the procedure might end up seriously injured and defamed as well. Unfortunately, much real-life lie detection shares these drawbacks.

In our own society confidence in the efficacy of the polygraph often leads to confessions. In fact, I have been told by several experts in the field that there are a sizable number of polygraph practitioners who have never learned to operate the instrument at all, but who successfully use it to solve criminal cases. Their technique consists of putting the suspect through the routine of a polygraph examination, meanwhile ignoring the cryptic tracing of the instrument's pens. When the test is finished, the examiner looks the suspect dead in the eye and says, "The machine says you lied!" A surprising number of felons break down and confess at this point, but the person who indignantly stands his ground is judged by the examiner to have told the truth.

In such cases the polygraph acts as nothing more than an expensive stage prop, and some interrogators have been able to achieve the same result without even producing the instrument. A leading text on criminal interrogation advises the following:

Regardless of the unavailability of Polygraph test facilities, much can be gained by telling a subject, "All right, if you're telling the truth, as you say you are, then you're willing to take a lie detector test!" Without waiting for an answer, the interrogator should then say, "I'll immediately arrange for a test," and at the same time the interrogator should pick up a telephone directory or go to the door and direct someone to phone "the lie-detector laboratory." A guilty subject is likely to voice some objection or ask a question about the test or give an excuse for not wanting to be tested at that time. On the other hand, truthful subjects ordinarily will welcome the opportunity to take such a test. This customary difference in reactions to the suggestion of a Polygraph test provides a very helpful indication as to whether the interrogator has before him a guilty or innocent subject."[3]

Such tactics may seem sneaky and contemptible, but perhaps a policeman investigating a serious crime may be forgiven if he takes a pragmatic approach to his job. He is, after all, only trying to find the truth. The danger, of course, is that he will come to believe this method infallible.

The employment of this kind of sham by police and other polygraph examiners is partly responsible for the bad name the instrument has earned. However, defenders of the polygraph are quick to point to the many instances in which the instrument has worked on the side of civil liberty.

Even cases which are investigated thoroughly and conscientiously by the police occasionally lead to the conviction of an innocent person. Perhaps the largest single reason for such miscarriages of justice is mistaken identity. Eyewitness testimony is notoriously unreliable, but often it is the only evidence available; and more than one innocent person has been given a long prison sentence or even the death penalty, simply because he bore a superficial resemblance to someone else. In such situations, lie detection may be the last and only hope of the accused.

Unlike eyewitness testimony, the results of lie-detector tests have, until recently, been inadmissible as evidence in federal courts. The earliest attempt to exonerate a defendant through a lie detector examination was in the case of *Frye* v. *United States* in 1923. An appellate court refused to admit the test results as evidence because the technique had no scientific standing[4] The defendant lost his appeal and began serving a life sentence for murder. Fortunately, three years later the actual killer confessed to the crime and the innocent man was released from prison.[5]

During the half-century since the Frye case, federal courts have steadfastly resisted the admission of the lie detector as evidence. Recently, however, there has been a weakening of this resolve. In 1972 a federal judge tried unsuccessfully to permit lie-detector results to be used as evidence for the defense in a criminal case.[6] In another 1972 federal case, *United States* v. *Ridling*, a defendant accused of committing perjury before a grand jury tried to have polygraph results confirming his innocence admitted as evidence. The court, in what may be a landmark decision, decided that polygraph examinations were acceptable scientific evidence as are fingerprints, voice identifications, and blood analyses because "the state of the science is such that the opinions of experts will assist the trier of fact to understand the evidence," an implicit reference to one of the rules of evidence for U.S. District Courts.[7] The *Ridling* decision is under appeal, however, and the status of polygraph evidence in federal cases remains uncertain.

Many state courts have been admitting lie-detector tests as evidence for several years under a condition known as "stipulation." This means both the prosecution and defense stipulate, before the test is administered, that the results will be admitted as evidence, regardless of the outcome. Also there is prior agreement on the conditions under which the examination will be given, who will actually conduct the examination, and similar matters. Recently, some state courts have admitted polygraph evidence without stipulation, that is, over the objection of the prosecution. While there seems to be little danger that the lie detector will ever replace the jury system as a means of deciding guilt or innocence, it has clearly gained considerable legal respectability during the five decades since the *Frye* case.

Scientific lie detection is based on the fact that the act of lying produces certain momentary changes in the body. This is not surprising; we are all familiar with certain nonverbal clues that suggest a speaker is not telling the truth. If he blushes, hesitates, fails to look us straight in the eye, or swallows hard, we are inclined to doubt him. It's not proof, but it's enough to make us suspicious.

Effective lying is an adult talent; children make the worst liars because they lack experience, but as they get older, they learn by observing grown-ups. It's basically a matter of self-control, and some learn to be better at it than others. In fact, some people become master liars; they can look you in the eye and, without blush or hesitation, convince you of the most improbable fictions. Yet even such a virtuoso will experience subtle, transient bodily changes as he delivers his falsehood, and with the right instrument these can be detected.

The first modern scientific attempt to detect the physiological effects of deception was made in the last decade of the nineteenth century. It involved a somewhat primitive device used to measure the blood pressure of criminal suspects during interrogation.

Later, researchers discovered that deception was accompanied by certain characteristic changes in respiration patterns. In the 1920s they developed an instrument that could simultaneously record pulse, respiration, and blood pressure. The instrument was later improved by adding a galvanometer to record slight changes in the electrical resistance of the skin (known as the galvanic skin reflex, or GSR), and this device became the prototype of the modern polygraph.[8]

Physically the polygraph has changed little since the 1930s. The subject sits in a chair, and the examiner stretches a ten-inch corrugated rubber tube across his chest. The rubber expands and contracts as the subject breathes, resulting in measurable changes in the air pressure inside the tube. The subject's arm is encircled by an inflatable blood-pressure cuff, and a pair of electrodes are attached to his fingers. The readings from these "sensors" are recorded by pens on a moving chart in view of the examiner.[9]

The apparatus is usually compact and portable, but considerable care is exercised in selecting and preparing the room in which the polygraph is to be used. An examiner would not, for example, set up the instrument and attempt to test a subject in a crowded corridor. The environment must be free from anything that might startle or distract the subject during the examination. Typically, polygraph examinations are conducted in small, windowless rooms. The walls are bare, except, in some cases, for a one-way mirror through which the subject can be observed from an adjacent room. Normally only the subject and the examiner are present during the test.[10]

While the polygraph equipment has changed very little over the years, there has been considerable development in the way the instrument is used. Obviously the bodily changes recorded by the polygraph can result from factors other than deception; anxiety and general nervous tension will produce similar chart patterns. But successive refinements in the questioning technique have enabled the polygraph examiner to discriminate between deception and these other factors with increasing accuracy.

The essence of polygraph testing is the comparison of the subject's bodily reactions as he responds to different questions. The test is a highly structured series of questions calculated to produce a pattern of physiological responses that will distinguish the truthful subject from the one who is lying. There are a variety of testing procedures in use, all of which are based on three elementary techniques: the relevant-irrelevant technique, the control question technique, and the peak of tension technique.

The relevant-irrelevant technique consists of asking the subject a series of questions, some which bear directly on the matter under investigation and others which do not.[11] For example, a prospective employee might be asked the following questions in an attempt to verify his application for a job:

1. Are you wearing a wristwatch?
2. Do you have a high school diploma?
3. Is today Thursday?
4. Were you honorably discharged from the service?*

A truthful applicant is expected to show no greater reaction as he answers questions 2 and 4 than he does on questions 1 and 3. High school diplomas and honorable discharges are not subjects that most people find particularly stressful. However, a person who is lying

*Actual polygraph tests would involve more questions than this example.

about either of these matters would very likely show a significantly stronger reaction to the relevant question.

If the applicant did show such a reaction, would the polygraph examiner immediately brand him a liar? No, at least, a competent and responsible examiner would not. There could be many reasons for the stress other than deception. The examiner would discuss his findings with the applicant to see if he could determine whether some outside issue had affected the test. He might discover, for example, that the applicant was made to repeat his last year in high school before he was given a diploma and felt angry and frustrated about this subject. The examiner would probably give the applicant another polygraph test, asking him such questions as, "Do you intend to tell me the truth about your high school diploma?"

The relevant-irrelevant technique is used when the issue under investigation is not, in itself, a stressful matter, for example, the details of an employment application. However, it is of limited effectiveness in criminal cases, because such questions as, "Did you take the missing money?" are likely to produce stronger polygraph reactions than irrelevant questions, regardless of the truthfulness of the suspect. The control question technique was devised to deal with this problem.

The objective of the control question technique is to get the suspect to lie about a matter unrelated to the matter under investigation and then compare this response to his reaction when questioned about the main issue.[12] Suppose, for example, a polygraph examiner knows that the suspect he is testing once stole a car and got away with the crime. Now he is trying to find out if this same individual stole a missing sum of money. He would ask the suspect, "Have you ever stolen an automobile?" The suspect would, of course, deny it, producing a strong reaction on the polygraph. Then the examiner would ask, "Did you take the money?" If the polygraph shows an equal or stronger reaction to this second denial than was produced by the control question about the automobile, the examiner would conclude that the suspect was lying. If the response was weaker, the person would be cleared of stealing the money.

In most cases, however, the polygraph examiner will not have the advantage of knowing of outside issues that the suspect is likely to lie about. Instead, he will use a control question such as, "Have you ever taken anything that did not belong to you?" instructing the suspect to answer this in the negative. (Nearly every polygraph examiner I've spoken to believes that absolutely everyone has, at some time in his life, stolen something.) Other control questions will be included in the test, such as, "When you were a child, did you ever knowingly lie to your parents?" or, "When you were in school, did you ever cheat on an examination?"

Not surprisingly, there are many individuals who will show a very strong polygraph reaction when responding to any question of an accusatory nature. Polygraph examiners refer to such a person as a "guilt-complex responder." Guilt-complex responders will show deception-like reactions to questions such as, "Did you shoot Abraham Lincoln?" or, "Did you take the Holy Grail?" To reduce the margin of error, examiners will usually include one or more questions in the examination about crimes which are completely fictitious, but which the suspect believes to be real.[13]

For example, the examiner investigating the theft of some money from a strongbox might tell a suspect that he is going to be questioned about the money and a missing watch, when, in fact, the watch is entirely imaginary. The examiner will observe the suspect's reaction to, "Did you take the missing money?" and compare it to his reaction to, "Did you take the missing watch?" Even if the suspect reacts strongly to the question about the money, he will be cleared by the examiner if he shows an equally strong reaction to the guilt-complex question about the fictitious watch.

The peak of tension technique is intended to determine whether or not a suspect has certain incriminating knowledge of a crime.[14] Suppose, for example, that the robbery of a private home has been reported in the newspapers, but only the burglar, the victim, and the police know that a valuable ruby necklace was the only item stolen. The polygraph examiner will construct a list of questions such as, "Do you know about the diamond ring?" and "Do you know about the gold cufflinks?" inserting among them the question, "Do you know about the ruby necklace?"

While testing a suspect, the examiner will explain that the purpose of the test is to determine whether he knows what was taken from the home. Before the actual test, he will show the suspect the list of questions and may even leave it in view during the test. The reactions of the suspect having guilty knowledge of the burglary are expected to increase with each question, peaking on the question about the ruby necklace and dropping off rapidly on the subsequent questions.

A peak of tension test in a murder case might consist of asking the suspect about a variety of weapons, such as a gun, a knife, a rope, and so forth. In theft or embezzlement cases the questions might concern different sums of money. In some peak of tension tests, the suspect is not even asked to respond to questions; his polygraph reactions to the subjects introduced by the examiner are enough to show if he has more than casual knowledge of the matter under investigation. In one homicide case the murderer was correctly identified simply by observing his polygraph reactions to a series of photographs of young women, one of whom was the victim.

Knowing how the polygraph is used in lie detection, one may be inclined to doubt that it works at all, except as the mule did in the darkened hut. What the instrument seems to be measuring is anxiety, and that is a very individual thing. Of course, the peak of tension technique would be expected to work under the proper circumstances, but that does not, strictly speaking, seem to be lie detection; a murderer who reacts when shown a picture of his victim is responding to a matter of life and death, not truth and falsity. It is difficult to believe that general rules can be established about the way everyone's pulse or respiration will react to the experience of telling a lie.

This is the crux of much of the controversy over lie detection: Does the polygraph, in fact, work? The only way to settle the question is to try it and see.

This, however, is more easily said than done. The experience of a policeman or investigator using the polygraph in the field may convince him of the instrument's validity, but this is really not scientific proof. Scientific knowledge is discovered in the laboratory, where cause and effect can be separated neatly in a controlled experiment, but there is a vast distance between the laboratory and the police interrogation room. It has proved extremely difficult to duplicate in a controlled experiment some of the important elements in a real-life polygraph examination.

Typically, scientists trying to evaluate the polygraph will recruit college students as volunteer subjects, stage a mock crime—one of several subjects might "steal" a ten-dollar bill left in another room out of sight of the experimenter—and then attempt to identify the "guilty" person through a series of polygraph examinations. Experimenters also play a number game with their subjects: a subject picks a number, and the experimenter tries to determine which one he picked by interrogating him with the polygraph. Obviously, a volunteer subject in this kind of experimental situation is going to show a much milder polygraph reaction than would someone lying about an issue of personal importance.

Remarkably, such experiments have confirmed the polygraph as a lie-detection device. Experimenters no longer try to determine whether or not the polygraph works; the only question that remains is how well does it work? The answer found by most researchers is that the polygraph works very well. Reports of its accuracy in the laboratory range from 73 percent to 97 percent, with several other studies falling somewhere in between.[15]

Since the polygraph performs so well in the laboratory, it might be expected to achieve even higher levels of accuracy in real-life field situations, and this has been the experience of the few researchers who have attempted to study it in such an environment. The problem inherent in this kind of study is that it is usually difficult or impossible to establish with certainty whether the results of any given polygraph examination are correct, so less data are available from field studies than have been produced by laboratory experiments. However, researchers who have done systematic studies of the polygraph in the field report that it is an effective and accurate lie-detection device.[16]

Given that the polygraph technique works, why it works remains to be established. Why is a lie invariably accompanied by these momentary changes in the body? Can they be suppressed? What about drugs and hypnosis? Is there, in fact, any way to "beat the box"? All of these questions can be reduced to one: what is the psychological and physiological basis of the polygraph technique? There are so many different and contradictory answers to this question that it appears that none of the polygraph practitioners really knows exactly why his technique works.

Truth and Deception by Inbau and Reid, which is the standard text on the polygraph, offers the following explanation:

> Concern over possible detection appears to be the principal factor accounting for the physiological changes that are recorded and interpreted as symptoms of deception . . . unless a person is concerned over the possibility that his deception will be detected, his Polygraph records will not disclose that deception.
>
> Consciousness of wrongdoing, or remorsefulness, may serve as contributing factors, but their effect upon the physiological changes seem to be of minor importance when compared with the concern over detection.[17]

In other words, the bodily changes detected by the polygraph are not produced by the lie; they result from the subject's fear that the lie will be detected.

This theory seems to be the working hypothesis of many polygraph examiners. Before every polygraph test, the examiner interviews the subject. There are several objectives of the pretest interview, but one of the most important seems to be the "conditioning" of the subject to believe, beyond any doubt, that the polygraph works and will show if he is lying.

Before conducting the actual polygraph test, many examiners will also conduct an "acquaintance test," or "card test," to demonstrate the instrument's effectiveness to the subject. The examiner offers the subject a deck of cards and tells him to pick one. The examiner then conducts a polygraph test consisting of questions about the card, and the subject is instructed to lie to the examiner. When the examiner looks up from his charts and correctly identifies the card, the subject is conditioned to believe that the polygraph is going to catch him if he lies about anything else.

However, this kind of card trick is not the easiest thing to accomplish with a polygraph; similar tests in the laboratory achieve only 90 percent success. If the examiner fails to make a correct call, the subject will be counterconditioned and will be less inclined to fear that the polygraph is going to detect his lies. Success in the card test seems to be so important to an effective polygraph examination that the leading polygraph text offers this advice: use a marked deck.[18]

Another variation of the card test is the number game, in which the subject picks a number, say, between one and ten. The examiner leaves the interrogation room, and the subject is instructed to write the number on a piece of paper and put it in his pocket while the examiner is absent. Then the examiner returns and proceeds to give the subject a "polygraph test" to learn the number he picked. The popularity of the number game with examiners is one reason that so many polygraph examination rooms are equipped with one-way mirrors.

While many polygraph examiners feel that they must persuade their subjects of the instrument's infallibility, there is at least one laboratory study which indicates that such dramatics make no measurable improvement in the accuracy of the test.[19] Moreover, it is a commonplace of the polygraph profession that the very best subjects for the test are those people who are most familiar with the instrument's capabilities and limitations, the polygraph examiners themselves. Familiarity with the polygraph seems not to breed contempt.

If fear of getting caught is what makes the polygraph work, can someone defeat the instrument by convincing himself that it won't catch him? The answer is that he might be able to do it if he learned the technique developed by Soviet intelligence. The Soviets have never made much use of the polygraph themselves, but they perfected a method of indoctrinating their agents with the belief that the polygraph could not catch them, and for a time this countermeasure proved very effective.

Good information on polygraph countermeasures is scarce, because if someone invents a way of beating the box, he isn't likely to advertise the fact. Polygraph specialists won't publicize anything that would reduce the effectiveness of their instruments, and the successful liar can probably resist the urge to boast about his triumph. But there are many reports of countermeasure techniques that have been tried and either didn't work very well or failed completely.

Probably the oldest trick in the book is to attempt to distort the polygraph reading on an irrelevant or control question so that it cannot be distinguished from a deceptive response to a relevant question. The crudest way of doing this is by flexing the leg or back muscles or the anal sphincter while answering, but some polygraphs come equipped with a special chair that will cause the instrument to register even the slightest bodily movement. This also catches the subject who tries to achieve the same result by putting a tack in his shoe and pressing his foot down on it. Actually, most attempts of this kind will be noticed by a good polygraph examiner even if he is not equipped with the special chair. They only makes his job easier, because he knows, even before he asks the relevant question, that the subject is going to lie about it.

Drugs and hypnotism are among the more exotic polygraph countermeasures. It is impossible to generalize about the effects of drugs on the polygraph test, because there is such a wide variety of drugs which can produce many different kinds of changes in the body. Some research has been done on drugs and the polygraph,[20] but much yet remains unknown. For a drug to be completely effective as a polygraph countermeasure, it must, in addition to suppressing the subject's reactions when lying, produce no other physiological effects which would show up on the polygraph and make the examiner suspicious, and it must be undetectable in a urinalysis. If any pharmacologist has been able to fill this tall order, he has, as we should expect, kept it to himself.

Hypnotism seems like a more effective way of beating the box, but, as with so much other lie-detection lore, there are conflicting reports of its use as a countermeasure. One source told me that self-hypnosis can be used to control such otherwise involuntary physical processes as pulse, blood pressure, and perspiration, which are recorded by the polygraph. Another indicated that hypnotic suggestion can be used to instill in a subject absolute confidence that the polygraph cannot catch him, thus removing the fear of detection some think necessary for the polygraph to work. (This may be the technique used by Soviet intelligence.)

Regardless of whatever limited success intelligence services may have achieved with sophisticated countermeasures, polygraph experts say most liars get caught when they try to fool the instrument. And, paradoxically, a very few aren't caught precisely because they don't try to beat the instrument.

Polygraph examiners have long known of what they call "wash out." The more often a subject lies, the less distinct is his reaction on the polygraph.[21] If the test is repeated often enough, the polygraph chart will look as though he is telling the truth. For this reason polygraph examiners will not usually test a subject immediately after he has been interrogated because he may have washed out his anxiety by repeating the lie over and over again.[22] Also, sheer fatigue may produce a condition known as "adrenal exhaustion," which also makes it impossible to read deception in the polygraph chart.[23] An examiner will wait until the subject is well-rested and has not discussed the issue under investigation for several hours.

Strangely, a subject may unintentionally wash himself out by giving up all hope of beating the polygraph. In a few cases a criminal suspect has taken a polygraph test with the absolute conviction that he would be caught by the instrument, but for some reason he lied anyway. His belief in the polygraph was so complete that his lies didn't generate enough emotional effort to register on the instrument, and to his astonishment the examiner called the test "inconclusive" or, in some cases, cleared him.[24]

The most celebrated polygraph beater of recent years was the writer Clifford Irving. Irving and his researcher, Richard Susskind, concocted a bogus autobiography of Howard Hughes and convinced a book publisher, McGraw-Hill, and *Life* Magazine that their manuscript was the billionaire's own story as told to Irving in a series of interviews. Irving collected $650,000 for the manuscript, a sum the publishers thought they were paying, through Irving, to Howard Hughes.

Clifford Irving was a master liar. Typical of the consummate skill with which he promoted his hoax was his adroit handling of a cross-examination by CBS reporter Mike Wallace on the television program "Sixty Minutes." At one point Wallace asked Irving if there had been any witnesses to his alleged meetings with Hughes. Irving replied that his researcher, Susskind, had accidentally been present at one meeting in a hotel room. According to Irving, Hughes arrived early for a planned interview and was startled to find Susskind in the room. Irving said that Hughes introduced himself to Irving and

> then after a moment of awkward silence, Hughes reached into his pocket and pulled out a bag—we still disagree; I say it was a

cellophane bag, Susskind says it was a paper bag—and he said to Dick Susskind, "Have a prune."[25]

Hughes's bag of prunes was the virtuoso touch. It was a beauty mark, the faintest of blemishes on the face of an anecdote which might otherwise seem too perfectly pat. If the story were a fabrication, why would its author deliberately create a question about a minor detail? Irving and his researcher might disagree on whether the bag was paper or cellophane, but who could doubt that there was a bag of some kind and that the man who proffered it was Howard Hughes?

Despite Irving's skill as a prevaricator, however, there were enough little flaws in his story to cause some *Life* executives to question it. Irving sought to put the doubts to rest with a bold move: he volunteered to take a lie-detector test. To his horror, his publisher took him up on the offer.

By Irving's own account of the affair[26] his proposal had been pure bluff, and he never expected to have it accepted. But within a couple of hours after making the offer, he was riding an elevator to the thirty-second floor of the McGraw-Hill building where the polygraph examiner waited with his instrument. Irving says that he mumbled a complete confession during that elevator ride but that the publishing executives escorting him to the test couldn't make out what he said.[27]

Irving may have known something of polygraph countermeasures. Although he doesn't say so, his mumbled "confession" could have been an effective ploy to wash out some of the anxiety he might later experience when lying during the exam, and Irving seems to understand the relevant-irrelevant technique. When he was asked, "Is your name Clifford Irving?" he answered, "Yes," but told himself over and over, "My name is Clifford Holmes." However, he says that he experienced tremendous stress when he answered negatively to the questions, "Have you conspired with anyone else to defraud McGraw-Hill of any sums of money?" and, "Have you taken any or all of the $650,000 meant to go to Howard Hughes?"[28]

The written report by the examiner was not shown to Irving, nor was it ever made public, but, as with any other polygraph examiner's report, it had to reach one of three possible conclusions—deception indicated, no deception indicated, or inconclusive. According to Irving, the examiner's remarks to him immediately after the test suggest that the verdict was inconclusive. In any case, it does not appear that the test led to a conclusion of deception indicated.* The test was administered to Irving on December 22, 1971, and he was not unmasked until the middle of the following February. "And," said Clifford Irving, "the subject of the polygraph, as well as the results, was never again mentioned in my presence."[29]

Irving's celebrated victory over the polygraph caused understandable consternation in lie-detection circles. No one claims 100 percent accuracy for the technique, and errors, when they happen, are more often made in the suspect's favor, since most examiners won't accuse a suspect of lying if they think there is the slightest cause to doubt that conclusion. Still, failure in such a famous case is terrible publicity for the polygraph profession. As might be expected, several of the instrument's apologists have offered explanations for the failure of the Irving test.

The most plausible theory is that the polygraph examiner had been influenced, consciously or otherwise, by what he knew about the case before administering the examination. Irving had produced several handwriting samples to support his claims. These included what Irving claimed was Hughes's signature on some cancelled checks and letters and his handwritten notes in the margins of some manuscript pages. The New York firm of Osborn Associates, one of the world's most prestigious experts in the matter of authenticating handwriting, examined these documents, compared them with some authentic samples of Hughes's handwriting from 1936 and 1938, and stated

*Irving's examiner was Mr. Rudolph R. Caputo of the Smith and Wesson Company. Caputo's version of the Irving polygraph test was published in a *New York Times* article on lie detection (James Lincoln Collier, "Again, the truth machines," New York *Times*, November 25, 1973, 6:107–108.) According to Caputo, Irving's responses seemed deceptive, but he had insufficient time to retest the writer, who had to leave to catch a flight back to Ibiza. Caputo says he was therefore forced to call the test inconclusive. The fact that Irving used the impending flight to put a time limit on the test is confirmed by his own account of this incident.

confidently that all were unquestionably written by the same hand.[30] The polygraph examiner may have known this, and, if he did, he may simply not have believed what his instrument seemed to be telling him.

Whether or not this second theory is true, it illustrates the supreme importance of the human element in lie detection. Advocates of the polygraph correctly point out that one can never beat the instrument (assuming it has no electrical or mechanical malfunction), because all it does is record certain physiological variables. The person using the polygraph is the "lie detector," and, if the test is defeated, it is he who was beaten.

Whenever someone sits down to take a polygraph test with the intent of beating it, he enters into a duel of wits with the person on the other side of the instrument. His chances of success are directly proportional to how much he knows about polygraph countermeasures and how well he can apply them, and they are inversely proportional to the skill, knowledge, and experience of the examiner.

In most criminal investigations, the game is weighted heavily in favor of the examiner, because the typical suspect has never even seen a polygraph before the examination. But in the world of international espionage the situation is completely different. The subject may know as much about beating the test as the examiner does about catching liars. The degree of skill and cunning of both participants may rival that encountered in a world chess tournament. A seasoned veteran of military intelligence told me of the continuing lie-detector war that is waged out of public view by the Communist and Western intelligence services.

The Soviets, my informant told me, had beaten the polygraph by thoroughly indoctrinating their agents against fear of detection. After Soviet tanks crushed the Hungarian uprising in 1956, Western Europe was flooded with refugees from the East, and Western intelligence began recruiting from among their ranks. Many were excellent agent material, but it was impossible to check their backgrounds, since all records of their personal histories and nearly everyone who might vouch for them were still on the other side of the mine fields and barbed wire. The Communist intelligence services saw a golden opportunity to plant a few ringers on the opposition, and they took it. Not realizing the Soviets had developed an effective countermeasure, Western intelligence relied entirely on the polygraph to screen recruits, and the Communists soon succeeded in infiltrating the entire Western European intelligence apparatus with double agents.

Fortunately, several of the interlopers had their covers blown through bad luck or carelessness. Western counterintelligence people realized that polygraph screening hadn't worked and quickly learned how the trick had been managed. They now had a hard choice of either developing an effective countercountermeasure or abandoning nearly every one of their operations in Eastern Europe. They began working around the clock on the first alternative.

The Western polygraph specialists solved their dilemma and, in the process, learned things they had never dreamed of about the psychology and physiology of deception. In fact, they accomplished a major breakthrough in the craft of lie detection.

The experts learned that the changes in the human body which result from telling a lie take place on several different levels. On the grossest level there will be symptoms of anxiety if the subject feels real fear of being found out. These are relatively easy to read on a polygraph chart and have always been the established basis of most polygraph lie detection. But, whether or not the deceptive subject feels he is in jeopardy, there are also more subtle changes in his pulse, respiration, and other polygraph variables when he lies, and this happens for reasons quite different from fear.

Simply stated, telling the truth is easier than lying. Is your name John Smith? Were you born in Chicago? If we answer these questions truthfully, we do so with almost no intellectual effort; the response is automatic. But if we are going to lie, we have to do just a little more intellectual work. First of all, we must gag that blabbermouth inside and keep him from blurting out the truth, which is his natural inclination. Then we must quickly review the lie: Is the alias we are using John Smith, or is it Jim Smith? Did we say "Chicago," or did we tell the examiner we were born in Cleveland? We've got to think a bit harder than if we were telling the truth simply to keep from being tripped up. And ever so slightly the brain draws on the body's resources to sustain the effort: the lungs draw a little more oxygen, the heart pumps a bit more blood. And the best of polygraph examiners can read it all in their charts.

But the lie-detector war didn't end with this discovery. The Communists continued to try to find new ways to beat the box, and Western intelligence tried to build better boxes. After the Western services neutralized the Communists' self-confidence countermeasure, the Soviets came up with a new wrinkle, mental arithmetic. It was simple and ingenious. They realized that in spite of the discovery of this new, subtle level of polygraph response, the essence of lie detection was still the comparison of polygraph reactions. If the mental effort of a lie made it stand out on a polygraph chart from the irrelevant and control questions, then the trick was to produce equal mental effort when telling the truth. Every Soviet agent was trained to divide or multiply a pair of numbers in his head immediately after giving a truthful answer during an examination. After a lie, he would let his mind rest. The trick worked: there was absolutely no difference shown on the polygraph charts between true and deceptive responses.

Did our side ever work out a counterploy to defeat this new Soviet trick? Yes, but I don't know what it is. My informant refused to tell me, so I assume the ball is still in the Communist side of the court. If he ever tells me, I'll know that the Soviets have pulled ahead once again and that our own people are working day and night to catch up. The game continues.

Competition between the intelligence services of the East and the West has drawn lie detection out of the shabby world of card tricks and psychological ploys and developed it into an accurate and reliable investigative technique. Through successive refinements, it has dramatically increased the effectiveness of the standard polygraph, although the instrument itself has remained essentially unchanged for over a quarter of a century.

But the lie-detector war has also produced advances in the hardware of lie detection. The research and development sections of intelligence agencies have been experimenting with the use of brain waves, skin temperature, and a host of other physiological variables which can be used to increase the effectiveness of the polygraph. And out of this work has come one of the most dramatic developments in the long history of lie detection: the discovery that the stress accompanying deception causes subtle, inaudible changes in the speaker's voice at the very moment that he is telling a lie. The instrument that can measure this stress is the ultimate lie-detection device, the psychological stress evaluator.

4 THE PSYCHOLOGICAL STRESS EVALUATOR

Give every man thy ear, but few thy voice.
—*Hamlet*, Act II, Scene 3.

No one denied that Riley Brooks killed his friend. Even Brooks admitted that he had gone to the man's house and emptied a pistol into his body. But he insisted that it wasn't murder. The Maryland police didn't believe him, nor did the twelve members of the jury that convicted him of first-degree murder. The jury's verdict was upheld on two appeals and the case was rejected by the United States Supreme Court. Riley Brooks was sent to the Maryland state penitentiary for the rest of his natural life. He would still be there today if it weren't for the psychological stress evaluator.

Brooks had been free on bail during his appeals and, due to an administrative error, he was not picked up afterward. For two years he lived the life of a free man, working at the Bethlehem Steel plant and running a small carry-out shop. His wife had a child, then another. But finally the clerk of the circuit court discovered the arrest order that had never been served. The police came for Brooks that night. They took him from his family and brought him to the state penitentiary. Next morning the sun rose on the first day of Riley Brooks's life sentence.

Brooks was a black working man and his resources were limited, but he kept on with his struggle within the prison walls. After serving two years, he contacted Donald McIntosh, a Baltimore attorney. Like everyone else, McIntosh believed Brooks was guilty, but the cruel way the man had been snatched from his family and thrown into prison disturbed the lawyer. Brooks and his family had suffered because of the court's mistake. McIntosh thought he might be able to use this to get Brooks's sentence reduced.

Donald McIntosh visited his new client at the state penitentiary. To the lawyer, Brooks seemed a gentle person, unlikely to commit a premeditated murder. McIntosh listened carefully to Riley Brooks's side of the story.

On the day of the shooting, the victim had invited Brooks and several other friends to a barbecue at his home. Brooks brought the steaks and picnic supplies and the host supplied the drinks. In fact, the man had been drinking heavily before the cook-out, and Brooks and the other guests arrived to find him in an angry and unpleasant mood. A short time later, in a drunken rage, he produced a gun and drove everyone from his home, shooting at, and barely missing, several of the guests.

Brooks had known the man for years. He went home and telephoned him, pointing out that the steaks, which he had left behind in his hasty departure, were his own property, and if the barbecue was off, he wanted them back. The man told Brooks to come and get them.

When Brooks returned to his friend's house he found the man in the bedroom. The effects of the alcohol were wearing off, and the two men talked for more than an hour. During the conversation the man started drinking again and once more became enraged and drew his gun. The two struggled, a shot was fired into the ceiling, and Brooks succeeded in wrenching the gun from his friend's hand. He started to leave, but the man dove for his bed and drew a second pistol from under the mattress. In fear of his life, Brooks turned and fired. The man was hit, but he still clutched his gun and tried desperately to get his visitor into its wavering sights. Brooks fired again, then several times more. He threw the empty pistol on the floor and fled.

McIntosh was inclined to believe his client, and, if Brooks was telling the truth, it was clearly a case of self-defense, not premeditated murder. Yet there was a damning circumstantial case against him and only Brooks's word that things had happened as he said. Brooks volunteered to take a lie-detector test, but McIntosh was skeptical of the polygraph and its practitioners.

McIntosh had heard of a new type of lie-detection device which was supposed to detect deception in a suspect's voice. McIntosh knew nothing more about the instrument except that it was being used by Lt. Mike Kradz of the Howard County, Maryland, police.

The lawyer knew that Kradz had an impressive reputation for fairness and honesty and was recognized as an expert in lie detection, fingerprinting, handwriting, and nearly every other technique of criminalistics. If Kradz was using the new device, then it must be reliable. McIntosh arranged for a postconviction hearing and proposed to the state's attorney that Kradz give his client a test with the psychological stress evaluator and that the results be admitted as evidence. The prosecutor agreed.

On the appointed day McIntosh and Brooks met with Lieutenant Kradz for the test. The lawyer was pleased to discover that the PSE testing procedure was simple and quick. The policeman reviewed the facts in question, switched on a tape recorder, and began his interrogation of Brooks. He asked the prisoner few more than a dozen questions, stopped the recorder, and rewound the tape. The test was over, Kradz announced, except for the results.

Kradz opened an ordinary-looking attaché case. Set into a panel inside the case were several buttons and switches and a chart drive similar to an electrocardiograph. This, Kradz explained, was the psychological stress evaluator.

The policeman connected the PSE to the tape recorder with a length of electronic cable. He played the tape and stopped just before Brooks's first answer, then switched the recorder to a slower speed and turned it on again. The tape reels turned slowly and Brooks's words became a long, low rumble. The PSE stylus danced back and forth across the moving chart paper, leaving a ragged trail in its wake.

Kradz repeated this procedure for each of Brooks's responses, then switched off the recorder and PSE, tore the strip of chart paper from the instrument, and spent several minutes studying the traces left by the stylus. Finally, he put down the chart and turned to McIntosh. Riley Brooks, said Lieutenant Kradz, was telling the truth.

The lawyer was incredulous; it all had seemed too simple. Could Kradz be certain? The police officer nodded. With the polygraph there was such a thing as an inconclusive result, he said, but not with the PSE. Kradz had personally conducted more than one hundred investigations using the device, and his findings had been positively confirmed by confessions, convictions, or exonerations in almost every case. There was no doubt in Kradz's mind: Riley Brooks shot his friend in self-defense.

McIntosh reflected on this for a moment. If his client's story were true, then the dead man had had a second gun. What happened to it? Why was it never found by the police? He put these questions to Mike Kradz. The policeman shrugged. He couldn't answer them, but, he pointed out, the postconviction hearing was still some weeks off. He suggested they reinvestigate the case.

The two men learned that one person had visited the scene of the shooting after Riley Brooks had fled but before the police arrived—the dead man's widow. After some difficulty they located the woman. The story she told cleared up the mystery.

When she heard the shots, the wife rushed to the bedroom. Brooks was gone and her husband lay mortally wounded, but still alive. She telephoned for the police and asked them to send an ambulance. While she was waiting, she tried to do what she could for her husband. He thrust the second pistol into her hands and told her to hide it and say nothing about it to the police. When the police arrived they found only the gun Brooks had fired. As the ambulance attendants lifted him onto the stretcher, the dying man told the police that Riley Brooks had come into his home and shot him. He was dead on arrival at the hospital emergency room.

At first the widow told the police only what her husband had ordered her to say. On the basis of this and the dying man's accusation, Riley Brooks was arrested and charged with first-degree murder. But after her husband died, the woman felt free to speak the truth, and she told the police about the second gun. However, the state's attorney brought Brooks to trial anyway. When he put the widow on the stand, he failed to ask her any questions that might lead to the revelation of the existence of the second gun or her husband's final instructions. Curiously, Brooks's defense attorney didn't pursue the matter either.

Armed with this information, McIntosh no longer needed to offer lie-detection evidence in his client's behalf. During the years that passed since the trial, a new state's attorney had taken office, and McIntosh had no difficulty in getting his cooperation. The case was promptly taken to Maryland's governor, Marvin Mandel, who granted Riley Brooks a full pardon.[1]

If the PSE evidence had been used in court as planned to reverse Riley Brooks's conviction of first-degree murder, it would have been a dramatic endorsement of the legal status of the new instrument. As it happened, the PSE results fulfilled the more common role of lie detection: they led to the discovery of other physical evidence and testimony that were enough to solve the case. But beyond any doubt, the psychological stress evaluator was the key that freed an innocent man wrongly convicted of murder.

The PSE is the brainchild of three retired army intelligence officers, Allan Bell, Jr., Charles McQuiston, and Wilson Ford. The three men are typical of a very rare breed of modern intelligence officer who practices the ancient cloak-and-dagger craft of espionage using the newest developments of space-age technology.

Colonel Bell is part James Bond and part Thomas Edison. At forty-eight he is a lean, wiry man of medium height. He is entitled to wear the Silver Star, the Legion of Merit, two Bronze Stars, and a chestful of other medals earned during the course of his twenty-six years as soldier and spy. He holds a fifth degree black belt in karate, is an accomplished swordsman and small-arms expert, and is qualified in Chinese knife fighting. He has practiced his trade in sixteen countries around the world.

But Bell is also an inventor with well over a dozen inventions to his credit, including a miniature microdot camera, concealed lock-picking equipment, and a device for neutralizing burglar alarms. Several of the items Bell developed while serving in the army are still classified, and he describes them only as "special-purpose tools."

The idea of a "remote lie detector" or "invisible polygraph" has been a commonplace item on the dream lists of United States intelligence agencies for many years. It's the kind of thing the operational people ask the research and development types for, partly to keep them out of their hair, but also because it would come in very handy if anyone ever figured out how to do it. Government planners rarely give any serious attention to anything more than five years in the future, and the remote lie detector is the kind of thing they say they hope to have in ten years.

Colonel Bell has demonstrated an unusual talent for removing items from these dream lists and translating them into field-ready equipment with a minimum of money and personnel. When he learned of the requirement for a remote lie detector, he considered several alternative ways that it might be done and concluded that, with a modest research and development effort, he could probably build one. He proposed the idea to the army but received a much less than enthusiastic response.

The layman who hears of bugged martinis and spy satellites might believe that intelligence services always use the most advanced technology in everything they do. This is not completely true. Intelligence agencies are very keen on improving their existing functions—the spy satellite of the 1960s and 1970s is essentially an improvement on the U-2 and other reconnaissance planes of the 1940s and 1950s, and these, in turn, were merely a logical extension of the nineteenth-century observation balloon—but when it comes to the kind of innovation which will revolutionize the way they do business, they are as resistant to change as anyone else. Army intelligence wanted a remote lie detector, but not right now, thank you.

Bell and his two associates retired from the army in 1970 and formed Dektor Counterintelligence and Security, Inc. The principal activity of the new company was to develop, manufacture, and sell antibugging equipment for private customers, primarily to combat industrial espionage. But Bell had not forgotten his ideas for a remote lie detector; at Dektor, he carried out the research and development that the army had declined to support.

Bell had already decided that odor and voice were the two media which seemed most promising for the covert detection of emotional stress. Sensitive instruments had been developed which could detect the physical presence of a human being through the odors emanating from his body, and it seemed possible that further refinement would permit the measurement of anxiety by this means. But Bell chose to explore the possibility of detecting stress in the voice because it offered the means to a truly remote device, especially if the stress characteristics could be transmitted over the telephone or other voice-communication medium.

Bell's hunch paid off. The early experiments he and his partners conducted confirmed that emotional stress does indeed produce a detectable change in the human voice. Once they understood the kind of sound pattern they were looking for, the Dektor team was able to design and build an instrument to measure it. This breadboard prototype was the first psychological stress evaluator.

The three inventors decided that the best place to test their new instrument was in front of a television set in Bell's living room as they watched the popular program, "To Tell The Truth." Most television watchers are familiar with the format of this show. A trio of contestants is brought on, each claiming to be the same person, usually someone with an interesting experience or accomplishment, but without a well-known face. A panel of celebrities tries to determine through questioning which of the three is actually the person he claims to be. After the questioning, each panel member makes his choice, and then "the real So-and-So" identifies himself. Bell and his associates decided to play the game with the help of the PSE.

This was an especially difficult test of the PSE for several reasons. First, the "lies" told by the contestants are part of a socially acceptable game-playing situation and would not be expected to produce severe psychological stress. The nervousness that even the truthful contestant experiences during what is likely to be his first appearance on national television should result in comparable stress.

Second, the rules of the game leave the two imposters free either to lie or tell the truth during the questioning by the panel. The comparison of different responses by the same subject—the essence of lie detection—would be a very uncertain procedure, since no one answer could be confidently used as a "true-irrelvant" response.

In fact, the experimenters chose to analyze only the contestants' inital statement, "My name is ———," and to attempt a judgment of truth or deception based solely on the degree of stress exhibited there. The success they reported was phenomenal: out of the seventy-five cases they ran on the PSE, they correctly identified "the real So-and-So" seventy-one times.[2] In other words, the PSE, when used in the most difficult of artificial lie-detection circumstances, had an accuracy of 94.7 percent.

The three inventors conducted a second series of tests of the new instrument, using it instead of a polygraph in 24 conventional lie-detector examinations (that is, relevant-irrelevant, control, and peak of tension tests). These were low-stress experiments with volunteer subjects. The PSE gave the right answer in 22 of the cases, an accuracy of 91 percent.[3]

There was no longer any doubt about it. Bell, Ford, and McQuis ton had accomplished exactly what they set out to do. The remote lie detector was no longer merely an item on someone's dream list; it was a solid reality. It took the three men some time to absorb the idea, and when they did, they were a little frightened.

"We thought about it for a long time," Bell later told me. "At one point we almost decided to break it up, burn our files, forget the whole thing. But then we thought, nobody has the inalienable right to lie, cheat, or steal. So we went ahead with it."

It remained only to field test the PSE in actual criminal cases. The opportunity to do so soon presented itself in the person of Lt. Mike Kradz. One of Kradz's duties as a policeman was to conduct polygraph examinations. He had used the polygraph for years and believed that the instrument was a valuable investigative aid, but there were some things about it he didn't like. For instance, Kradz absolutely refused to perform the theatrics some examiners use to convince a suspect that the polygraph is infallible. He felt that it was hypocritical to lie and then ask others to tell the truth. Kradz always used the polygraph as a lie-detection instrument, never as a stage prop. But without the help of the pretest conditioning mumbo-jumbo, he sometimes came up with inconclusive results. Kradz, a life-long criminologist, felt that there ought to be some scientific way to improve the accuracy of the polygraph. When he heard about the PSE, he thought that might be it.

Kradz obtained one of the first PSEs from Dektor and began using it in conjunction with the polygraph. Whenever he was called upon to give a polygraph examination, he also tape recorded the suspect's answers and ran them through the PSE, then compared the results from the two instruments. In general, the PSE and the polygraph agreed, but the PSE results were clearer. In some cases, however, one instrument indicated truthfulness and the other showed deception. Kradz followed up on every case. Some suspects confessed after the lie-detector tests, some were convicted on the basis of other evidence or testimony, and some were acquitted or the charges against them were dropped.

Kradz ran forty-two examinations with the PSE and polygraph in parallel. The polygraph gave the right answer in thirty-eight of the cases but was inconclusive in the other four. The PSE results, however, were corroborated in every case.[4] Kradz put away his polygraph. During the next year he ran more than one hundred cases with the PSE—everything from homicide to forgery—and was able to confirm his results in almost every instance. Kradz had set out to augment the polygraph; he ended up replacing it.

Word of Kradz's success with the new instrument spread throughout legal and law-enforcement circles around Howard County, a rural and residential area between Baltimore and Washington, D.C. Kradz was already known as an expert in criminalistics, the application of the physical and behavioral sciences to criminal investigation, and he was often "borrowed" by attorneys and nearby police forces to give expert testimony in court or assistance in solving a particularly difficult case. News of his work with the PSE brought a sharp increase in demands for his help.

One of Kradz's biggest customers for PSE examinations was Bernard F. Goldberg, the Howard County public defender. Often when a defendant claimed innocence and asked the public defender's office for help, Goldberg would suggest a PSE examination. Richard J. Kinlein, the local state's attorney, accepted the validity of Kradz's PSE tests and would usually move for dismissal of charges if the examination confirmed that the suspect was innocent.[5] In fact, Kradz's PSE results were accepted by Howard County courts on three occasions—two cases of forgery and one case of assault, attempted murder, and burglary—and resulted in dismissal of charges each time.[6] The three former defendants are no doubt thankful that Bell did not decide to destroy his files and suppress the PSE.

Even if Colonel Bell had burned his files and suppressed his discovery, within a few years other scientists would have come across the principle that is the basis of the PSE. The effect the Dektor inventors discovered is related to a phenomenon that has recently received close attention from biological researchers—physiological tremor. One of the leading investigators of the phenomenon describes it thus:

> The contraction of a voluntary muscle is accompanied by tremors of the muscle in the form of minute oscillations. In an electrical recording of the muscle's activity the tremor can be seen as a trace

of very fine rhythmic movements superimposed on the record of the contraction itself. The amplitude of the oscillations is about a hundredth or a fiftieth as large as that of the total movement produced by the contraction, and the predominant frequency in man is about 10 cycles per second.[7]

In other words, every muscle in the human body, when in use, vibrates minutely ten times each second. The vibrations are too slight to be apparent, but they can be detected with the proper instruments.

Bell and his associates discovered that physiological tremor can be detected in the voice. The vibration of the muscles we use to stretch our vocal cords when we speak causes the pitch of the sound we produce to shift slightly about ten times per second. The effect is exactly what would happen if we plucked a guitar string, then twisted the tuning key back and forth rapidly. Instead of a single note, we would hear an alternately rising and falling tone. In the voice the effect is so slight as to be inaudible, but with the right electronic instruments it shows up as a frequency modulation in the basic vocal formative frequencies.

The key to using this phenomenon in voice lie detection is Bell's discovery that physiological tremor and its effect on the voice disappear under conditions of fear, anxiety, excitement, or, in other words, stress. The voice of an individual under stress does not carry the normal ten cycle per second frequency modulation component, but only the pure vocal formative frequencies. What the polygraph does through its cumbersome measurement of pulse, blood pressure, respiration, and perspiration, Bell and his associates were able to accomplish by electronic analysis of the voice.[8]

The polygraph is, in fact, far from the ideal means of detecting psychological stress, since the variables it measures are at several removes from the source of anxiety, the brain and central nervous system. A deceptive polygraph response shows up on the chart only after several seconds have elapsed from the moment the subject tells a lie: it takes that long for the effect to reach the respiratory and circulatory systems. Meanwhile other, irrelevant factors may move the pens across the polygraph charts. Polygraph examiners have to learn how to establish base lines for each of the variables and must pause several seconds after the answer to one question before asking another.

Physiological tremor, on the other hand, is the terminus of a much shorter path from the central nervous system. Stress patterns appear in the voice at the same moment the subject experiences the stress. PSE examiners don't have to pause between questions and, also unlike polygraph, long narrative answers are permitted. Stress is often seen to appear in a single word or phrase, and this gives the examiner a much sharper picture of the subject's psychological set.

However, the American Polygraph Association disapproves of the PSE for several reasons. The first objection raised by the APA is an irrefutable fact: "The PSE-1," declared the association in its August 1973 declaration, "is not a polygraph."[9] The instrument, says the APA, "does not record the pneumographic and cardiosphygmographic patterns held to be minimal by the APA and by several of the states which license polygraph examiners."[10]

The APA's objection that the PSE does not measure pulse, blood pressure, and respiration is not based on the poetic conceit that all lies originate in the heart, but upon a principle which, at first, seems more substantial. The polygraph measures four physiological variables, while the PSE measures only one. Thus, argues the APA, polygraph results will be more reliable than PSE results. But this argument emphasizes quantity and ignores quality.

Consider, by analogy, the problem of forecasting the weather at some particular location—an airport, for example—over a short time period, say, ninety minutes. The weatherman could use a barometer to measure air pressure, a thermometer to measure air temperature, a hygrometer to measure relative humidity, and an anemometer for wind speed and direction. Armed with these different readings, the forecaster could make an educated guess about the chance of rain during the next hour and a half. However, if he chose instead to use weather radar, he could watch the formation of precipitation areas, observe their location, and track their paths. His forecast would certainly be more accurate based on a single, twentieth-century electronic instrument than if he relied on four different nineteenth-century devices.

The analogy with the PSE and polygraph is exact. When Mike Kradz discontinued parallel operation of the two instruments in his police work and began to use the PSE alone, he did so not only because the PSE was giving him the right answers, but also because the polygraph sometimes gave him the wrong answers. Kradz found that a single physiological variable, the voice, is a more accurate indicator of truth and deception than all of the combined variables monitored by the polygraph.

In addition to its inherently greater accuracy, the PSE has several other advantages over the polygraph. From the suspect's viewpoint, the PSE examination is a much less unpleasant experience than a polygraph test. The mere physical appearance of the polygraph with its straps and wires seems sinister and suggests some exotic means of executing the death penalty. This impression is heightened when the breathing tube is strapped across the suspect's chest, the blood pressure cuff is clamped on his arm, and the GSR electrodes are attached to his hand. The experience itself produces stress. In contrast, a PSE examination is nothing more than a tape-recorded interview. The suspect need not even be aware that it is taking place.

The first actual instance of covert use of the PSE occurred early in the instrument's history, just after Dektor entered into an agreement with another firm which proposed to sell and service the PSE. The Dektor people began to suspect that their new associates were not entirely honest. Colonel McQuiston phoned the president of the other company and recorded the conversation. When he ran the tape through the PSE, his suspicions were confirmed. Being cheated was bad enough, Bell told me later, but lying to the inventors of the PSE was really stupid, and the Dektor people were insulted as much as they were outraged.

Another early covert PSE examination also involved a business deal. One of Dektor's clients, a company, was selling something to another company. What that something was must remain unspecified, but, whatever it was, it was expensive: the buyers said that three million dollars was their final offer. PSE analysis of the tape of a telephone bargaining session indicated that this wasn't true, that the buyers would be willing to pay three and a half million. With some misgivings, the selling company called the buyer and named that figure on a take-it-or-leave-it basis. Half an hour later the buyer called back and took it.

The possibility of covert use of the PSE is the most frightening thing about the invention, and it is one of the major objections raised by the American Polygraph Association as the basis of their opposition to the PSE. In its declaration concerning the PSE, the APA board of directors said:

> The APA is deeply disturbed by published reports that the PSE-1 is capable of utilization, *without the knowledge and consent of the person being examined,* by means of surreptitious recordings, telephone transmissions, and video or radio signals, since such utilization would contravene constitutional guarantees in regard to self-incrimination and the unlawful invasion of privacy.[11] (Emphasis in original.)

The APA's concern over the PSE's threat to civil liberties may seem less than sincere to the labor unions and congressmen who have opposed the use of the polygraph on similar grounds. The association membership is mainly composed of private investigators, industrial-security officers, and law-enforcement officials, all law-and-order hardliners who have argued that the constitutional safeguards against self-incrimination apply only to court trials and other legal proceedings and have no bearing on the use of the polygraph as an investigative tool.

In fairness to the APA, it should be noted that its standards and principles of practice forbade involuntary polygraph tests long before the PSE became an issue.[12] Such benevolence costs nothing, however, since it is physically impossible to give a polygraph examination to a subject who refuses to cooperate. The crux of the issue is how one defines "voluntary," and here the polygraph people seem to be playing with words.

It's difficult to imagine why anyone, given a completely free choice, would ever volunteer to take a lie-detector test. The innocent person falsely charged with a crime "volunteers" to take the test because it provides an opportunity to exonerate himself, and the alternative is to be punished for an offense he did not commit. A job applicant "agrees" to take a preemployment polygraph examination because he wants the job more than he doesn't want to take the test. An employee may submit to a lie-detector test to clear himself of suspicion of theft and keep his job. A liar takes the test in the hope

of beating it, and an honest person submits to it because he wants
to prove his truthfulness, but both would obviously prefer to have
their word accepted at face value, without mechanical endorsement.

The reference to "unlawful invasion of privacy" in the APA declaration seems to imply that surreptitious recording of telephone or
other conversations is against the law. This is a popular misconcep-
tion which is largely untrue. Only five states* have laws which forbid
surreptitious recording; it's perfectly legal in the other forty-five and
the District of Columbia. Many people erroneously believe that federal law requires—under threat of criminal penalties—anyone recording a telephone conversation to transmit a "beep" tone over the line
every few seconds to let the other party know that his words are being
recorded. This just isn't true; telephone companies prefer that their
customers follow this practice, but the only relevant federal law is the
Omnibus Crime Control and Safe Streets Act of 1968, which prohib-
its surreptitious recording of conversations unless at least one party
is aware that the conversation is being recorded. Most APA members
know all this from their backgrounds in security and investigative
work.

The American Polygraph Association also objects to Dektor's
three-day course in PSE operation, which the APA considers inade-
quate.[13] Unlike polygraph manufacturers, Colonel Bell requires all
prospective purchasers of the instrument successfully to complete a
short course in its use. When I asked him if he would lend me a PSE
to experiment with for the purpose of writing about the device, he
agreed on the condition that I first take the course. Thus I came to
have first-hand experience with the object of this particular APA
complaint.

The course was held in the conference room of a Falls Church,
Virginia, motel. The eight other students were employees of customers who had purchased PSEs. These included a private detective
agency in Pennsylvania, a New York chain store, and the security
service of an East African country. Most of the students had some
training and experience in using the polygraph.

The instructor was Mike Kradz, the Maryland policeman who first

*California, Hawaii, Maryland, Massachusetts, and Pennsylvania.

field tested the PSE, now retired and with Dektor as its director of training. I knew Kradz by reputation, but this was the first time I'd met him. He is of middle age and height, physically fit, energetic, and full of enthusiasm for his job. He is almost totally bald and trims his remaining hair close to the scalp, creating the shaved-head image of a tough cop. In reality, Kradz is nothing like that stereotype. He seems to draw at least as much satisfaction from exonerating the innocent as from nailing the guilty. Kradz is a student of people, especially those who commit crimes. His twenty-two years as a cop were spent studying the traces they leave, finding ways to use the minutiae of human life to find the truth. Kradz is the kind of policeman found more often in fiction than in the station house. Bell's reason for recruiting him is obvious: Kradz is the best.

The first morning of the course was devoted to the physical operation of the PSE. The instrument is used in conjunction with a Uher 4000 tape recorder, selected because it has four speeds and can be manually wound back to locate a particular point on the tape. The interrogation is recorded at a tape speed of 7 1/2 inches per second, then it is played back and stopped at the suspect's response. The recorder is switched to a slower speed, usually 1 7/8 or 15/16 inches per second. Playing the suspect's answer at an extremely slow speed permits each cycle of the vocal sound to be processed and charted by the PSE.

The PSE is built into a large metal attaché case. At first glance, the array of buttons and knobs mounted on a panel set into the case suggests that the instrument is more complicated to operate than it really is. One row of buttons is used to select one of the four modes in which the PSE can be operated. These are roughly analogous to the different power lenses that can be swung into position on a microscope, each providing an increasing degree of magnification. The four PSE operation modes are used to examine the human voice for signs of emotional stress with four increasing degrees of sensitivity. The remaining controls on the PSE panel turn the instrument on and off, adjust the stylus, and operate the chart drive.

While the tape recorder plays back the suspect's response at a very slow speed, the signal is transmitted to the PSE by means of a cable, filtered through the instrument's circuits, and traced on the moving chart paper. The result is a strip of paper with a squiggly line. The rest is up to the human eye and brain.

On the afternoon of the first day, Kradz showed us what to look for. The unstressed voice looks like an untrimmed hedge, with stalks of different height sticking up (and down) at irregular intervals. But add some stress, and the hedge begins to appear trimmed. The greater the stress, the smoother and more regular the shape. If the suspect is experiencing the hard stress which accompanies deception, the overall outline of the figure takes on the rectangular shape of a concertina as seen by the player. Kradz showed us slide after slide of PSE charts made during actual police interrogations. He gave us the background of each case and pointed out the tell-tale signs of deception whenever they were present.

The next day, Kradz reviewed the theory of polygraph interrogation, which applies equally to the PSE. For most of the students this was a brief refresher course in familiar material. Kratz covered the major polygraph interrogation techniques, then presented the one recommended by Dektor for use with the PSE, a modification of the zone comparison technique. The technique consists of a series of irrelevant, relevant, control, and guilt-complex questions.

There was homework. At the end of class that day, Kradz gave each student a small reel of tape. Each reel contained several recorded interrogations. These were actual criminal investigations with the names and other identifying references removed to protect the privacy of the suspects. Each of us hurried back to his motel room with the tape and the PSE equipment. We had spent the past two days in the theory and mechanics of the PSE. Here, finally, was a taste of the real thing.

One of the cases I was assigned concerned a young man who had been accused of stealing money from his father's store. I recognized the voice of the interrogator, Kradz. He started by asking an "outside-issue" question,

"Are you afraid I'm going to ask you a question we have not discussed?"

Almost everyone, Kradz had explained to the class, has some deep secret he doesn't want anyone to know. Unless it relates directly to the investigation, the examiner couldn't care less what it is, but the suspect may be afraid that it's going to come out in the lie-detector test. The examiner must put him at ease, go over the questions he intends to ask before the actual exam, and assure the suspect that those are the only questions he will be asked. The outside-issue question is aimed at finding out whether the examiner has been successful.

The young man answered the question in the negative. Then the following exchange took place:

"Do you live in Howard County?"
"Yes."
"Do you suspect someone of having taken the money?"
"No."
"Are you wearing a white shirt?"
"Yes."
"Do you know who took the money?"
"No."
"Are you wearing a ring?"
"Yes."
"Did you take the money?"
"No."

There were also a few guilt-complex questions about fictitious crimes. The questions about wearing a white shirt and a ring and living in Howard County were the irrelevant questions, and the questions about the missing money were, of course, the relevant ones.

I ran the tape again and charted it on the PSE. All but two of the young man's responses were unstressed. The question about suspecting someone of taking the money produced a fair amount of stress, enough to indicate deception. But the other question that produced stress was one of the irrelevants, "Are you wearing a ring?" Curiously, his positive response produced the total stress I had seen only once or twice in the class slides.

The next morning Kradz called on me. Did the suspect take the money, he asked. I said I didn't think so. Kradz nodded. Did he know who took the money? Yes, I thought he did. Very good, said Kradz. Did I notice anything else about the interrogation? Well, yes, there was this business about the ring. Perhaps the suspect had stolen it. Kradz smiled. No, the kid hadn't taken the ring, but he was gay. He had exchanged rings with another guy. Nobody knew about it. The kid didn't really expect to be asked about it when the test began, because Kradz had gone over all the questions with him beforehand. Still, when the ring was mentioned, he panicked. It was almost as though we had read the young man's mind.

No one had made any serious mistakes in doing his homework assignment, so we were all feeling satisfied with ourselves. After only two days of instruction, we had successfully run actual criminal cases on the PSE. Everyone was ready to pack up his instrument, go home, and start doing some lie detection. Mike Kradz, however, wasn't quite finished with us.

The excop turned off the classroom lights and switched on the slide projector. On the screen there was a chart with ten PSE waveforms. Kradz explained that this was a number game, in which a subject had picked a number between one and ten and then been interrogated by Colonel McQuiston. Looking at the chart, could anyone in the class say which number the subject picked and lied about?

There was silence in the classroom. All of the responses looked alike. There seemed to be a little stress in all of the waveforms, but not very much in any one. One of the students tentatively offered a guess, which was seconded by another member of the class.

"Nope," said Kradz. "Anyone else? No? Then let's look at this."

He advanced the projector to the next slide. This, he explained, was the same test run in a different PSE mode and at a different tape speed. On the second chart two of the subject's responses showed more stress than the other eight. The class was about equally divided, half picking one number, half the other. Kradz showed more slides —the same test, different modes, different tape speeds. Gradually, a majority of the class settled on one candidate. Right, declared Kradz. He ran through the charts again and pointed out the subtle clues that McQuiston had used to zero in on the right answer.

The rest of the third class day was just like that. Kradz trotted out all of the monsters—the number guessing games, some of the charts from the "To Tell The Truth" television program, and several particularly tough criminal cases. By the end of the day, every one of us had had the experience of looking at a PSE chart, drawing a conclusion, and being wrong.

Kradz didn't have to say it, his message was clear· the PSE is a great investigative instrument, but don't ever confuse it with a crystal ball. It won't give you the answer, but if you keep your eyes, ears, and mind open, it will lead you to the answer nearly every time. And the Dektor three-day course taught you how to operate the PSE and read the charts, but it didn't invest you with the power to leap tall buildings with a single bound. Kradz shook hands with each of us and handed us our diplomas. The engraved certificate was impressive looking but conservative in its claims. It merely said that the student had "satisfactorily completed the PSE–1 Orientation Course." It wasn't a license to slay dragons.

A seasoned polygraph examiner who learned the psychology of the lie-detection game by training, apprenticeship, and experience would graduate from the Dektor course equipped to resume the practice of his craft with a superior instrument. A novice, however, was encouraged to take it easy and, whenever there was the slightest doubt about a PSE chart, to ask for help. Where? At Dektor. Each Uher tape recorder was equipped with a telephone coupling device to transmit recordings over the telephone. Any PSE user with a problem could phone Mike Kradz or another of the Dektor staff and transmit the problem tape. On the Dektor end, the tape would be copied and run through the PSE, then the user would be called back and given the opinion of one of the most experienced PSE examiners in the world. Almost everyone who graduates from Mike Kradz's course makes that telephone call sooner or later.

Kradz's final lesson made such an impression on me that I felt I had to prove to myself that I could, in fact, use the PSE effectively. One opportunity for experimentation was to play the number game with friends, but Kradz had demonstrated that this was among the most difficult tasks for the PSE user. Nonetheless, I decided to try.

I phoned a friend, told him about the PSE, and asked if he'd be willing to play a little game to test it. He agreed and picked a number between one and ten, then I proceeded to question him: "Is the number one?" "Is the number two?" and so on. He answered no each time. I recorded his responses, ran them through the PSE, and called him back. The number he picked, I told him, was five.

He was dumbfounded. He had not heard of the PSE before, and he thought that I might have been concocting some elaborate joke at his expense. But when I called him back and correctly identified the number he had picked, he realized I was serious. And he was shocked.

My initial success was not consistently repeated. I tried the same experiment with others and found that in some cases I could narrow it down to two numbers but had to toss a coin to choose between them, and in other cases I couldn't read any differences in the PSE waveforms. However, my overall hit rate was around 50 percent, not particularly impressive but five times better than chance.

I tried my PSE skill on broadcasts of the "To Tell The Truth" show, which I taped from my television set. After the three contestants had each announced, "My name is _____," I would run the recording through the PSE and try to make a call before the "the real _____" stood up and identified himself.

At first, I found this nearly impossible to do. Almost every contestant seemed to show the same moderate degree of stress, the obvious effect of finding himself speaking before television cameras and a studio audience. There seemed to be no less stress in the truthful statement than in the two lies. Then I noticed a pattern.

I compared the PSE waveforms of several of the truthful contestants to those of the others. All of them showed moderate stress when they began speaking, but the truthful contestant relaxed as he spoke his own name, and the liars didn't. "My name is John Doe," would contain stress throughout if the speaker were lying, but, for the *real* John Doe, stress dropped off after, "My name is _____."

When I applied this rule to the programs, I had much better results. My success rate climbed to 60 percent, twice what I could expect from random guessing and not bad at all for a novice running an artificial, low-stress experiment.

Although PSE charts can be difficult to read in low-stress, experimental situations, they are much easier to interpret in real cases. This was borne out in a study made by Gordon Barland of the University of Utah, one of the leading academic researchers in the field of lie detection. Barland conducted two experiments using the PSE and polygraph in parallel as Mike Kradz did. In one of his experiments he tested college students in an artificial number guessing game. His PSE results were unimpressive. Then he tested criminal suspects referred to him for examination by police departments, prosecutors, and defense attorneys in Utah and Nevada (in addition to being a member of the University of Utah Psychology Department, Barland is a licensed polygraph examiner with a military intelligence background). In the high-stress circumstances of an actual criminal interrogation, Barland demonstrated the PSE's effectiveness. In the one instance where the PSE and the polygraph disagreed, the polygraph indicated that the suspect was telling the truth. Barland investigated this case further, giving a polygraph examination to another person involved in the matter. The second test showed that the earlier polygraph results had been wrong and confirmed the PSE's indication that the first suspect had lied.[14]

Because it is highly accurate and effective in real criminal cases, the PSE has rapidly gained acceptance by police forces around the world. In little over a year since Dektor's first public announcement, PSEs have been put to use by more than nineteen American law-enforcement agencies.[15] The instrument is also used in thirteen foreign countries—Canada, the United Kingdom, Australia, West Germany, Greece, two countries in West Africa, and six in the Middle East. It has been reported that King Hussein of Jordan, who has been the target of repeated assassination attempts, has equipped his security force with five PSEs.[16]

Security and law enforcement are not the only areas in which uses have been found for the PSE. Because the device is an accurate instrument for measuring stress, it has been successfully applied in medicine, psychotherapy, and behavioral research. Dr. John W. Heisse, Jr., a Burlington, Vermont, physician, uses a PSE to study the relationship of his patients' anxieties to their physical problems.[17] Dr. Heisse was one of a score of medical and behavioral scientists who attended an August 1973 conference in Springfield, Virginia, to discuss their work with the PSE.

Heisse presented some of the work he had done in using the PSE to assess a patient's psychological readiness for surgery. Another researcher[18] described his use of the PSE in the treatment of a patient with a pathological compulsion to shout obscenities. A psychiatrist[19] reported on the way the standard word-association test could be enhanced by using the PSE to measure the stress in a patient's responses. Several scientists attending the conference made informal presentations of work in progress involving the PSE in a variety of research applications.

From the first my own interest in the PSE centered on its potential use in historical research, especially in probing the JFK assassination. People who knew what happened in Dallas had talked about it in front of microphones, and somewhere those recordings had been preserved. But could the PSE really be used this way? After all, the zone-comparison interrogation technique recommended by Dektor for use with the PSE is a highly structured series of irrelevant, relevant, control, guilt-complex, and outside-issue questions. Could a narrative statement or a differently structured interview be used to achieve the same result? I asked Kradz and Bell.

The answer was "maybe." They told me about a particularly vicious murder case they had helped solve using the PSE exactly the same way I proposed to do. Two suspects who had been questioned by the police refused to take polygraph tests but permitted their statements to be recorded. The detectives investigating the case sent the tapes to Dektor and asked if they could be analyzed by the PSE. Bell listened to the recorded statements. The suspects explained why they were in a certain place at a certain time and denied specific actions that had been elements of the crime. Bell discovered that the statements contained most of the relevant, irrelevant, and control issues of a structured PSE examination. He isolated those portions of the tape and ran them on the PSE. The results were so clear that he advised the police that these suspects were very probably the murderers. The detectives focused their investigation on the men and obtained additional evidence and, finally, confessions.

Bell and Kradz explained that the feasibility of using the PSE this way depended on how close the recorded statement resembled a structured test. It was something like the early days of photography in the nineteenth century. If you brought your subject into a studio, made him sit very still, and used a lot of light, your results would be almost as sharp as the best that is done today; but when you used a camera outside the studio, the pictures would be sharp, blurred, or useless, depending on the amounts of light and motion involved.

There would be no problem, they explained, in detecting stress in an old recording, if it were there. The difficulty lay in interpreting the cause of the stress, which might be deception but could be something else. But if the recorded statements contained elements which amounted to irrelevant, relevant, and control issues, then I could be confident of my results. And, they pointed out, conspiracy was an especially apt target for this kind of PSE probe: if several witnesses showed deception-like stress while talking about the same event, this greatly increased the chances that some or all of them were lying.

I decided to try an experiment to see if I could use the PSE on a previously recorded statement. I needed a case in which someone was lying about a matter of some importance to himself, and I had to be sure that he was, in fact, lying. I had to know the outcome of the affair. So I chose the man who had beaten the polygraph test, Clifford Irving.

I obtained an audio tape of Mike Wallace's "Sixty Minutes" interview with Irving. Most of Wallace's questions related directly to the matter of Irving's alleged biography of Howard Hughes, and I knew that Irving's responses were lies, but I found a few of the author's statements that were true and could be used as irrelevant issues. I charted them on the PSE.

"When you travel, you don't talk," said Irving. He was trying to explain why, if Hughes's physical condition precluded long interviews (as Irving claimed), the billionaire was able to make the long journeys to their alleged meetings. It was an abstract generalization, and Irving probably felt it was true, yet Wallace's grilling had produced a fair amount of situational stress, and it was apparent in the PSE waveforms. If Irving's lies were going to show up on the PSE, they would have to produce total stress.

They did. Were there any other witnesses to his meetings with Howard Hughes? "Yes," replied Irving, "a researcher, a man named Richard Susskind." Irving then related the bag of prunes anecdote. Where, asked Wallace, did Irving really get the transcripts of his alleged meetings with Hughes. "I got the transcripts from Howard Hughes," Irving replied calmly. I charted his statements on the PSE.

Nearly every one of Irving's lies produced the smooth, rectangular, "trimmed hedge" waveform that signals maximum stress, and there was a clear difference between the relevant and the irrelevant issues. Irving had deceived the wordly-wise editors of *Life* Magazine and McGraw-Hill, the handwriting experts at Osborn Associates, and the polygraph. But he would have been caught by the PSE.

I showed my results to Colonel Bell. He smiled and nodded.

"We knew at the time that Irving wasn't telling the truth," he said, "but nobody asked us, so we stayed out of it."

"You ran Irving on the PSE?" I asked.

"No," he said, "we ran Hughes. That's why we were so sure."

Bell explained that at the height of the controversy someone claiming to be Howard Hughes held a news conference over the telephone with a group of television newsmen. The conference was broadcast, and Dektor recorded it and charted it on the PSE. The person on the other end of the line showed absolutely no stress when he said he was Hughes, nor when he said that he had never heard of Clifford Irving.

"Stress has to be interpreted," said Bell. "It may mean deception, but it could also be due to a guilt complex or an outside issue. But the absence of stress is unambiguous. If someone is talking about something of personal importance to himself and he shows absolutely no stress, then he must be telling the truth. If we had run Irving and gotten these results," he pointed to my charts, "there still would have been some small margin of doubt about why he was stressing. But we were certain that the man who said he was Howard Hughes believed what he was saying." Later, when I made the one most important discovery of my investigation into the assassination of President Kennedy, I had reason to remember Colonel Bell's words.

In writing the exposition of the polygraph and the PSE contained in this and the preceeding chapter, I have emphasized the physical and psychological facts of lie detection and made only passing reference to problems of ethics. Unquestionably, lie detection, especially covert lie detection with the PSE, raises ethical problems. While I did not try to avoid these issues, neither did I explore them in depth. The technical facts of lie detection are not simple to explain or understand, but the philosophical questions are even more complex, and powerful arguments, both pro and con, have been advanced by others more qualified to debate the issue. My own position is that lie detection is ethically neutral with enormous potentials for both good and evil depending on how it is used. But this is merely a personal opinion and would be out of place in this exposition. However, when a journalist uses the PSE as I did, a special kind of ethical question is raised, and I feel I must address it here.

As it happened, all of the assassination tapes I analyzed with the PSE were recordings of people talking to journalists. In some cases I was the journalist and, in those instances, the people I interviewed knew that I planned to use the information they gave me in order to write about the assassination of President Kennedy. Of course, I did not tell them about the PSE nor what I was really trying to do. But no privileged, confidential, or off-the-record conversations were involved. The voices on the assassination tapes are people willingly telling their fellow Americans their version of what happened in Dallas.

This, in itself, could be an unfortunate precedent for the profession of journalism. If public figures knew that their statements to writers and reporters would be analyzed electronically for signs of deception, a "chilling effect" might result which could impede the free flow of information. Even a truthful person would be reluctant to gamble his credibility on the accuracy of some piece of gadgetry.

I have tried to guard against this by claiming no more for the PSE than I can justify by my own experience. I have explained, as best I know how, what lie detection really is, how the PSE is used to detect deception, and the limitations of the technique. Many of us are all too ready to believe in the infallibility of a machine unless we understand how it works. I have tried to convey this understanding.

It could be argued that a journalist has a duty as well as a right to verify the information given him by his sources and that my use of the PSE was merely an unusual extension of a time-honored tradition. I do not offer this argument. My reason for employing lie-detection equipment and techniques in the investigation of President Kennedy's assassination is much more straightforward.

The president of the United States was shot down in the street in full view of his wife, the Secret Service, and hundreds of American citizens. The government investigated the case for ten months and published a report that raised more questions than it answered. The assassination may have changed our lives more than any other event in living memory, yet few of us believe that we know how or why it happened. The government has closed the case and the files have gathered ten years of dust in the National Archives. The truth has been hidden from us and may soon be obscured by the shadows of history.

The psychological stress evaluator was a last resort. That is my only justification.

5 TAPES FROM THE ARCHIVES

. . for murder, though it have no tongue, will speak with most miraculous organ.
—Hamlet, Act II, Scene 2.

"It would have been beneficial to everyone concerned," said former Dallas police chief Jesse Curry. "The Warren Commission was rather concerned about why we didn't do it."

The time was May 1973 and the place was Curry's office, high in a new, glass-walled, air-conditioned building called One Main Place, four blocks from the Texas School Book Depository and Dealey Plaza. Curry, now vice-president and security director of a Dallas bank, had granted me an interview. He was explaining why ten years before the Dallas police had not tape recorded their interrogation of Lee Harvey Oswald.

"When we remodeled the City Hall," he said, "we requested that certain rooms be equipped so that we could tape interrogations, but because of the money involved, the city turned us down."[1]

Oswald was in Dallas police custody from about 2:00 P.M. on November 22 until he was pronounced dead at about 1:00 P.M. on November 24. During that period he was questioned by the police, the FBI, and the Secret Service for a total of twelve hours: seven hours on Friday, three hours on Saturday, and two hours on Sunday morning.[2] Not a word of the interrogation was tape recorded.

In 1963 tape recorders were not as commonplace, inexpensive, or easy to operate as they have become in the last ten years. The now ubiquitous cassette recorder did not come onto the market until 1964. But, while the tape recorder was not a common consumer item in 1963, neither was it a rarity, and it had been in widespread use by law-enforcement agencies for many years. Although it may be plausible that the Dallas police were not equipped with a single recorder

in November 1963, it is difficult to understand why none of the FBI
and Secret Service agents present arranged to tape at least some of
those twelve hours of interrogation. If the Warren Commission expressed its concern about this to Chief Curry, it did not raise the
question in the Report. The commission may have been reluctant to
criticize other agencies on this point for a very simple reason: of the
552 witnesses who gave testimony to the commission, apparently only
one was recorded.*

The most extensive criminal investigation in American history was
conducted by the most sophisticated law-enforcement and intelligence agencies in the world, yet virtually no official electronic record
was created. History must rely on the stenotypists' account of what
was said before the commission, and the official transcript in the
twenty-six volumes of testimony is often rent by the phrase "(discussion off the record)," mysterious and unexplained gaps in the testimony where the commission and its staff chose to conduct its questioning away from the scrutiny of history and the American people.

Some of the events of November 22–25, 1963, were recorded on
audio and videotape by the national television networks, but, with a

*In July 1973 Robert Smith of the Committee to Investigate Assassina-
tions discovered the existence of some sound recordings among the material
turned over to the National Archives by the commission and obtained permission to listen to them. Smith and I went to the archives and were
presented with a set of plastic disks from an office dictating machine. We
found that they contained some of Marina Oswald's testimony in Russian
before the commission. The dictating machine, which was not designed for
this use, seems to have been placed near the commission members examining
Mrs. Oswald, because their questions are fairly audible, as is the voice of the
interpreter who translated the questions and answers. Marina Oswald's voice,
however, is very faint. Background sounds, which seem to be a commercial
radio broadcast, are also audible behind the testimony and may have been
picked up by the recording machine through the electrical wiring in the
building in which the examination was conducted. These technical problems
resulting from the careless and amateurish way the recordings were made
discouraged me from attempting a PSE analysis of them. However, our trip
to the archives yielded at least one discovery: there are significant discrepancies between the recorded testimony and the corresponding transcript published by the government.

few notable exceptions, these recordings shed little light on the mysteries of the Kennedy assassination. Most of the network coverage was concerned at first with reaction to the tragic news from both people in the street and national leaders, then later with the solemn ceremonies in the Capitol Rotunda and Arlington National Cemetery. The television cameras were outside of things on the street and in the press conferences at Washington and Dallas. A more telling drama was being played out, unrecorded, in the interrogation rooms of the Dallas police station.

However, on the evening of Sunday, September 27, 1964, the CBS television network broadcast a two-hour news special to coincide with the publication of the Warren Report. The press had been given copies of the Report two days earlier, but the CBS program obviously had been in preparation for weeks or months. The news special, "November 22 and the Warren Report," was narrated by CBS anchorman Walter Cronkite and included interviews with eyewitnesses, Dallas police officers, Oswald's family, and others who had testified before the Warren Commission.

Three years later, CBS News broadcast a program entitled "CBS News Inquiry: The Warren Report" in four one-hour segments on the evenings of June 25–28, 1967. Prompted by the rising chorus of public doubt about the assassination, the inquiry attempted to probe some of the major questions raised by the critics. In the course of the program there were interviews with more eyewitnesses, policemen, and former associates of Oswald, as well as ballistics experts, medical examiners, and members of the Warren Commission and its staff.*

Regardless of whether the two CBS programs achieved their goals of exposition and investigation, they constitute the most comprehensive audiovisual record of the assassination inquiry in existence. Early in 1973 I contacted CBS and learned that these programs (and nearly every other piece of news film produced by CBS cameras) had been carefully indexed and stored in the CBS News archives in New York City. With the cooperation of CBS News, I obtained tape recordings

---

*The 1964 program, while not openly challanging the Warren Report, seemed to carry strong undercurrents of doubt about the official conclusions. The 1967 program, however, came out squarely behind the Report.

of the full six hours of sound track from the two programs. The CBS tapes were of excellent technical quality, and I had no difficulty processing them with the PSE.

Before presenting my findings, several general observations are in order. No precise numerical index of stress in PSE charts has yet been devised, since stress is identified by the presence of as many as seven different characteristics in the PSE waveform; there is no meaninful way now available to look at a PSE chart and say, for example, that it shows 79.3 percent maximum possible stress. But the experienced eye can easily distinguish between different degrees of PSE stress, and some researchers who work mostly with one-syllable, "yes-no" responses are able to identify as many as ten different stress levels.

In analyzing longer, narrative utterances, as I have often done with the assassination tapes, I have noticed that the degree of stress may vary somewhat during a statement. Therefore, to describe the amount of stress present in an entire statement, I have chosen a set of four categories—none, moderate, good, and hard—which cover the range from the complete absence of stress to the presence of maximum stress. Sometimes, when a statement seems to fall between two adjacent categories, I have described it in terms of both, for example, "moderate-to-good." Thus, in effect, I have characterized narrative statements in terms of seven distinct levels of stress.

In studying the PSE charts of a variety of "known lie" statements, I have observed that deception regarding a matter of importance to the speaker almost always produces a minimum of good stress and usually some hard stress. Therefore, I have interpreted moderate stress to mean that the speaker is probably telling the truth.

The presence of good or hard stress is a necessary, but not sufficient, indication of deception. As I have noted earlier, the essence of lie detection—polygraph or PSE—is the comparison of the stress experienced by the subject when speaking about two or more distinct issues. In the cases of some of the speakers on the assassination tapes, the only statements recorded were relevant issues, so no such comparison was possible. In these instances, the most that can be said when good or hard stress is found is that the PSE cannot confirm that the speaker is telling the truth.

Other cases on the tapes seem to provide almost classic examples of relevant-irrelevant responses, and in some of these there is good or hard stress in the relevant statement and moderate or no stress in the irrelevant. Such instances are strongly suggestive of deception but do not constitute absolute proof that the speaker is lying. It must be recalled that in processing a prerecorded tape, such as a television news sound track, the circumstances under which the recording was made are not only beyond the control of the PSE analyst, they are unknown to him. The sudden movement of a cameraman, for instance, would go unrecorded on either the audio or video elements of the program, yet it could produce a brief moment of stress in a speaker at a critical point in his statement.

The question has been raised as to whether the very experience of being televised might produce good or hard stress in someone unaccustomed to microphones and television cameras. The answer seems to be no, at least for most people. For example, analysis of the "To Tell The Truth" contestants, who are not professional actors or performers and who are appearing for the first time not only before television cameras, but in front of a live audience and a panel of celebrities on national TV, demonstrates that such experiences produce only moderate levels of stress in most individuals. And, of course, a person who did experience high stress levels as a consequence of appearing on television should exhibit that stress constantly, during irrelevant as well as relevant statements.

Another problem that has been raised is the possibility that the subject of President Kennedy's assassination might produce stress in most Americans. This issue confuses stress and distress. The psychophysiological condition measured by the PSE and referred to as "stress" is not yet completely understood, but it is not directly related to the emotions of grief, despair, or sadness, which are likely to be stimulated by thoughts of the Dallas tragedy. PSE stress is produced by fear, the "fight or flee" syndrome. It seems also to be associated with intense mental concentration. The stress found in the assassination tapes may be the result of something other than deception, but it is very probably not caused either by the experience of being televised or the subject of national tragedy.

But if stress in a prerecorded interview cannot be equated with deception with 100 percent certainty, of what use is the PSE analysis of such tapes? The answer is that my objective is not to establish whether any one individual is lying, but to determine the truth about the Kennedy assassination. A pattern of stress characteristic of deception in the statements of one individual implies some probability that he is not telling the truth. When deception is indicated in the statements of several different people who are witness to or have knowledge of the same event, the probability becomes very high that at least some of them are not telling the truth. The presence of deception in the accepted account of the event is often of much greater significance than the question of whether any one individual lied.

This is especially so, as will be seen, in the case of eyewitnesses. If the people who say they saw Lee Harvey Oswald shoot the president and Officer J. D. Tippit are not telling the truth, this would not necessarily link them to an assassination conspiracy. Eyewitnesses often, after some reflection, realize that they are no longer certain about what they believe they saw. Some are reluctant to equivocate because of police pressure or the fear of appearing foolish, but many admit their uncertainty when the suspect is actually brought to trial and other doubts are established about his guilt. But in the case of Lee Harvey Oswald, the suspect was dead and his guilt confirmed by the official stamp of a tribunal of respected men. Telling the world what it wanted to hear may have seemed an innocent way of claiming a footnote in history.

While the PSE, when used on a prerecorded, unstructured interview, cannot determine with complete certainty that someone is lying or why he is lying, the instrument sometimes can confirm with a high degree of accuracy that a speaker is telling the truth. Most lie-detection specialists who have worked with the PSE are convinced that the absence of stress is a very reliable indicator of truthfulness. If someone is talking about a matter of considerable personal importance to himself and if there is no stress or the stress on the relevant statement is much less than that on irrelevant declarations, then it is almost certain that the speaker is telling the truth. It should be noted, however, that this truth is limited by what the speaker knows or believes, that is, no lie-detection technique can determine that a subject is sincere but mistaken.

These principles are illustrated by an analysis of the statements of eyewitnesses regarding the direction from which the assassination shots seemed to have come. One witness, a railroad worker named S. M. Holland who watched the assassination from the tracks on the triple underpass at the bottom of Dealey Plaza, reported seeing a puff of gunsmoke behind a picket fence at the top of the grassy knoll. He also said that the sound of a rifle shot seemed to come from that direction. Charles Brehm, another eyewitness, said he believed that no shot was fired from the grassy knoll. Officer Hurchel Jacks of the Texas State Highway Patrol was driving Vice-President Johnson's limousine, and he denied that any of the shots sounded as though they came from the grassy knoll. Another policeman, Officer J. W. Foster, said there was no doubt in his mind that the shots came from behind the motorcade.

Holland may have embellished his story a bit, because the PSE showed good stress in his statement that he heard a shot coming from the direction of the grassy knoll, but there was only moderate stress associated with his report of seeing gunsmoke: Holland did believe he saw smoke coming from behind the picket fence. However, Charles Brehm showed no more than moderate stress when he said that no shot came from that direction. Thus, the PSE results confirm the conflicting testimony of two witnesses.

Officer Jacks's statement showed hard stress, but so did an irrelevant statement he made. The PSE does not confirm that he is telling the truth, but neither does it give a clear indication that he is not.

No irrelevant statement by Officer Foster was available, but there was good stress in his relevant statement. The reason for Foster's stress may be revealed by a careful examination of what he actually said:

> INTERVIEWER: Officer Foster, was there any doubt in your mind about the direction from which those shots came?
>
> FOSTER: No, sir, there wasn't, *not after I had moved to the railroad.* There was no doubt that the shots were coming from back of the motorcade toward Elm and Houston.[3] (Emphasis added.)

Immediately after the shooting, several policemen ran to the top of the grassy knoll with their guns drawn, and Officer Foster was one of them. Obviously he thought there was a sniper on the grassy knoll. He may have changed his mind when he found no gunman there or in the railroad yard beyond, but he might be expected to show good stress when saying "there was no doubt" that the shots came from somewhere else. Yet, if Officer Foster actually had doubts about the source of the shots, does this suggest that he was a conspirator? No, it merely implies that the Dallas policeman may have seen no point in rocking the boat. As to the actual direction from which the shots were fired, the PSE, unfortunately, seems to shed very little light on the matter, beyond confirming that Holland really believed he saw a puff of smoke on the grassy knoll. "Earwitness" testimony, even when confirmed by lie detection, is not very useful. Estimates of the direction of a brief sequence of rifle reports would be unreliable under the best of circumstances; in the sudden blaze of violence in Dealey Plaza accurate observation seems even less likely.

But the eyewitness testimony of Howard L. Brennan is much more substantial. Brennan, a forty-five-year-old steamfitter, witnessed the assassination from a vantage point directly across the street from the book depository. He reported that minutes before the shooting, he saw a man in the southeast corner window of the depository's sixth floor. Immediately after the first or second shot, Brennan stated, he looked up and saw the same man taking aim and then firing the final shot. Brennan described the gunman to the police immediately after the shooting, and his report may have been the source of the police description broadcast a few minutes later* which the police claim was the basis upon which they located and arrested Oswald in the Texas Theatre.

Brennan testified before the Warren Commission that the gunman he saw was Lee Harvey Oswald. The commission seems to have had mixed emotions about Brennan's testimony. On the one hand, Brennan offered apparently irrefutable evidence that Oswald was the assassin—the section of the report that discusses Brennan's testimony is entitled "Eyewitness Identification of the Assassin"—but, on the other hand, there were serious problems with Brennan's identification.

*The police broadcast described the suspect as "white, slender, weighing about 165 pounds, about 5′ 10″ tall, and in his early thirties."

The Report admits that, although Brennan identified Oswald in a police lineup as the person who bore the closest resemblance to the gunman in the window, he had seen Oswald's picture on television before making the identification. The Report further notes that Brennan did not positively identify Oswald in the lineup but tells us that Brennan says he could have done so but didn't because he felt the assassination was "a Communist activity" and feared for his own safety.[4] The commission concluded, "Brennan saw a man in the window who closely resembled Lee Harvey Oswald, and that Brennan believes the man he saw was in fact Lee Harvey Oswald."[5]

Jesse Curry seems much less impressed with Brennan's testimony. Curry wrote:

> Brennan was unable to make a positive identification of Oswald in the lineup. He was willing to admit that Oswald resembled the man in the window, but that was all. Brennan's later testimony to FBI Agents apparently varied from month to month after the assassination. Brennan was later to become the Warren Commission's key witness. At the time of the Warren Commission Hearings Howard Brennan was willing to positively identify Oswald as the man he saw in the window.[6]

On the CBS tapes Brennan said, "I noticed this one man on the sixth floor of the Texas book store by himself. Well, he left the window a couple of times in the course of seven or eight or ten minutes. . . ." Then the shooting began, and, said Brennan, "I looked directly across and up, possibly at a forty-five-degree angle. And this man—the same man I had saw prior to the President's arrival—was in the window and taking aim for his last shot."[7]

There is only one statement by Brennan on the tape that can serve as an irrelevant issue: "The Secret Service man asked me for a description," which, presumably, is true. Brennan shows moderate-to-good stress on this. Everywhere else, the stress is hard, nearly the maximum stress level that can be exhibited in a PSE waveform. Unfortunately, the CBS tape does not include a statement by Brennan that he is certain the man in the window was Oswald, but the stress patterns in Brennan's recorded statements raise serious doubts that he saw anyone in the window.

Three of the eyewitnesses who identified Lee Harvey Oswald as the man who shot J. D. Tippit were interviewed on the CBS tapes. Among these was Domingo Benevides, who witnessed the shooting from a distance of no more than twenty-five feet. I was particularly interested in the PSE analysis of Benevides's statements because of the questionable circumstances surrounding his identification of Oswald as the murderer.

Benevides witnessed the Tippit shooting from his pickup truck as he was driving near the murder scene. When questioned later by the police, he said that he would not be able to identify the killer; therefore, he was not asked to identify Oswald in a police lineup. However, when Benevides testified before the Warren Commission several months later, he said that the pictures of Oswald he had seen on television resembled the man who shot Officer Tippit.[8] Some critics of the Warren Commission have speculated that Domingo Benevides may have changed his story out of fear after the death of his brother, Eddy Benevides, who was shot in the head in February 1964.[9]

By the time the CBS News inquiry was broadcast in June 1967, Domingo Benevides had become even more emphatic in his identification. It was no longer a question of Oswald resembling the murderer of Tippit:

> INTERVIEWER: Is there any doubt in your mind that Oswald was the man you had seen shoot Tippit?
> BENEVIDES: No, sir, there was no doubt at all. I could even tell you how he combed his hair and the clothes he wore and what have you, all the details.[10]

Benevides also gave the interviewer a lengthy account of how he happened to witness the shooting, seeing the gunman flee, and other details. I selected some of the best-established details in this account to use as irrelevant statements. The PSE showed good-to-hard stress on most of them. The whole subject of the shooting seemed to cause Benevides severe anxiety, so I held little hope for a clear PSE result from his statements. Nonetheless, I ran his reply, "No, sir, there was no doubt at all." To my amazement, I found the stress in this statement to be little more than moderate.

On November 22, 1963, Domingo Benevides could not identify the killer of Officer Tippit, yet nearly four years later he had no doubt that it was Oswald, and his memory seemed so vivid he could give a detailed description of Oswald's appearance. While it is difficult for me to accept his story, the PSE confirms that it is what Benevides himself believes. Why did Benevides change his story? It was apparently not done out of fear. But this writer believes an equally powerful psychological force may have been involved—suggestion.

Ted Calloway, the manager of a used-car lot in the neighborhood of the shooting was another eyewitness who linked Oswald to the Tippit shooting. Calloway didn't see the shooting, but he testified that he heard the shots and saw a man running from the scene of the murder. Calloway later picked Oswald out of a police lineup.[11] Meagher has pointed out that, according to other testimony before the commission, the police lineups in which Oswald was identified by Calloway and several other eyewitnesses were biased: unlike the other men in the lineup (all police employees), Oswald's face was cut and bruised from the scuffle in the Texas Theatre, and he was audibly protesting his presence in the lineup.[12]

On the CBS tapes, Calloway describes the identification:

> CALLOWAY: Yes, sir, I saw him that night in the police lineup. They asked me to come down to police headquarters, and I identified him in the lineup as the man that I had seen running with the pistol in his hand.
> INTERVIEWER: Did you have any trouble identifying him in the lineup?
> CALLOWAY: None whatsoever.[13]

Calloway's statement, "None whatsoever," shows good-to-hard stress. Most of the rest of his statements during the interview show no more than moderate-to-good stress.

The eyewitness who provided the commission with the most detailed account of the Tippit shooting was Mrs. Helen Markham. Mrs. Markham said she saw the whole thing from start to finish: Oswald was walking along the sidewalk, a police car pulled up and stopped, Oswald walked over to the car, leaned against it, and talked with the officer through the window on the passenger side. Suddenly, Oswald backed away, the policeman got out and started to walk around the front of the car, and Oswald shot him several times and fled.

Mrs. Markham's testimony before the commission contained many self-contradictions, and her accuracy and credibility have been challenged so extensively that the problems cannot easily be summarized here.[14] One especially striking problem with her version of the Tippit shooting is posed by the photographic evidence and the testimony of other witnesses who arrived immediately after the shooting, establishing that the passenger-side window of Tippit's car was rolled up.[15] If Tippit had been talking to someone through that window, it would have to have been rolled down; and, if he suddenly decided to get out of his car and apprehend this individual who was allegedly backing away, it is not likely he would have paused to roll the window up. As with Howard Brennan, the commission seemed a little queasy about Mrs. Markham's testimony, and it admitted that she changed her story while testifying. The commission concluded that Mrs. Markham was "reliable," but added, "even in the absence of Mrs. Markham's testimony, there is ample evidence to identify Oswald as the killer of Tippit,"[16] presumably referring to the other witnesses who picked the battered and protesting Oswald out of the Dallas police lineup.

Since nearly all of Mrs. Markham's story has been called into question, there was nothing in her interview on the CBS tapes that could be assumed true for the purpose of relevant-irrelevant comparison. The stress in her statements varies from none all the way to hard. Some of the hardest stress appeared in her account of identifying Oswald in the lineup: "And I kept looking at [Oswald], and I had him turn to the side, then back, and then I knew that it was him, because of the way he looked."[17]

Thus, of three of the eyewitnesses who linked Oswald to the shooting of Officer Tippit, the PSE confirms the truthfulness of only one, Domingo Benevides, and in his case, other evidence strongly suggests that his certitude was the result of hearing the "official truth" repeated again and again for more than three years.

Three of the people who found physical evidence linking the Mannlicher-Carcano rifle to the assassination were interviewed on the tape: Deputy Constable Seymour Weitzman, one of the two police officers who found the rifle and thought it was a Mauser; Darrell C. Tomlinson, the senior engineer at Parkland Hospital who said he found the intact rifle bullet—exhibit 399—on the floor beneath a stretcher in a hospital corridor; and Sgt. Gerald Hill, who supervised the search of the book depository that led to the discovery of the empty rifle shells near the sixth-floor window.

Weitzman described finding the rifle hidden behind a stack of cartons and added:

> To my sorrow, I looked at it, and it looked like a Mauser, which I said it was. But I said the wrong one because just at a glance I saw the Mauser action, and—I don't know—it just came out words, it's a German Mauser, which it wasn't. It's an Italian-type gun. But from a glance it's hard to describe, and that's all I saw it was at a glance. I was mistaken, and it was proven that my statement was a mistake, but it was an honest mistake.[18]

PSE analysis revealed hard, near-maximum stress throughout. Weitzman's account of the circumstances of finding the rifle contain the same high level of stress:

> . . . I stumbled over it two times, not knowing it was there . . . went right by it. And Mr. Boone was climbing on top, and I was down on my knees looking, and I moved a box, and he moved a carton, and there it was. And he in turn hollered that we had found a rifle.[19]

There is no reason to doubt Weitzman's story of finding the rifle: if he had been part of a conspiracy to plant the Mannlicher-Carcano in the book depository, he would not have immediately announced that the weapon was a Mauser. The issue of interest is whether he really believes he was wrong and that the rifle was "an Italian-type gun." Unfortunately, the consistent level of hard stress throughout his statements prevents any conclusions from being drawn regarding his truthfulness. What is apparent from the PSE charts and from simply listening to his voice, is that Seymour Weitzman was experiencing a high degree of anxiety while discussing the question of the rifle.

It seems likely that at the time of the CBS interview Weitzman was no longer sure of the kind of rifle he found in the book depository. Although his reference to the Mauser inspired doubts in both the Warren Commission and its critics, there is no record that he was ever asked to examine the Mannlicher-Carcano and confirm that it was the weapon he discovered. The commission's failure to do this may be attributable to general carelessness, but it is more probable that this measure was omitted because of the very serious problems that would have arisen if Weitzman denied that it was the same weapon.

Whether or not Weitzman was mistaken, his identification of the rifle as a Mauser caused problems for the Dallas authorities, and he probably was severely reprimanded. Whatever was said to him about the matter, it appears to have caused him extreme anxiety while discussing it nearly four years later. When I visited Dallas in May 1973, I was unable to contact Weitzman. He was no longer with the sheriff's department. Some of the local private assassination researchers told me that he had changed his name and moved away. I tried to locate him elsewhere in Texas but failed.

Darrell C. Tomlinson described at length on the CBS tapes his finding of the rifle bullet at Parkland Hospital. According to Tomlinson, he moved one of several stretchers stacked in a hospital corridor, he heard a rattle, and then he saw the bullet. Tomlinson said that he was sure the stretcher had been taken off the elevator that carried Governor Connally to the operating room but that he couldn't be certain that the stretcher he moved had actually borne Connally.[20]

There was some stress in Tomlinson's statements, but I would classify the stress level as moderate-to-good—not enough to indicate deception. More importantly, the level of stress was constant throughout all of Tomlinson's statements, irrelevant and relevant. The PSE provides a clear indication that Tomlinson was telling the truth about finding the bullet in the hospital corridor. However, in view of the ballistic and photographic problems with the single bullet theory, how it got there remains a mystery, and the PSE cannot, unfortunately, shed any light on that question.

The bullet found by Tomlinson at Parkland and the bullet fragments found in the presidential limousine were ballistically matched to the Mannlicher-Carcano by several of the Warren Commission's

firearms specialists. One of them, Dr. Joseph D. Nichol, Superintendent of the Illinois Bureau of Criminal Investigation, was interviewed
on one of the CBS programs.[21] He stated his findings, and there was
virtually no stress in his voice.

Sgt. Gerald L. Hill, the officer who commanded the team of
policemen that searched the book depository immediately after the
assassination, described the discovery of the rifle shells that were later
ballistically linked to the Mannlicher-Carcano. "We saw a bar-
ricade," he began, referring to the stack of book cartons which
shielded the "Oswald window" from the rest of the sixth floor.
Initially, Hill's voice shows moderate stress, but the level rises as he
speaks and reaches the good-to-hard category when he says, "Immediately under the window that was later determined to be the actual
spot that the shots were fired from, there were three rifle bullet
hulls."[22]

The PSE analysis of Sergeant Hill's statements is especially interesting because of the major role he played in several of the events of
November 22. Not only was he in command of the first team of police
to enter and search the book depository immediately after the assassination, he was also in the second squad car to arrive on the scene of
the Tippit shooting; and he was one of the officers who wrestled
Oswald to the floor of the Texas Theatre and brought him back to
police headquarters.[23] The three events took place in different parts
of the city several miles apart but within a span of less than ninety
minutes. Apart from his remarkable ubiquity during that crucial hour
and a half, Hill is also interesting because of his long-time acquaintance with Jack Ruby.[24]

Hill was still on the Dallas police force—advanced to lieutenant
—when I visited Dallas in 1973. I interviewed him several times, and
these conversations are discussed in Chapters 8, 9, and 10.

One of the most important witnesses interviewed on the CBS
tapes was Capt. James J. Humes, the pathologist who presided over
the president's autopsy at Bethesda Naval Hospital.[25] Before the
interview Humes had visited the National Archives and had been
permitted to examine the autopsy photographs and x-rays. During the
interview he produced a sketch of the president's body, representing
wounds in the number and locations described in the official autopsy

report. The interviewer asked, "Your reexamination of the photographs verify that the wounds were as shown here?"

"Yes, sir," he replied. There was almost no stress.

Were there any other wounds except the one at the base of the neck and the one in the skull?

"No, sir, there were not." There was moderate-to-good stress, not quite enough to suggest deception.

Was there any doubt that the wound at the back of the president's head was an entry wound?

"There is absolutely no doubt, sir." Again there was moderate-to-good stress.

All together, how many wounds were there?

"There were two wounds of entrance and two of exit." The stress was now good-to-hard.

Where were the entry wounds located?

"Posteriorly, one low in the right posterior scalp, and one in the base of the neck on the right." This showed good stress.

"Could he be absolutely certain that what he said was an entry wound was, in fact, that?

"Yes, indeed we can." This showed hard stress.

The interview with Humes was one of the longest and most detailed on the CBS tapes, and I charted most of it with the PSE. It was clear that he believed much of what he was saying, but the frequent flickerings of moderate-to-good stress and the occasional flashes of hard stress suggested that he wasn't nearly as confident of his testimony as he claimed to be. The two subjects that nearly always elicited good or hard stress were entry wounds and the matter of how certain he was.

The PSE confirmed Humes's statement that he had absolutely no doubt that the wound at the back of the president's head was an entry wound, yet nearly every other statement about the location and number of entry wounds seemed to produce considerable stress. The problem seems obvious—the wound in the throat. Humes did not even know of its existence until the telephone conversation with Dr. Perry in Dallas, after the president's body was already lying in state in the Capitol Rotunda and there was no possibility of a second examination. The autopsy photographs would only have shown

Humes the tracheotomy, which obscured the size and shape of the wound. Humes had been unable to probe the back wound to link it up with the throat wound, which he should have been able to do if both were caused by the same bullet.

Since he had not examined the throat wound during the autopsy and since his autopsy examination was not completely consistent with the belief that the shoulder bullet had completely traversed the body, some residue of doubt about the throat wound should have remained in Humes's mind. Yet the PSE confirms that Humes is confident the shoulder and head wounds were entry wounds. Assuming the x-rays showed no bullet still in the body, how could the throat wound be anything but an exit wound? The answer that occurs to this writer and may have worried Humes is that the massive entry wound in the back of the head, caused by the final shot, might have obscured a smaller exit wound caused a few seconds earlier by a shot from the grassy knoll striking the president in the throat.

In any event, the PSE results clearly contradict the theory that Captain Humes was part of a conspiracy systematically to misrepresent the real autopsy results. If Humes was covering up anything, it was his own doubt. The CBS interviewer asked him one good "bottom line" question,

"Do you have any different conclusion, any different ideas, any different thoughts now, after seeing [the autopsy photographs] again, than you had at that time?"

"No," replied Humes, "we think they bear up very well and very closely our testimony before the Warren Commission." The stress was hard.

PSE analysis of the case against Lee Harvey Oswald, as represented by the recorded statements of the Warren Commission's witnesses, raises an appalling number of fresh doubts. But what of the members of the commission and its staff? Did those learned lawyers and statesmen believe the conclusions they presented in their own report? For the answer, we must go to the recorded voices of the Warren Commission, its staff and its counsel.

6 THE COMMISSION

> The rulers of the state are the only ones who should
> have the privilege of lying, either at home or abroad;
> they may be allowed to lie for the good of the state.
> —Plato: *The Republic*

The Warren Report's strongest claim to credibility is presented at the beginning of that document, on the page listing the members of the Warren Commission and its staff. The chairman was the chief justice of the United States Supreme Court and, in the view of many historians, one of the greatest Americans ever to occupy that position. Four of the commission members were eminent legislators; the other two had distinguished themselves in government service and international law. A mixture of Democrats and Republicans, liberals and conservatives insured political balance. The twenty-seven members of the commission's legal counsel and staff included some of the most respected lawyers in America. It is commonly believed that the Warren Report was the product of ten months of investigation in which each commission and staff member fully participated. This, however, is not exactly what happened.

In June 1966 Edward Jay Epstein published his study of the Warren Commission entitled *Inquest.*[1] Epstein wrote his book as a master's thesis in government at Cornell University. His objective was to examine the functioning of a government organization in an extraordinary situation in which there were no rules or precedents to guide it, and he chose the Warren Commission as a case study. Through Professor Andrew Hacker of Cornell, Epstein obtained interviews with several members of the commission and its staff including former assistant counsel Wesley Liebeler.[2] Liebeler gave Epstein access to his personal files on the commission's investigation on the mistaken belief that the same information was also available to the public at the National Archives.[3] Epstein's study provided the first inside view of how the Warren Commission reached its conclusions and wrote its report. Publication of *Inquest* caused a mild sensation.

Epstein's window on the inner workings of the commission presented a picture completely contrary to the one popularly imagined. The investigation did not last ten months, but barely half of that period; the early months were taken up by organizational and procedural matters, the final months were consumed by the writing of the report. The six commissioners had little or no participation in the investigation, which was really conducted by the staff.* The experienced senior members of the commission's legal staff were paid $100 per day for their services—much less than their usual fees—so most of them worked only a few days for the commission, even though their names appear on the Report. The greatest part of the investigation was carried out by the junior members of the staff. After July 1964 all of the senior attorneys had returned to private practice, and only three of the junior men continued working full-time for the commission.

Epstein also revealed that the commission had no investigators of its own in the field. It relied on the Federal Bureau of Investigation, the Central Intelligence Agency, and the Secret Service to collect and analyze evidence, to conduct the field investigation, and to locate and interview witnesses. When the commission received a report from the Texas authorities that Oswald may have been an employee of the FBI, it assigned the FBI itself to investigate this matter and accepted the FBI's assurance that there was no substance to the report. The handful of staff members who were actually conducting the investigation were required to communicate with the FBI and the CIA through a Justice Department lawyer assigned to the staff as liaison; all direct requests to these agencies for information were refused, and the requestor was told to "go through channels." Simi-

*Meagher notes that less than one-fourth of the witnesses who gave testimony actually appeared before the commission; the others were examined by the staff. She observes that in none of the cases in which witnesses did testify before the commission were all seven members present during the entire examination. (*Accessories After the Fact*, p. xxx).

larly, all communication between the commission and the staff had to be funneled through J. Lee Rankin, the commission's general counsel. Such communication was, in fact, quite limited, and to the commission staff, Chief Justice Warren was the commission.

Epstein's most disquieting revelations concerned the attitude of Warren and the other commissioners regarding the purpose of the investigation. He presents persuasive evidence that the commission's primary objective was to dispel rumors at home and abroad regarding the assassination, rather than to make a thorough and objective investigation of what really happened. The staff was directed to complete their work by June 1, and a June 30 deadline was initially set for releasing the report. When these dates could not be met, the White House and the commission exerted increasing pressure on the staff to finish. The commissioners considered it essential that the work be completed well before the presidential election in November to prevent the assassination from becoming a campaign issue.

While Epstein's account of the Warren Commission's procedures will not appear especially sinister to anyone familiar with government operations, it is clear that the investigation of President Kennedy's assassination was carried out by a handful of lawyers—most of them junior—in rigidly bureaucratic circumstances, under intense political pressure to complete their work in much less time than they actually required to do a thorough job. This is a far cry from the popular image of the Warren Commission and falls considerably short of what was necessary to establish beyond reasonable doubt the truth about the events in Dallas.

Epstein's study was well-documented, and his sources were the commissioners, the staff members, and their unpublished files. I interviewed Wesley Liebeler in May 1973, and he told me, "Shortly after Epstein's book came out, I was in Washington and I talked to Chief Justice Warren. He was a little critical of me, and he put it very bluntly. He said, 'It looks like you wrote about half of Epstein's book.' "[4]

Liebeler had not, in fact, written any of Epstein's book, although he had made his private files available to the writer. But Warren's comment confirms that Epstein's study was a fairly accurate inside view of the Warren Commission at work.

Epstein's thesis was not that the Warren Commission had been a part of some dark assassination conspiracy, but that it had selected testimony and evidence to support a lone gunman theory and ignored equally valid and persuasive indications that there had been a second assassin. Epstein summarized his position in the final paragraph of *Inquest:*

Why did the Commission fail to take cognizance in its conclusions of this evidence of a second assassin? Quite clearly, a serious discussion of this problem would in itself have undermined the dominant purpose of the Commission, namely, the settling of doubts and suspicions. Indeed, if the Commission had made it clear that very substantial evidence indicated the presence of a second assassin, it would have opened a Pandora's box of doubts and suspicions. In establishing its version of the truth, the Warren Commission acted to reassure the nation and protect the national interest.[5]

But if the commission did bias its Report to support its preestablished conclusion that Lee Harvey Oswald was the assassin and that he acted alone, the question remains: Did the commissioners and staff members themselves believe that conclusion? To find an answer, I used the PSE to analyze some of their recorded statements.

Arlen Specter, one of the junior attorneys who was most involved in the commission's work, was interviewed on the CBS tapes. He stated that the case against Oswald fitted together very well and, "seldom would you find a case which was as persuasive."[6] There was some stress in Specter's statement, but it never rose above the moderate-to-good level. The PSE seems to confirm that he believed what he said.

John McCloy, a member of the commission, was also interviewed on the CBS program.[7] He said much the same thing as Specter and added that he had seen no credible evidence to contradict the findings of the commission. There was virtually no stress in any of this. In speaking of the Report, however, McCloy added, "There was nothing fraudulent about it," and showed good-to-hard stress.

Specter and McCloy appear to belive in the essential validity of the commission's findings, although the sudden onset of hard stress in McCloy's denial of fraud in the Report suggests that he may feel the document was somewhat slanted to support these findings.

Bob Smith of the Committee to Investigate Assassinations lent me a tape recording he made of the Louis Lomax television program in October 1966 on which Wesley Liebeler was interviewed.[8] Apparently Mark Lane had been on an earlier Lomax program, and now Liebeler was on to rebut him. It was apparent, even without PSE analysis, that Liebeler was under heavy stress, and, in view of the circumstances, this is not particularly remarkable. The interview was conducted before a studio audience which seemed to be composed primarily of people hostile to Liebeler and his point of view.* It was obvious that in appearing on the Lomax program, Liebeler was representing a very unpopular position, and the PSE showed that he was experiencing a high general level of stress.

Most of the exchange between Liebeler, Lomax, and the audience was argumentative and did not deal with specific points of fact. However, I found two key statements by Liebeler and charted them.

The first statement, in response to a question by Lomax, was, "I have no doubt about the conclusions of the Report." The stress was good-to-hard, but Liebeler's general stress was at the good level. I could draw no conclusion about the slight increase in stress accompanying this statement.

The second statement related to those commission documents that were still classified and held in the National Archives. Lomax asked Liebeler if there was anything in them which would alter Liebeler's opinion. Taken literally, it was a strange question, since Liebeler had presumably seen the documents, and if they could alter his opinion, they would already have done so. Lomax probably meant to ask if the documents conflicted with the conclusions of the Warren Report. Whatever Liebeler thought the question meant, he quickly replied, "Oh, none, none at all." PSE analysis showed hard stress in this answer, but I didn't know what to conclude from that fact.

* Around the time of the Lomax interview, Liebeler appeared on campuses in the Los Angeles area to debate Mark Lane and represent the Warren Commission's viewpoint. During those appearances, he was often the target of the same extreme abuse directed at most Establishment representatives by college students during the 1960s.

In May 1973 I interviewed Liebeler at his home in Los Angeles
(he was then a law professor at UCLA). He was candid and open in
our conversation, and he made some effective points in response to
my questions about the commission. For instance, when I pointed
out that Sen. Richard Russell, a member of the commission, had
stated in 1970 that he never believed Oswald acted alone and that
Warren had refused to let him state his dissent in the Report, Liebeler noted that of all the commissioners, Russell had been least
involved in the investigation.* He also pointed out that Warren and
Russell were ideological adversaries and that it was difficult to imagine how Warren could have coerced Russell into signing the Warren
Report against his will.

Liebeler admitted that most of the commission's work was done
by the junior lawyers on the staff, but he offered this as proof that
the Report was not a cover-up. A group of young attorneys, he said,
would gain nothing by suppressing evidence of an assassination conspiracy but could greatly enhance their reputations by exposing it.
Liebeler summed up:

> The people who wrote the Warren Report were human beings
> just like everybody else, and they make mistakes. You can only
> know things to a certain degree of certitude; beyond that, you take
> it on faith and you live your life.
>
> We did the best goddamn job we knew how to do, given the
> limitations. The only problem was that we didn't have enough
> time. There was too much pressure to get the job done. I thought
> that after we finished we should have gone off on a couple of weeks
> vacation, then taken another look at it. If we had done that, it
> would have been much more difficult to criticize.
>
> The Report wasn't the kind of thing I would like to have filed
> with the Supreme Court: I would have liked to have spent more
> time working the thing over, but I don't think there is anything
> that we could have found, and I don't think anybody has found
> anything since then, that would suggest that there was anything
> involved other than what was indicated in the Report.

*Meagher reports that Russell was present for the testimony of only six
of the witnesses who appeared before the commission.

Naturally, I had to know, and shortly after the interview I returned to my motel room, set up the PSE, and played the recording of my conversation with Liebeler. Liebeler's voice was remarkably lacking in stress, and the PSE confirmed that, in general, he really was as candid as he seemed to be. Some stress of the moderate-to-good variety appeared whenever he categorically disclaimed any doubt about the conclusions of the commission, but it was clear that he harbored no serious reservations. This is no more nor less than what might be expected: Liebeler is an astute attorney, and the defects in the commission's case cannot have escaped him, but it would be imprudent of him to discuss whatever misgivings he has in a casual interview with a journalist. The PSE analysis made it apparent that Liebeler believes the Warren Report is the most probable explanation of the assassination.

There were only a few instances of hard stress on the tape. One of these occurred when I asked Liebeler if the staff received full cooperation in the investigation from the FBI and the CIA. He replied that he had only asked the CIA for assistance once and that the agency was not very helpful, but the matter involved was of small importance. He noted that the FBI is a highly bureaucratic organization, hence, inconvenient to work with, but added, "The FBI did everything we asked them to do that I can recall, and we never had any problem about that." On this last statement, the stress level shot up from none to hard.

I was, of course, curious about the reason for the great stress accompanying this statement, but I saw no way to pursue the matter at the time. Sometime later I received a photocopy of the following letter Liebeler wrote to a man in Irving, Texas, two years after the Warren Report was published, and this helped to clear things up.*

The letter reads as follows:

* I do not know specifically how my source obtained a copy of this letter, but I am certain that it was not done illegally. The letter is written on UCLA School of Law letterhead, and from its contents it is apparent that Liebeler was not acquainted with the addressee. Since it was not, therefore, an intimate personal message and because it bears directly on the questions discussed in this chapter, I see no reason not to include it.

October 12, 1966

Mr. Charles Klihr
2046 Rosebud
Irving, Texas
Dear Mr. Klihr:

I am a former assistant counsel to the President's Commission on the Assassination of President Kennedy. My interest in some aspects of the events of November 22, 1963 has been rearoused by some of the books that have been recently published about the Commission and its Report.

One of the pictures that Oswald took of the area around General Walker's house showed a car parked behind the General's house. The picture was multilated by someone in such a manner that the license plate is no longer visible. When we noticed this during the investigation we asked the FBI to determine whose car it was. They asked Mr. Surrey about it and he told them he thought it was your car. I find no indication that FBI agents talked to you about the matter, however.

When I asked General Walker about it, he was not able to identify the car, which appears to be a 1957 Chevrolet.

I would appreciate it very much if you would let me know whether or not the FBI did interview you about this and if you were able to identify the car as your own. I enclose a copy of the exhibit in question so that you can determine now whether it is your car or not, if the FBI did not interview you about it.

As this matter is of some importance to me, I hope very much that you will be able to extend your cooperation.

Sincerely,
Wesley J. Liebeler
Professor of Law

Even to the casual reader, this letter will seem extraordinary. To the student of the assassination and the Warren Report, however, it speaks volumes.

Like so many other loose ends, the question of the mutilated photograph is not mentioned in the Warren Report but is buried in the twenty-six supplementary volumes. The photograph was report-

edly found by the Dallas police after the assassination when they
searched the home of Mrs. Ruth Paine, with whom Marina Oswald
was living at the time. It was turned over to the FBI and later to the
commission. It is not clear when Liebeler noticed the mutilation, but
he seems to have taken an interest in the question in July 1964, about
seven months after the photograph was discovered, because of the
testimony of Marina Oswald:

> MARINA OSWALD: When the FBI first showed me this photo-
> graph I remember that the license plate, the number of the license
> plate was on this car, was on the photograph. It had the black and
> white numbers. There was no black spot that I see on it now.
> When Lee showed me this photograph there was the number on
> the license plate in this picture. I would have remembered it if
> there were a black spot on the back of the car where the license
> plate would be.
>
> LIEBELER: The original of this picture, the actual photograph,
> has a hole through it. That's what makes this black spot. . . . you
> remember, then, that the license plate was actually on the car
> when you saw the picture?
>
> MARINA OSWALD: This black spot is so striking I would have
> remembered it if it were on the photograph that Lee showed me
> or the FBI.[9]

Liebeler asked General Walker if he could identify the automobile
in the photograph, but the General replied that he was "not very
good on cars."[10] Robert Surrey, an associate of General Walker, told
the commission he thought the auto belonged to Charles Klihr,
another Walker follower and the man to whom Liebeler addressed
his October 1966 inquiry.*[11]

The photograph was one of the pieces of evidence used to link
Oswald to the Walker shooting incident, and Mark Lane has suggested that the year on the license plate might have shown that the

---

*Surrey was established by the commission to be the author of the
"wanted for treason" handbill, which bore a photograph of President
Kennedy and a list of inflammatory accusations against him and was distributed in Dallas the day before the assassination.

picture was actually taken when Oswald was out of the country.[12] The real significance of the hole in the photograph, however, is that, based on Marina Oswald's testimony, evidence material to the commission's investigation was destroyed after it came into the possession of the FBI and the commission. The FBI interviewed Dallas detectives Stovall and Rose—two of the policemen present when the photograph was discovered—who stated that the hole was present when the photo was found in Mrs. Paine's home,*[13] but most of the commission's case that Oswald tried to shoot Walker is based on other testimony by Marina Oswald. If Liebeler and the commission considered her a truthful and reliable witness, they should have given considerable weight to her definite denial that the hole had been present when the FBI showed her the photograph.

The possibility that the license plate was punched out of the photo after it was given to the FBI raises a strong suggestion of deliberate obstruction of justice. Regardless of whether there was such obstruction, one would expect the FBI and the commission to make a special effort to solve this mystery or, at the very least, to settle the question of whose automobile it was. It seems very strange that the FBI did not even bother to ask Klihr about it.

Liebeler's letter to Klihr reveals several things about the affair. First, it tends to confirm that he was not party to a cover-up; if he were, he would not have been investigating the matter more than two years after the Report was published and the commission dissolved. Second, Liebeler's letter suggests that he continued to harbor some degree of doubt about the assassination; his interest in the matter may have been prompted merely by a desire to neutralize one of Mark Lane's debating points, or he may have had more serious suspicions, but he obviously felt that an important question remained unanswered. Third, the letter strongly suggests that Liebeler was not entirely candid when he told me, "The FBI did everything we asked them to do . . . ," a conclusion I had already reached after examining the PSE chart of this statement. Finally, the fact that Liebeler chose to contact Klihr indicates that the commission's former assistant

*Stovall and Rose pop up again in the mysterious affair of the phantom polygraph test in Chapter 10.

counsel could not or would not rely on the FBI to tie up this loose end. One can hardly blame him.

There was one more thing I found interesting about the letter: it was dated October 12, 1966, just four days before Liebeler appeared on the Louis Lomax show and said, "I have no doubts about the conclusions of the Report," a statement that showed good-to-hard stress on the PSE.

Liebeler's assigned role in the commission's investigation was "to explore Oswald's life and to delineate factors which might have caused him to assassinate the President."*[14] Thus, Liebeler's familiarity with the investigation was necessarily narrowed, and, as he readily admitted, neither he nor any of the other staff members acquired a synoptic view of the evidence and testimony that filled the twenty-six volumes. In fact, with the possible exception of J. Lee Rankin, who acted as liaison between the staff and the commission, the only individual who was in a position to acquire a total picture of the investigation was the chairman, Chief Justice Earl Warren. Liebeler's belief in its essential validity is an impressive endorsement of the Warren Report, but it would be far more valuable to know what Warren himself believed.

Warren declined to be interviewed by CBS News when it presented its 1967 program,[15] but on May 3, 1972, he appeared on a television program in Boston, part of a series called "The Brandeis Television Recollections." I was able to obtain a tape of the audio portion of the program.

The interview was an hour long, but the subjects of the Kennedy assassination and the Warren Commission came up only once. The interviewer, Abram Sachar, chancellor of Brandeis University, was friendly and deferential. I charted some of Warren's remarks unrelated to the assassination and found that he showed little stress. Sachar raised the subject of the commission obliquely, and Warren volunteered several rather lengthy statements about it.

*This assignment was made in January 1964, before the investigation had begun. It is worth noting that a major conclusion of the commission—that Oswald was the assassin—seems to have been assumed by the commission to be true before even a single witness was called to testify.

Warren said that immediately after the assassination there were two theories, one that Khrushchev and Castro were behind the killing, the other that a group of right-wing Texas oil men was responsible. He said, "We explored both of those theories for ten months and found no evidence that either of them was involved in it." There was good-to-hard stress in the statement.

Warren continued, ". . . we found no evidence of any kind that there was any conspiracy." The stress was still good-to-hard, and it was hardest on the words, "no evidence."

"I have read everything," said Warren, "that has come to my notice in the press, and I read some of the documents that have criticized the commission very severely, but I have never found that they discovered any evidence of any kind that we didn't discover and use in determining the case as we did." The stress was good-to-hard, and it peaked on the word "never."

"I have found nothing since that time," he continued, "to change my view, nor have I heard of anything that has changed the view of any member of the commission since that time." Again the stress was good-to-hard, and it peaked on the words "nothing" and "member." Apart from the PSE analysis, this statement is remarkable in itself, since it is not credible that Warren was unaware of Senator Russell's public statement two years earlier.

Warren made one general reference to the relationship between the commission and the other government agencies involved in the investigation. He said that President Johnson had directed the heads of every department of the government to withhold nothing from the commission, no matter how classified the information might be. "And," he added, "we got everything, as far as we know, and as far as we believe, everything that any of those departments had bearing upon it." The stress was good-to-hard, mostly hard.

Perhaps it is advisable at this point to recall that stress, even hard stress, such as that in former Chief Justice Warren's statements, is not necessarily indicative of deception. Warren was certainly one of the greatest Americans of our time, a distinguished and courageous man who, perhaps more than anyone else of his generation, advanced the causes of justice and civil liberties. Because of his leadership in these causes, he has been the target of vicious public slander. Even to entertain the possibility that he was not telling the truth seems abhorrent.

Students of history will readily admit that great men sometimes lie in a noble cause, but it seems hard to imagine a motive so noble that a man of Warren's character would dissemble about the assassination of a president. In fact, many believe the Warren Report in the face of its defects simply because it is inconceivable that Justice Warren could have been a party to covering up a political murder, no matter who was responsible for it. The improbabilities of the official explanation are outweighed by the endorsement of a man beyond reproach.

But suppose for the moment that Warren had as many grave doubts about the commission's case as the harshest critic of the Report. What options would have been open to him? He could, of course, have gone to the FBI and demanded that the doubtful questions be reinvestigated, but suppose he did that and still came out with more questions than answers. What then?

As Warren said in his television interview, there were two general conspiracy theories. One theory attributed the assassination to Khrushchev or Castro, the other blamed it on a domestic right-wing group. The commission developed huge amounts of evidence which could be used to support either of these theories: Oswald, the presumed gunman, had defected to Russia, lived there for three years, returned and joined the Fair Play for Cuba Committee, and was said to have visited the Soviet and Cuban embassies in Mexico City less than two months before the assassination. But he also attended meetings of General Walker's right-wing group and was reported to have been seen in the company of anti-Castro Cubans. And Dallas, the scene of the crime, was the center of much extreme right-wing political activity, including a campaign of virulent anti-Kennedy propaganda. If the assassination was the work of more than one person, then one or the other of these two theories was almost certainly correct. But which one?

The assassination occurred at a time when the country was threatened by Communist aggression abroad and racist violence at home. The murder of Medgar Evers and the bombing of a black Sunday school in Birmingham had taken place only months before. The Cuban missile crisis had occurred little more than a year earlier. And even as the commission deliberated, three civil-rights workers were brutally murdered in Mississippi. The Bay of Pigs and the crises in Berlin were still fresh in our memory. If Warren equivocated, if the commission offered us anything less than certainty, then the pressure of our hates and fears would have rushed in to fill the vacuum of doubt. A tornado of national violence might have been spun.

But perhaps the most terrifying nightmare to torture Warren was the possibility that doubt would give voice to that darkest of all suspicions—the *cui bono* theory. The vice-president was a powerful Texan, and the president was murdered in Texas. Lyndon Johnson was surely not insensitive to the whisperings which began even before Air Force One returned from Dallas, and his appointment of a commission headed by Justice Warren to investigate the assassination was an eloquent statement that he had nothing to hide. But Warren certainly realized that an open verdict by the commission would fuel these rumors. As the commission's investigation progressed, the 1964 presidential campaign moved into high gear. The candidate nominated by the Republicans in August was a man of integrity, but, as our recent history has confirmed so dramatically, there are ruthless people in American politics who will not hesitate to use the most vicious slander against an opponent. The Warren Report was released five weeks before the election.

Justice Warren may have had doubts as he brought the commission's work to a close in the early autumn of 1964, but he surely had no alternatives. It is one thing to suspect, quite a different thing to know, and yet a completely separate thing to have a case with which to obtain indictments and convictions. And no one would know this better than the chief justice of the United States Supreme Court. A report admitting that the case against Lee Harvey Oswald was less than airtight, that the assassination may have been the work of a conspiracy, that the commission had been unable to determine definitely what had happened was an option closed to any person who put his country's interest above all else.

If this was, in fact, Warren's dilemma, the situation was almost classic in its ironic tragedy: a man who had devoted his life to justice was, in the twilight of his career, confronted with the realization that truth and the national good had become opposing interests. A good and wise man may have lied as an act of profound self-sacrifice in the service of his country.

7 THE MAN WHO DID NOT KILL THE PRESIDENT

The shots which killed President Kennedy and wounded Governor Connally were fired by Lee Harvey Oswald.

—Report of the President's Commission on the Assassination of President John F. Kennedy

"I didn't shoot anybody."
—Lee Harvey Oswald

Throughout that long afternoon and evening of November 22, the reporters came to Dallas. Nearly every major newspaper, wire service, and television network was represented. In the homicide and robbery bureau on the third floor of Dallas police headquarters, a police captain and agents of the FBI and Secret Service were questioning Lee Harvey Oswald. Outside in the corridor television cameramen were setting up their equipment, and newsmen were beginning to assemble. As the evening wore on, more than one hundred reporters jammed into the narrow third-floor hallway.

Inside the homicide and robbery bureau—according to reports of the Dallas police, the FBI, and the Secret Service—Oswald was advised of his right to legal representation, of his right to remain silent, and that any statement he made could be used against him in a court of law.[1] Sometime during the night, Oswald was asked about the shootings and he emphatically denied killing either President Kennedy or Officer Tippit.[2] He refused to discuss the assassination with the FBI agents until he was represented by an attorney.[3] When he was asked to submit to a polygraph examination, he refused to do so until he had an opportunity to consult a lawyer.[4]

Several times during the evening Oswald was taken under guard from the third-floor office to appear in lineups and to be arraigned for the murder of Officer J.D. Tippit. At midnight he was taken to the basement for a brief and and confused "press conference." Whenever Oswald was brought out of the third-floor office, the reporters elbowed forward, vying with each other to get a statement from the prisoner. In answer to their shouted questions, Oswald expressed bewilderment at his situation and protested that he had not been allowed legal representation. When asked if he had killed the president, Oswald replied that he had not. Although nothing he said in the police interrogation room was recorded, the newsmen's microphones captured Oswald's statements in the corridor and at the press conference. At least two of his claims to innocence were recorded on tape.

He could not have known it at the time, but when Oswald spoke those words, he was taking a lie-detector test. Eight years would pass before the lie detector would be invented that could test for the subtle and inaudible vocal clues that are evidence of truth or deception. Another two years would elapse before anyone used the psychological stress evaluator to test Oswald's denials that he killed President Kennedy. In 1973, I obtained copies of those recordings and processed them with the PSE.

The CBS tapes contained this brief exchange between Oswald and the newsmen, recorded at the midnight press conference in the basement of police headquarters:

OSWALD: I positively know nothing about this situation here. I would like to have legal representation.

REPORTER: (unintelligible)

OSWALD: Well, I was questioned by a judge. However, I protested at that time that I was not allowed legal representation during that very short and sweet hearing. I really don't know what this situation is about. Nobody has told me anything, except that I'm accused of murdering a policeman. I know nothing more than that. I do request someone to come forward to give me legal assistance.

REPORTER: Did you kill the president?

OSWALD: No, I have not been charged with that. In fact, nobody has said that to me yet. The first thing I heard about it was when the newspaper reporters in the hall asked me that question.[5]

The press conference was held under circumstances very unfavorable for stress-deception analysis. Oswald was shackled between two policemen. He had been brought into the basement lineup room to face a battery of television lights and cameras and a surging mob of newsmen. Each reporter was trying to outshout his fellows in the competition for a statement. I expected to find a uniform level of hard stress in both relevant and irrelevant statements, but I discovered that this was not the case.

The first statement, "I positively know nothing about this situation here," showed good-to-hard stress. The stress was moderate-to-good in, "I would like to have legal representation." It remained at that level until he said, "I protested at that time," when it went back up to hard. The stress dropped back to good, then moderate-to-good in the phrase, "I really don't know what this situation is about." It continued good until he said, "I know nothing more than that," at which time it turned hard again. "I do request someone to come forward to give me legal assistance" was moderate-to-good, except for the word "someone," which was hard.

The statement, "No, I have not been charged with that" showed an unusual range of stress. It began with almost no stress, but there was hard stress on the word "that." On listening repeatedly to the recording, I noticed that Oswald ran the words "no" and "I" together, producing the same phonetic effect as "know why." Electronically, it was a single, two-syllable word, and it produced a single waveform on the PSE chart. The waveform began with almost no stress but ended with good stress. Obviously, it was important to discover how much of the stress had been present during the "no" part of the utterance.

I played the tape several times at a reduced speed until I was able to identify the point at which the o vowel ended and the i sound began. I made a small visible mark on the tape at this point then switched the recorder to the even slower speed required by the PSE.

I backed up the tape, switched on the PSE, and played the statement again. When the mark on the tape reached the recorder's playback head, I switched off the machine. The PSE stylus dropped back to the zero line. I looked at the waveform.

The stress was none-to-moderate.

I asked Mike Kradz of Dektor to look at the charts. I told him that the speaker was a young man accused of murdering a policeman and an executive, who had been interviewed by reporters under chaotic conditions in a police station. I showed Kradz the transcript of the tape, but I had altered the question, "Did you kill the president," to read, "Did you kill him?" As Kradz inspected the charts, he did not know that the speaker was Lee Harvey Oswald or that the murdered executive was John Kennedy.

Kradz studied the charts carefully and said it seemed the speaker was telling the truth when he denied the murder. While he was impressed with the low level of stress in the "no," which I had separated electronically from the rest of the statement, he felt that even considering the increased stress that appears later in the sentence, there was a strong indication that the young man wasn't lying. Kradz pointed out that the stress, although considerable, was not equal to the consistently hard stress shown in the phrases, "I positively know nothing about this situation here," and "I know nothing more than that." The young man may have been lying when he made those statements, or there may have been some other reason for the stress. But whatever the case, Kradz pointed out, that subject seemed to mean a great deal more to the speaker than the matter of murdering the executive. The indication was that he didn't do it.

After he announced his conclusion, I told Kradz that the speaker was Lee Harvey Oswald and the murdered executive was President Kennedy. The excop stared at me for a moment, then picked up the charts again and examined them minutely. Finally he put them down and shook his head in disbelief. "I wonder who he thought he killed," he said.

Kradz's incredulousness was only natural; the charge that Lee Harvey Oswald killed President Kennedy has gained widespread acceptance, even in the face of public doubts about the Warren Report. During the first few years after the assassination, Oswald was de-

scribed in the press as "the alleged assassin," an implicit reference to
the fact that he had not lived to be convicted of the crime in a court
of law. But, as propagandists have often demonstrated, repetition of
a charge gradually leads to its public acceptance. Ten years after the
event, even most skeptics doubted only that "Oswald acted alone."

I was too familiar with the weaknesses in the case against Oswald
and had seen too many indications of deception in the recorded
statements of the witnesses against him to be very surprised at this
new discovery. I remembered the words of ex-FBI agent William
Turner in his book, *Invisible Witness:* "While in police custody
Oswald's demeanor was not that of a wanton assassin. He steadfastly
denied the crime and some newsmen were struck by the appearance
of genuine shock when he was told he was accused of the assassination."[6]

But Kradz's skepticism led him to think about the chart and
transcript I had shown him, and he finally raised a point which, I was
forced to agree, made the PSE results less than 100 percent conclusive: it is not completely clear what Oswald meant when he responded to the question, "Did you kill the president?" The Warren
Report contains the following transcription of his reply: "No. I have
not been charged with that."[7] If the statement is read as two distinct
sentences, Oswald seems to be denying his guilt and then adding that
he has not been charged with the crime (which, at the time of the
midnight press conference, was the case). But, as I knew from listening to the tape, Oswald sounded as though he were saying, "No, I
have not been charged with that," in one sentence, not two. Was
"no" a specific denial of guilt or merely a rejection of the question,
a way of saying, in effect, "Don't ask me that; even the police haven't
accused me of that"?

Of course, if Oswald had been the man who killed the president
only hours earlier, he might be expected to show hard stress while
making any reference to the shooting, no matter how oblique, and
it certainly should have been a more stressful subject than what he
knew about the circumstances of his arrest. But Oswald's denial
seemed ambiguous, and the PSE results, however interesting, could
not be called absolutely conclusive. It seemed likely, however, that
Oswald was asked the crucial question by newsmen again during the
night of November 22, and his answer was probably recorded on tape

somewhere. I set out to find a recording of a categorical denial, and several weeks later I succeeded.

Ironically, my search ended in Dallas. I was visiting Al Chapman, one of the hundreds of private citizens who do not believe the Warren Report and continue to investigate the case. Chapman has compiled a small library of materials relating to the assassination, including some sound recordings. Among these I found a long-playing record called *Probe*, which was released several years ago by Columbia Records. *Probe* is an audio documentary on the assassination (and one of the bitterest attacks on the critics of the Warren Report), and it contains many excerpts from news recordings made during the weekend of the assassination.

Lee Harvey Oswald speaks only once on the record, apparently while he is being led along the crowded third-floor corridor of the police station:

> OSWALD: These people have given me a hearing without legal representation or anything.
> REPORTER: Did you shoot the president?
> OSWALD: I didn't shoot anybody, no sir.

I transferred the segment to tape. Later, I processed the recording with the PSE.

Oswald's protest that he has been given a hearing without legal representation shows good-to-hard stress. His categorical denial that he shot anyone contains almost no stress at all.

I remembered Colonel Bell's words when I showed him the Clifford Irving charts. Bell told me he had known that Irving was lying, not by analyzing Irving's claim that he had interviewed Howard Hughes, but by analyzing Hughes's statement that he had never met Irving. Stress is a necessary, but not sufficient, condition of lying; it must be interpreted, and therein lies the margin of error. But the absence of stress is a sufficient condition of truthfulness. If someone is talking about a matter of real importance to himself and shows absolutely no stress, then he must be telling the truth.

Oswald denied shooting *anybody*—the president, the policeman, anybody. The psychological stress evaluator said he was telling the truth.

But, despite the many other indications that Oswald was innocent, the almost complete absence of stress in his voice is still remarkable, in view of the circumstances of his conversation with the press. The recording sounded clear and of excellent technical quality, and hard stress was apparent in his voice when he protested that he had been denied legal representation. Still, I wondered if some yet unknown recording phenomenon had managed to eradicate the stress in Oswald's statement of innocence. This didn't seem very likely, but I was uncomfortable with the fact that the tape had been made from a phonograph record, which, in turn, had been cut from another recording. None of my other results had come from phonograph records. Did something about this medium sometimes erase stress? I decided that I would have to obtain another tape of the statement, one that was not the result of a re-recording chain involving a phonograph record. Otherwise, I couldn't be certain.

Since the *Probe* album was produced by Columbia Records, it seemed possible that the original tape was in the CBS News archives, so I visited CBS News in New York. Unlike the other broadcast networks, CBS maintains a library of nearly everything that it has ever put on news film or videotape and a huge, carefully maintained card index to the collection. The CBS people I spoke to were cooperative and helpful, but they could not find reference in the index to the clip of Oswald that I needed. It was probably on one of the reels of videotape recorded in Dallas on November 22, but finding it would require tying up some very costly video playback equipment for hours. I felt there must be a simpler route. I found it at the John F. Kennedy Library in Waltham, Massachusetts.

Pending construction of the Kennedy Library in Cambridge, Massachusetts, the books, papers, and other materials relating to the presidency of John Kennedy are stored in a government warehouse in Waltham under the custodianship of the National Archives. The collection includes two thousand sound recordings and is available to scholars and researchers. Among the recordings, I found a stack of audio tapes that had been recorded from the television network coverage of the events of November 22–25, 1963. The librarians furnished me with a recorder, a set of earphones, and a corner in the researcher's room. After two days of listening, I found what I was looking for.[8] I connected the recorder to a second machine and duplicated the brief interview with Oswald.

The Kennedy Library copy sounded the same as the recording I had found in Dallas, with one exception. On the Dallas recording Oswald says, "I didn't shoot anybody, no sir." On the Waltham recording he can be heard to say, "No, I didn't shoot anybody, no sir." The two recordings were probably made from two different microphones. Many photographs of Oswald in custody show several newsmen holding up microphones in front of him. The reporter who asked him, "Did you shoot the president?" was probably at Oswald's side, and Oswald may have been turning to face the man as he answered. Thus, some of the microphones would have missed the "no."

I ran the Waltham recording on the PSE. The initial "no" showed moderate stress. The PSE waveforms for the rest of Oswald's statements were virtually identical to the ones I made from the Dallas tape: there was good-to-hard stress on, "These people have given me a hearing without legal representation or anything," and almost no stress on, "I didn't shoot anybody, no sir." There was no longer any question of distortion from the phonograph record. The evidence that the Waltham tape had been recorded from a different microphone from the Dallas tape established that the two tapes were the end points of two completely separate transmission and recording chains. And both tapes yielded identical PSE results. It was not some strange sound-recording fluke; Lee Harvey Oswald was telling the truth.

I returned from Waltham and visited Mike Kradz at Dektor. I showed him the second set of transcript and charts. No prolonged examination was necessary: the utter lack of stress in Oswald's statement was immediately obvious. It was hard to accept, but Mike Kradz had run too many criminal cases on the PSE to have any doubts about the meaning of the PSE charts I showed him. There was no other possible explanation than that Oswald was telling the truth.

Kradz asked me if I would object to his showing the charts to someone else. I said that I wouldn't, and he stepped out of his office and returned in a few minutes with a wiry, middle-aged man whom he introduced as Rusty Hitchcock.

L. H. "Rusty" Hitchcock is a former army intelligence agent and one of the most experienced polygraph examiners in the country.

Since he graduated from the army's polygraph school at Ft. Gordon in 1954, lie detection has been his specialty. Besides conducting thousands of polygraph investigations, he has also carried out basic research in lie detection and is an expert on the phenomenon of the galvanic skin response and the effect of hypnosis on polygraph results. He is the author of many training manuals and procedural guides used by army polygraph examiners. Hitchcock is well-known in professional polygraph circles and, although he now embraces the heretical psychological stress evaluator, he is still held in high regard by most of his fellow members of the American Polygraph Association. He is retired and spends most of his time raising cattle on his Georgia ranch, but he occasionally serves as a consultant to law-enforcement agencies and private security firms.

Rusty Hitchcock was incredulous when Kradz showed him the PSE charts I had run on Oswald. He questioned me closely to assure himself that I had not made some procedural mistake in operating the PSE equipment. Convinced that I had not, he speculated that there might be a defect in the equipment I was using, and he also pointed out that I had run Oswald in only one of the PSE modes and at only one tape speed (varying the speed of the tape recorder or chart drive mechanism can sometimes reveal low-level stress which would otherwise go unnoticed). This was true, but the combination of mode and tape speed I had used was the one most often used in criminal cases, since it is completely sensitive to the levels of stress likely to be produced in such matters. Oswald had shown hard stress on the irrelevant issue and almost none on his claim of innocence.

I was certain the PSE and recorder I had used were working properly, and I was confident I would get the same results no matter what equipment, PSE mode, or tape speed I used. I offered Hitchcock a copy of the recording and suggested he check my findings with his own instruments. He replied by inviting me to his ranch, suggesting that we review the tape together. Several weeks later, I accepted his invitation.

Rusty Hitchcock lives on a quiet country road in northern Georgia. As I sat across from him in his study while he set up his PSE and recording equipment, I reflected that I had come to a strangely peaceful place to investigate a presidential assassination. Through the window, I watched some of Rusty's Black Angus cattle grazing in the pasture while he threaded the Oswald tape through his recorder and prepared to give a lie-detector test to a dead man.

We spent most of the morning and a roll of chart paper on it. I watched over his shoulder as Rusty tried each combination of PSE mode and recorder speed in turn. The answer was always the same. In the end he too was convinced. Rusty is no student of assassinations, but he is a specialist in the natural history of lying. Perhaps better than anyone, Rusty could read the message written over and over again that day by the stylus of his PSE. He had the courage of his convictions, and he gave me his findings in the form of a signed statement. It reads as follows:

Dear Mr. O'Toole:

As you requested, I have analyzed with the Psychological Stress Evaluator the tape recordings you provided of the voice of Lee Harvey Oswald. Oswald's comments regarding the circumstances of his arrest and his statements that he had been denied legal representation show considerable situation stress. When he is asked, "Did you kill the President," his reply, "No, I have not been charged with that," shows no harder stress than that found in his earlier comments. In replying to the question, "Did you shoot the President," his reply, "No, I didn't shoot anybody, no sir," contains much less stress than I found in his earlier statement regarding legal representation, made only moments before this.

My PSE analysis of these recordings indicates very clearly that Oswald believed he was telling the truth when he denied killing the President. Assuming that he was not suffering from a psychopathological condition that made him ignorant of his own actions, I can state, beyond reasonable doubt, that Lee Harvey Oswald did not kill President Kennedy and did not shoot anyone else.

/s/

Lloyd H. Hitchcock

Was Oswald a madman? The Warren Commission reported that it could reach no definite conclusion regarding Oswald's sanity in the legal sense of the word.[9] The commission included in its Report a lengthy and detailed biography of Oswald,[10] and the report of a psychiatrist who examined Oswald when he was arrested for truancy as a thirteen-year-old.[11] The psychiatrist found Oswald to be withdrawn and insecure, but not psychotic.[12] There is nothing in the commission's detailed record of Oswald's childhood and adult life to suggest that he was, in any sense, insane.

Rusty Hitchcock explained that he was not concerned about the possibility that Oswald was a pathological liar; the hard stress evident in some of his statements shows that he was responding normally to the situation in which he found himself. Rusty was allowing for the possibility that, for some reason such as temporary amnesia, Oswald was unaware of his recent actions. However, there is absolutely nothing in the official accounts of Oswald's statements while in custody that suggests he ever said he couldn't remember what he had been doing during the afternoon of November 22. There is no other plausible interpretation of the Oswald PSE charts than the explanation that Oswald was simply telling the truth.

But after ten years of repetition in books, magazines, newspapers, and the broadcast media, it is difficult to abandon the official doctrine that Lee Harvey Oswald was an assassin. Even the serious student of the Warren Report who is completely familiar with the defects in the commission's case against Oswald may be unable to resist the cumulative effect of "a well-known fact." The problems raised by skeptics with the testimony and evidence against Oswald tend to focus on the negative, to argue that the commission failed to prove its case. In debating the ballistic, photographic, and medical evidence, one tends to ignore the substantial positive arguments in favor of Oswald's innocence.

One of the strongest of these is the fact, established by the Warren Commission, that no more than ninety seconds after the president was shot, Lee Harvey Oswald was calmly standing in the lunchroom on the second floor of the book depository. Dallas motorcycle policeman M.L. Baker was riding in the presidential motorcade when the shots were fired. He got off his motorcycle and rushed into the lobby of the book depository, where he encountered Roy Truly, the depository manager. Baker and Truly ran up the stairs. On the second floor Baker saw someone going into the lunchroom. With his revolver in his hand, Baker followed. As he reached the lunchroom entrance, he saw that the room was empty except for one man, who was walking away from him. Baker called to the man, who turned around and walked over to the policeman. At this point, Truly entered the lunchroom and identified the man as Oswald.[13] The Warren Report describes the encounter:

> Baker stated later that the man did not seem to be out of breath; he seemed calm. "He never did say a word or nothing. In fact, he didn't change his expression one bit." Truly said of Oswald: "He didn't seem to be excited or overly afraid or anything. He might have been a bit startled, like I might have been if somebody confronted me. But I cannot recall any change in expression of any kind on his face." Truly thought that the officer's gun at that time appeared to be almost touching the middle portion of Oswald's body.[14]

The commission had Baker reenact his movements—getting off the motorcycle, meeting Truly in the lobby, and climbing the stairs to the second floor. Baker ran through the whole sequence twice and was timed by stopwatch. The first time he did it in one minute and thirty seconds, the second time in one minute and fifteen seconds.[15]

A Secret Service agent (and later several other people, including Chief Justice Warren) reenacted Oswald's supposed movements after firing the final shot—carrying a rifle from the southeast window to the northwest corner of the sixth floor, placing the weapon on the floor where it was allegedly discovered, descending the stairs to the second floor, and entering the lunchroom. Two trials were timed: the first, at a "normal walking pace" required one minute and eighteen seconds; the second, at a "fast walk" took one minute and fourteen seconds.[16]

There is no indication that the agent, in reenacting Oswald's supposed actions, stopped to wipe the rifle completely clear of fingerprints. (The FBI laboratory reported that there were no fingerprints on the rifle; the Dallas police claim to have found a palmprint, but on a portion of the rifle which could only be touched when the weapon was disassembled.) This might have added a few seconds to the test, although it is conceivable that the assassin could have wiped off the rifle as he walked across the sixth floor to the place where he secreted it.

Thus, the Warren Commission was able to establish that it was just barely possible for Oswald to have gotten from the southeast corner of the sixth floor to the lunchroom on the second floor between the time the final shot was fired and the moment at which Patrolman Baker and Roy Truly saw Oswald in the lunchroom. But while it was able to prove the physical possibility of its theory, it didn't even attempt to explain away the psychological problems of this version.

The absence of fingerprints on the rifle does not necessarily mean that someone wiped them off: contrary to popular opinion, weapons often do not "take" fingerprints, perhaps not even from the sweaty hands of a man waiting to murder the president of the United States. In fact, there would have been little point in Oswald wiping his prints from the rifle, since the weapon could easily be traced to him through the post-office box he had rented in his own name. But the question that the commission failed to answer, or even to ask, is why Oswald bothered to hide the rifle at all. He must have known that even if he had taken more pains than merely concealing the gun behind some cartons of books, a thorough police search of the book depository would have located it. Short of removing the rifle from the building, there was really no way in which Oswald could have hoped to keep the weapon out of the hands of the police.

If Oswald had been the assassin, then his supposed rush from the sixth-floor window to the second-floor lunchroom would have to have been for the purposes of establishing an alibi and facilitating his escape from the book depository. Time, then, would have been critical, and stopping to hide the rifle would have taken time. To carry the rifle across the sixth floor was to prolong the risk of being seen with the weapon by anyone who chanced to come upon the scene. If Oswald's plan was to avoid discovery and establish himself in the lunchroom as soon as possible, then the rifle should have been found near the southeast window, not hidden behind cartons in the northwest corner of the sixth floor.

Truly and Baker reported that when they saw Oswald in the lunchroom, he seemed calm, although a bit startled at being confronted by a policeman holding a gun. He was not, according to their account, out of breath, frightened, or excited. This would have been an extraordinary feat of self-control for a man who, ninety seconds before, pumped two bullets into the president, concealed his rifle, and hurried down four flights of stairs. If Oswald had been the assassin, if he had fled to the lunchroom to avoid detection, then confrontation by a uniformed policeman with a drawn gun should have at least suggested to him that the game might be over. But Oswald was not pale and shaken, merely startled. When his salvation arrived in the form of Roy Truly, who identified him to Baker as a depository employee, did he breathe a sigh of relief? None was reported. When Baker and Truly turned away to continue their search elsewhere, did Oswald hurry down that last flight of stairs and flee the building? He did not. According to the commission's reconstruction of events, Oswald walked over to the soft-drink machine in the lunchroom and bought a Coca-Cola.

Meagher cites some evidence that Oswald had, in fact, been drinking the Coke even before the confrontation with Baker, evidence which would support Oswald's claim that he was having lunch at the time of the shooting.[17] There is no question, however, that Oswald was drinking the Coke when he was seen, a few moments after meeting Baker, strolling through one of the offices on the second floor. Mrs. Robert Reid, a clerical supervisor at the book depository, saw him enter the office and told the commission, "I had no thoughts of anything of him having any connection with it all because he was very calm. He had gotten a Coke and was holding it in his hands and I guess the reason it impressed me seeing him in there I thought it was a little strange that one of the warehouse boys would be up in the office at that time, not that he had done anything wrong."[18] Oswald's casual presence in the second-floor office may have seemed strange to Mrs. Reid, but in view of the Warren Commission's charge that he was the assassin fleeing the scene of the crime, his pause for some leisurely refreshment seems downright incredible.

Yet another problem with the commission's reconstruction of Oswald's alleged dash from the sixth to the second floors is the testimony of an eyewitness who, during the critical seconds immediately after the shooting, happened to be on the same staircase Oswald was supposed to have used. Victoria Adams, who worked on the fourth floor of the book depository, told the commission that, within a minute of the last shot, she ran down the stairs from the fourth floor to the first floor. She said she neither saw nor heard anyone else on the stairs.[19] The commission concluded that she must have been wrong, that she really used the stairs several minutes after Oswald had already descended them.[20]

Shortly after he was seen by Mrs. Reid, Oswald left the book depository. Instead of continuing down the stairs in the northwest corner of the building adjacent to the area where he met Baker, Truly, and Reid and departing through the secluded back exit, Oswald strolled across the second floor and walked down the front staircase to the main entrance on Dealey Plaza.[21] Oswald left the building not as a murderer on the run, but like someone who had missed the excitement and was going outside to see what was happening.

Oswald never returned to the book depository but went to his furnished room in the Oak Cliff section of Dallas, and from there to a nearby movie theater. According to the reports of his interrogation, he claimed he felt that, under the circumstances, the book depository would close for the rest of the day; so, without waiting to be notified, he took the afternoon off, went home, and then went to the movies.[22] This story seems implausible,* but there is nothing in the commission's reconstruction of Oswald's trip from Dealey Plaza to his room which suggests flight. Traffic in the vicinity of the book depository had come to a standstill, and Oswald walked several blocks from the tie-up and boarded a bus. The bus went several blocks and then became stuck in the spreading traffic jam. Oswald got out and walked to the Greyhound Bus Station, where he got in a taxicab. The driver's account of what then transpired gives us a dramatic insight into Oswald's state of mind only minutes after the shooting:

> And about that time an old lady, I think she was an old lady, I don't remember nothing but her sticking her head down past him in the door and said, "Driver, will you call me a cab down here?"
>
> She had seen him [Oswald] get this cab and she wanted one, too, and he opened the door a little bit like he was going to get out and

*A more likely explanation for Oswald's afternoon moviegoing is suggested in Chapter 12.

he said, "I will let you have this one," and she says, "No, the driver will call me one."[23]

If Oswald was an assassin fleeing the scene of his crime, then he must also have been a man of remarkable chivalry.

Oswald took the taxi to Oak Cliff, went to his furnished room, changed his clothes, and went out again. Oswald's landlady, Mrs. Earlene Roberts, testified that Oswald spent only a few minutes in his room. After he left, Mrs. Roberts looked out the window and saw Oswald waiting at a bus stop in front of the rooming house.[24] Once again, Oswald is seen less than an hour after the assassination under circumstances suggesting neither furtiveness nor haste. There is, in fact, nothing in the commission's reconstruction of Oswald's movements during the ninety minutes between the assassination and Oswald's arrest in the Texas Theatre —apart from the very shaky evidence that he killed officer Tippit —to suggest that Lee Harvey Oswald had just committed the crime of the century.

The commission tried to assess the reasons for Oswald's presumed actions and devoted a chapter in the Report to "background and possible motives."[25] Even to the authors of the Report, the result was less than satisfactory. The commission concluded that it could not "ascribe to him any one motive or group of motives."[26] However, it stated that Oswald "sought for himself a place in history—a role as the 'great man' who would be recognized as having been in advance of his times,"[27] and implied that this was, at least in part, the motive for the assassination. To much of the public, this became the most plausible explanation. Oswald lost his freedom and then his life, and his name has come to surpass even that of Benedict Arnold as an American synonym for treachery. A place in history is the only thing he was awarded in exchange for this heavy price.

But one would expect such a man to demand at least a little more of history, and there were several easy options open to him through which he could have staked a claim to something more than he got. Somewhere, there should have been a manifesto, a long and boring specification of his grievances against the world, the system, and the man he is said to have killed. He could have drafted it and mailed it to the press on the morning of November 22, when he is alleged to have brought his rifle, concealed in a paper sack, to the book depository.* He could have carried it on his person and gone out in a blaze of glory by barricading himself in the book depository and shooting it out with the police and FBI. He could have surrendered himself to a local newspaper or television station where he would have received an immediate forum. He could have made his statement to the assembled newsmen and television cameras at the midnight press conference, or he could have delivered it when he was brought before a judge in the early hours of November 23 and formally arraigned for the murder of the president.

It has been suggested that Oswald had such a manifesto in mind and that he was waiting for the worldwide attention he would have received had he been brought to trial. But strolling around Dallas armed with a revolver, shooting a policeman, hiding in a darkened movie theater, and resisting arrest—if, in fact, he did any of those things—were not actions well-calculated to insure that he would live to stand trial. If the witness chair were to have been Oswald's soapbox, he should have surrendered himself in public view.

Captain Fritz of the Dallas police, who conducted Oswald's interrogation, wrote, "I asked him what he thought of President Kennedy and his family, and he said he didn't have any views on the President. He said, 'I like the President's family very well. I have my own views about national policies.' "[28] An FBI agent who was present wrote, "Oswald stated that he has nothing against John F. Kennedy personally; however, in view of the present charges against him, he did not desire to discuss this phase further."[29] A Secret Service inspector who was there wrote:

> Upon questioning by Captain Fritz, he [Oswald] said, "I have no views on the President." "My wife and I like the President's

*Recently, a would-be assassin was killed attempting to hijack an airliner and crash it into the White House to kill President Nixon. He had mailed his tape-recorded manifesto to a judge and a newspaper columnist the day before his abortive assassination attempt. Arthur Bremer, who wounded Gov. George Wallace of Alabama, left behind a diary detailing an earlier plan to assassinate Nixon.

family. They are interesting people. I have my own views on the President's national policy. I have a right to express my views but because of the charges I do not think I should comment further." Oswald said "I am not a malcontent; nothing irritated me about the President."[30]

From his remarks, Oswald clearly did expect to be brought to trial, but his statements are those of a man who plans to plead innocent and hopes to be acquitted, not someone who is waiting to shout his defiance to the world. Over and over again Oswald denied killing President Kennedy. He went to his death insisting that he had not done it.

The PSE evidence that Oswald was telling the truth, that he was not the assassin, is not my personal property. Anyone sufficiently interested is free to obtain the same recordings and subject them to the same electronic analysis. As the psychological stress evaluator becomes more familiar, not only as an investigative aid, but as an instrument of historical research, I expect others to do so, and they will obtain the same results. One noted researcher in the field of lie detection, Dr. Gordon Barland, has already done it.

Dr. Barland, who conducts lie-detection research in the Department of Psychology at the University of Utah, is well-known and respected among professional polygraph examiners. His work appears often in the Journal of the American Polygraph Association and related journals. Barland has conducted validation studies of both the polygraph and the PSE, and his work with the PSE was the first objective, scientific study to establish the effectiveness of that instrument. Barland's experience in lie detection is not limited to academic studies, however; he was a polygraph examiner in army intelligence and served on the Department of Defense Joint Working Group on Lie Detection. He is a licensed polygraph examiner in the state of Utah and is frequently called upon to aid in the investigation of criminal cases. Barland is a nationally recognized lie-detection expert, is often asked to give expert testimony on polygraph evidence in court, and serves as a consultant to the federal government on polygraph research.

Dr. Barland heard of my work on the Kennedy assassination

through his interest in the PSE, and he generously offered to review my results. I shipped a set of tapes to him in Utah and asked him to pay special attention to the Oswald denials. After spending a considerable amount of time analyzing the tapes with his own tape and PSE equipment, he called to report his results.[31]

Dr. Barland confirmed my findings of a complete lack of stress in Oswald's statement that he had not shot anyone and the presence of hard stress in the "irrelevant" statements regarding legal representation. He said that, based on the PSE charts he ran, Oswald appeared to be telling the truth when he proclaimed his innocence. Since Barland's experience with the PSE has been largely confined to controlled, polygraph-like examinations, he does not feel that he can make an absolutely conclusive judgment about any such uncontrolled interview as the exchange between Oswald and the reporter. Barland said that he thought it probably was impossible for someone to lie about such a matter, even in an uncontrolled situation, and show no stress. But, he added, he had not studied stress in uncontrolled interviews sufficiently to be categorical about it. In the interest of scientific accuracy he felt that he must use the word "probably." I asked him if he would be willing to make a numerical estimate of the probability, as he saw it, that Oswald was telling the truth. He promptly replied that he would certainly be willing to put the figure at 75 percent at the very least.

Except for my initial request of Mike Kradz that he look at the Oswald charts, I have not actively sought expert endorsement of my findings on Oswald. The psychological stress evaluator remains a controversial subject among polygraph professionals, and only a few have had the courage even to admit that the new instrument works and thus incur the wrath of their colleagues. I have not asked these few to go even further out on the limb and publicly support the thesis that Lee Harvey Oswald was not the assassin of President Kennedy. However, some of them have confidentially inquired about my work and, in every case, I have offered them my charts and tapes. Some have run the tapes on their own equipment. All who have seen the Oswald charts agree that—either certainly or very probably—Oswald was innocent. None has offered a contradictory interpretation, but only Mike Kradz, Rusty Hitchcock, and Gordon Barland have volunteered to be quoted. Yet in a court of law, any one of those three would be (and often is) accepted as an expert witness in the field of lie detection.

On Monday, November 25, 1963, John F. Kennedy was buried in Arlington National Cemetery. Presidents and kings escorted the flag-draped coffin to the grave. A squadron of jet fighters roared overhead, and a military guard fired a final salute. The bugler played taps.

In another cemetery near Fort Worth, Texas, there was another funeral. Lee Harvey Oswald's wife and mother, his brother, and his two small daughters were there, as well as newsmen and Secret Service agents. All of the clergymen Marguerite Oswald had approached refused to permit her son's body to be brought into their churches. None would even agree to conduct a graveside ceremony. A brief service was held by an official from a local church group. When he arrived, he left his Bible in his car. Reporters and Secret Service agents served as pallbearers. Later the grave was desecrated and the tombstone stolen.[32]

Oswald is one of the most hated figures in American history, and his guilt has become axiomatic. While critics of the Warren Commission sometimes find receptive and sympathetic audiences to hear their arguments, one proclaims Oswald innocent at his own peril. To offer a professional opinion in support of this thesis takes great courage. Those who have done so have earned my gratitude and admiration.

But there is more than a professional reputation to be risked in considering the PSE evidence of Oswald's innocence, there is one's peace of mind; and all who have dared to look over my shoulder have lost it. I remember vividly the emotions I felt during the afternoon and evening of November 22, as the reports came in from Dallas. In the stark tragedy of those hours there was some small consolation in knowing that the murderer had been captured. But whatever comfort there was in that belief, now it is gone. The president was killed by a person or persons unknown. Until the murderers are found, until the truth is known, until justice is done, there can be no rest and no peace. None for John Kennedy, none for Lee Oswald, and none for the rest of us all.

8 THE PHANTOM DOSSIER

Having made one lie, he is fain to make more to
maintain it. For an untruth wanting a firm founda-
tion needs many buttresses.
—Thomas Fuller: "The Lyer," *The
Holy State, The Profane State*

The National Weather Service had issued a tornado watch from 4:00
to 11:00 P.M., central standard time, and I could see the advancing
squall line on the western horizon as I drove down the Central
Expressway in the Dallas rush-hour traffic. I checked into a motel just
outside the downtown area and backed my car up to the door of my
room. An eerie greenish glow tinged the gathering clouds, and light-
ening crackled above the city as I unloaded my auto trunk. My
luggage included several dozen cassettes and reels of recording tape,
three tape recorders, and a variety of electronic odds and ends, such
as small microphones and the accessories one needs to tape record
telephone conversations. And, of course, I brought the compact
attaché case containing the psychological stress evaluator.

I had done about as much as I could with the tapes I'd managed
to retrieve from dusty storerooms across the country. A strange and
disturbing picture was emerging, but it was tantalizingly incomplete.
I was now convinced that Lee Harvey Oswald had not murdered the
president, yet a large (if defective) body of physical evidence and
testimony had implicated him. Someone had gone to a great deal of
trouble to make Oswald appear guilty, but who? The physical evidence against Oswald had been discovered by the Dallas police. Most
of the witnesses who testified against Oswald were rounded up by the
Dallas police. Some of the Dallas police officers spoke on the archives
tapes, but they had not been asked enough of the right kind of
questions. I would learn nothing more until I made some tape recordings of my own.

The tornado watch was extended until 1:00 A.M., and twisters tore through central Texas that night. Dallas was battered by high winds and severe thunderstorms. The violent Texas weather was an unwelcome omen of the danger that might still wait in this city for the outsider who happened upon a raw nerve. I knew that, during the three years following the assassination, seventeen people who had been involved in the investigation had died, some in violent and mysterious ways.[1] I had heard reports that the list continued to grow, and I planned to take every precaution to keep my name from being added to it. In the morning the skies cleared, and after a few hours' sleep I went out and began to build my cover.

It was May 1973, and my cover was that of a journalist working on a magazine piece to commemorate the upcoming tenth anniversary of the assassination. I was in Dallas to talk to those who remembered the event and to discover what, if any, lasting impact it had made on the city. I had a large camera bag slung over my shoulder, and around my neck dangled an impressive looking camera, an extra lens, and a small cassette recorder. My costume complete, I went down to Dealey Plaza and spent the day taking pictures and interviewing the tourists.

I had seen it once before, but still I felt a shock as I came upon the scene. One passes in front of the older buildings that stand along Elm Street on the western edge of the downtown section. Suddenly, one of the grim old hulks sparks a flash of recognition, the face of a famous murderer seen unexpectedly in a crowd. The Texas School Book Depository stands on the edge of Dealey Plaza, virtually unchanged during the past decade. It is empty now, locked up, and a sign warns off the curious. The vacant windows stare blindly out over the corner of Elm and Houston Streets, but the big Hertz Rent-a-Car sign on the roof still flashes the time and temperature. Below, a continuous stream of traffic passes over the spot where John Kennedy received his mortal wounds and moves past the grassy knoll, then through the triple underpass. Life and history go on, but when a sudden pause in the flow brings stillness to Dealey Plaza, there is a deep unquiet about the place.

In the Dal-Tex Building, across the street from the book depository, I found something called "The John F. Kennedy Museum." Inside there were exhibits, mainly blowups of front pages carrying news of the assasination, but there was also a Mannlicher-Carcano rifle mounted on the wall. The "museum" presented a color-slide show, with taped narration through a public address system, and a scale model of Dealey Plaza with little lights that went on and off at the right moments. Admission was $1.50 for adults, $.75 for children, and the brochure said that group rates were available on request. In the lobby there was a counter where picture postcards and commemorative ashtrays were sold. I interviewed the proprietor. He didn't trust me, but his principal worry seemed to be that I would take some unauthorized photographs in his establishment. Outside on Houston Street, a bus had unloaded a group of tourists, and business began to pick up. I left.

For the next week I continued to build my cover. I made repeated attempts to obtain an interview with the mayor, who had been a local television newsman at the time of the assassination. I had less interest in meeting him than he had in talking to me, and my efforts were fortunately ineffective. However, I got to repeat my name and story often enough to his secretary that, I assume, it had a chance to percolate throughout City Hall.

I obtained an interview with someone at the Dallas Chamber of Commerce. As it happened, he was a newcomer to Dallas who hadn't lived there in 1963. I walked into his office, shook his hand, and unharnessed myself from the dangling camera, tape recorder, and other paraphernalia. Of all the subjects I interviewed in Dallas, only he objected to having his remarks tape recorded. I was happy to spare the recorder's batteries, since the purpose of my visit was to plant my story and ask enough stupid questions to create the impression that I was harmless. I hoped that he would soon be repeating his account of the interview in some of Dallas's more fashionable watering places.

I interviewed Jesse Curry, former Dallas police chief, not because I suspected that he had any guilty secrets about the assassination, but because his prominent historic role in the event made him a logical subject for someone with the objective I claimed to have. Curry himself has raised public questions about the Warren Commission's case against Oswald,[2] a strong indication that he has no personal interest in the cover-up. And at the time of the shooting, he was riding in the motorcade immediately in front of the presidential limousine, hardly an intelligent choice of positions for anyone who knew that there was to be rifle fire from the book depository.

In any event, Curry's information could hardly have much bearing on the evidentiary matters in the case against Oswald. He was not an active participant in the investigation, which was supervised by Capt. Will Fritz, the head of the Dallas homicide and robbery bureau, and most of the legwork was done by Fritz's people and members of the identification bureau, working under the direction of Capt. George Doughty. Curry was at Parkland Hospital immediately after the assassination, then he accompanied Vice-President Johnson to the airport and stayed there during most of the afternoon. He was briefly present from time to time during the interrogation of Oswald, but he did not play a major role in the questioning. As would be expected, his principal task during that weekend was that of a police administrator dealing with the press, local officials, and the FBI and Secret Service. Because he was a witness to history, Curry is an interesting man to talk to, but the real value of my interview developed when, without any prompting, he suggested that I talk to some of the people who were already on my list. I had been worried that my cover story might seem insufficient reason to look them up. When I finally did, I told them that I had been referred by Mr. Curry, secure in the knowledge that he would confirm this if they happened to check.

I took some time out from my role playing to make contact with a few of the private assassination researchers in the Dallas area. This had to be done discreetly, and I drove to our meetings by circuitous routes, making frequent u-turns to clear my rear-view mirror. I was impressed by the courage and dedication of these people who continue to search for the facts at the scene of the crime. I was surprised to discover that they are typical Dallas citizens, boosters of Texas in general and Dallas in particular. Most are clearly to the political right and tend to view the assassination as a Communist conspiracy, but above all they want the truth to be known, regardless of the consequences.

One researcher, a woman who lives in a Dallas suburb, has amassed the largest collection of books, files, photographs, and other assassination materials I have seen. She stores the collection in an outbuilding behind her house, guarded by a pair of huge, snarling dogs which she held at bay with a broom while I scurried from her back door into her library. I asked her if she had any sound recordings relating to the assassination. She produced several, the most interesting of which was a radio interview with Officer Gerry Hill recorded during the afternoon of November 22.

Hill is the ubiquitous police sergeant who was in the book depository supervising the discovery of the rifle shells a few minutes after the shooting, next was in the second squad car to arrive at the scene of the Tippit shooting, and then a few minutes later was one of the policemen who dragged Oswald out of the Texas Theatre. I had already turned up hard stress in his account of finding the shells on the CBS tapes, so I was particularly interested in this interview, and I made a copy of it.

After another nervous trip past the snarling guard dogs, I brought the tape back to my motel room and analyzed some of Hill's statements with the PSE. He showed a fairly high general level of stress, so it was difficult to draw any firm conclusions from the charts. However, several of the statements Hill made were interesting in themselves. One pertained to the revolver alleged to have been in Oswald's hand when he was arrested in the theater, the same weapon linked to the Tippit shooting:

> INTERVIEWER: What kind of weapon did he use to kill the officer with, Gerry?
>
> HILL: A thirty-eight snub nose that was fired twice, and both shots hit the officer in the head.

Officer J.D. Tippit had been killed by four bullets[3], but Hill might not have known this at the time of the interview. He had been at the scene of the Tippit shooting, but the body had already been removed when he arrived, according to his own testimony before the commission.[4] But what Hill should have known was whether or not there were any spent shells in the gun's cylinder, since it was in his possession from the time of Oswald's arrest until he turned it in at headquarters. In Hill's arrest report, he wrote:

> As Officer Carroll started to get into the car, he pulled a snub-nosed revolver from his belt and handed it to me. He stated this

was the suspect's gun and that he had obtained it from Officer McDonald immediately after the suspect was subdued. When the pistol was given to me, it was fully loaded and one of the shells had a hammer mark on the primer.

I retained this gun in my possession until approximately 3:15 P.M., Friday, November 22, 1963, when in the presence of Officers Carroll and McDonald, I turned the weapon over to Detective T. L. Baker of the Homicide and Robbery Bureau . . . I marked the side of the casing on all the shells, which were also turned over to Detective Baker at the same time.[5]

If any doubt remains that Hill meant live ammunition, it is dispelled by his testimony before the commission:

BELIN: Now, you said as the driver of the car, Bob Carroll, got in the car, he handed this gun to you?

HILL: Right, sir.

BELIN: All right, then, would you tell us what happened? What was said and what was done?

HILL: Then I broke the gun open to see how many shells it contained and how many live rounds it had in it.

BELIN: How many did you find?

HILL: There were six in the chambers of the gun. . . .[6]

There follows a lengthy colloquy between Hill and the commission counsel in which the bullets are produced and examined by Hill, who identifies them as the ammunition he removed from the revolver. From the exchange, there is no doubt that they are talking about six live rounds. Hill had custody of the weapon, opened it in the car on the way to police headquarters and inspected the shells, then later marked them as evidence. Yet in the radio interview conducted no more than a few hours later, Hill said that the gun had been fired twice, which could only mean that the revolver had been found to contain two spent shells.

I charted Hill's statement on the PSE. The words "A thirty-eight snub nose that was" showed moderate-to-good stress; the words "fired twice" showed good-to-hard stress.

The revolver alleged to have been found in Oswald's possession was never linked to the Tippit murder with complete certainty. The FBI ballistic expert reported that he could not positively identify the bullets removed from the policeman's body as having been fired by the weapon, although another expert was willing to say that one of the four had come from that gun.[7] The commission relied on the fact that four spent shells found in some shrubbery near the scene of the Tippit shooting were positively matched to the revolver. Since the weapon was a revolver, the shells could only have gotten there if the weapon had been unloaded. A fleeing murderer might stop to reload his gun (although, if the revolver had been fully loaded before the Tippit shooting, two live rounds must still have been in the cylinder), but why would he hide the shells in nearby bushes, where the police would be sure to search? If the police lab had been able to link the slugs to the weapon, hiding the shells would be pointless; if it could not, leaving the shells behind would be foolhardy. Like the rifle "hidden" in the book depository, the spent shells seemed to have been put deliberately where they would be found after a brief search.

Hill clearly had not gotten the accurate details of the Tippit shooting at the time of his radio interview, since he reported that Tippit had been hit twice, not four times. But there should have been no confusion in his mind regarding the ammunition in the revolver, because he examined it and scratched his initials on each round. Why would he claim only a short time afterward that the gun had been fired twice but later testify that he had found six live rounds in the cylinder?

I wondered if the policeman interviewed on the tape was the same man who had testified to the Warren Commission. It was. The interviewer introduced him as Sgt. Gerald Hill, Dallas Police Department." And the voice on the radio interview tape was the same as that of the Sgt. Gerald Hill who appeared on the CBS tapes. It is a voice that I can now personally identify, because while I was in Dallas, I twice tape recorded interviews with Gerald Hill.

Hill is now a lieutenant in the Dallas Police Department. I reached him by calling the main police number, told him my story, and asked if I might interview him. He was agreeable and cooperative, suggested that we meet in the police station, and gave me detailed directions for getting there. As I drove to the meeting, I discovered that Lieutenant Hill works out of a station in an industrialized, semighetto area of South Dallas, rather than the downtown head-quarters.

Hill is a short, stocky, balding man in his middle forties. He seemed pleasant and friendly and proved to be quite articulate. I knew that he had served on the force since 1958, before that had been radio-television editor for the Dallas *Times Herald,* and worked as a news-man in the Dallas bureau of a Fort Worth television station. Hill is far from the stereotype of the gruff, taciturn Southern cop.

Hill came out into the tiny lobby of the station to greet me and ushered me inside to a small desk in a corner of the station. As I unloaded my recorder and other paraphernalia, I realized I was going to have a problem. The large, open area was filled with clusters of patrolmen, detectives, complainants, and suspects, and the chatter of a dozen separate conversations was loudly audible. Overhead on the wall, a public-address system was carrying the radio transmissions between the police dispatcher and the squad cars. Just to make things complete, someone was playing a radio tuned to a local rock station. The noise level was about that of a boiler factory.

Hill made no objection to my recording the interview, but I doubted that the resulting tape would be very useful for PSE process-ing. The recorder I was using was one of the very sensitive kind that will pick up a whisper across the room; PSE analysis is most reliable when the tape contains a strong, clear signal. The microphone I brought was omnidirectional, so I knew that it would pick up every-thing in the room and record it on top of Hill's voice. When I listened to the tape later that day, I discovered that things were even worse than I expected. On the recording the background noise sounded even louder than it did in the police station, and a few of Hill's words were completely drowned out by it. There were several lulls in the din where PSE analysis was possible, however. And some of the most interesting results of the interview didn't require any stress process-ing. There was, for example, the matter of Gerald Hill's involvement in the CBS television documentary that had provided me with so much material.

The program, which was produced in 1967 and consisted of four one-hour segments broadcast consecutive nights, was called a "CBS News Inquiry" and attempted to investigate the major disputed

points of the Warren Report. It was narrated by CBS newsmen
Walter Cronkite and Dan Rather and reached the same basic conclusions as the Warren Report: Oswald was the assassin, and he acted
alone. When it was broadcast during prime viewing time on the CBS
television network, the program probably reached more people than
the Warren Report and all of the dissenters combined. Critics of the
Warren Report were, of course, unhappy with this mass-media endorsement of the official account, and both Josiah Thompson and
Mark Lane devoted parts of subsequent books to refuting the arguments made in the CBS program.[8] But none knew that one of the
Dallas policemen who played a central role in the events of November 22 had acted as technical adviser to CBS News when it produced
the program.

The matter came out when I asked Hill if he had any doubts about
the official explanation of what happened. He didn't answer directly
but gave a long, circumlocutious reply saying, in effect, that Jack
Ruby had denied the police the chance to present their evidence in
court and settle the matter once and for all. Then he said:

> I think probably the most thorough and convincing incident
> that I have been a party to after the assassination was after the
> Warren Commission Report came out, the four-hour special that
> CBS did either proving or disproving the contested points of the
> assassination. They probably did more research into it than any-
> body ever has. . . . I worked with them for something like five or
> six weeks on this thing, and, had I not been convinced before, I
> would have been then.

It would have been interesting to know if Hill took five or six weeks
leave to assist CBS or if he had been assigned to the task by the police
department, but I thought it better not to ask. Of course, I don't
know exactly what role Hill played in producing the program, and it
would certainly be logical for the Dallas authorities to assign the
personable television newsman turned cop to help the New York TV
people in the interest of good public relations. But, considering the
many suspicions that had been voiced regarding the Dallas police, it
seems strange that broadcast journalists undertaking a full-scale investigation of the assassination would use a Dallas policeman as a techni-

cal adviser, if that was, in fact, his function.

The most interesting thing Hill said during the interview was that the Texas Department of Public Safety had compiled a dossier on Lee Harvey Oswald before the assassination. The matter came up when I asked him if he had known Oswald before the event:

> HILL: He was a statistic as far as we were concerned. We had a rather tight surveillance on some people who we suspected would be capable of doing something like this, and we received this information from the Secret Service and the FBI. We did not have any information on Lee Harvey Oswald from either source. But, immediately after the arrest, and after bringing Oswald to the station, we were in contact with the intelligence unit in the Department of Public Safety. They called us and asked us who the suspect was we had. And we told them what his name was. They immediately knew all about him and said this was one man we should have known about.
>
> O'TOOLE: This was the Dallas Department of Public Safety?
>
> HILL: No, the Texas Department of Public Safety.
>
> O'TOOLE: The state police, then.
>
> HILL: State intelligence. But we had no prior knowledge of the man at all. Although the FBI had contacted him while he was here, but the FBI knew he was here. The FBI had prior contact with him.
>
> O'TOOLE: I was misinformed. I thought that you had known him before.
>
> HILL: The only one I knew before was Jack Ruby.
>
> O'TOOLE: Oh, then that's how I got it confused—you knew Ruby.

Despite the background noise, I was able to chart parts of this statement and found good-to-hard stress in Hill's account of the Department of Public Safety's call and the phrase, "they immediately knew all about him." The story seemed manifestly implausible to anyone familiar with the ways of bureaucracies in general and intelligence services in particular. As Hill said, the FBI did know of Oswald before the assassination and received severe criticism from the Warren Commission as well as the Dallas police authorities for not having made their information known to the Secret Service and the police. If the Texas state police had a dossier on Oswald, kept it to themselves, and then found out that the man was the prime suspect in the assassination, they would have been more likely to have shredded the file on the afternoon of November 22 than to have called the Dallas police and announced that they had known all about Oswald. Yet if Hill was telling the truth, it cleared up one of the more serious questions about the case: the indications that the Dallas police knew of Lee Harvey Oswald well before the assassination.

If Oswald was framed for the murder of President Kennedy, then someone would have to have selected him for the role some time before November 22. Many skeptics have speculated that Oswald was selected from the Dallas police subversive files. But all of the Dallas police authorities stoutly denied that they had a file on Oswald or had even heard of him. On the CBS tapes in answer to the question, former Chief Curry said, "No, sir, we did not have any information on this man in our criminal intelligence file, and that's normally where it would have been."[9] And Capt. W.P. Gannaway, head of the special service (intelligence) bureau said, "The first time I heard the name Lee Harvey Oswald was on the afternoon of the 22 of November, 1963."[10] The PSE showed low levels of stress in both statements.

Yet on the afternoon of November 22, Lieutenant Revill of the special service bureau wrote a memorandum to Captain Gannaway about a conversation he had just had with an FBI agent concerning Oswald. Revill headed the memo, "Subject: Lee Harvey Oswald, 605 Elsbeth Street."[11] Oswald never lived at that address, but he had lived at 602 Elsbeth. However, he had not lived at the Elsbeth Street address since March 1963, a fact that the FBI agent, James Hosty, had established months earlier.[12] If the police did not have a file on Oswald, where did Revill get the Elsbeth Street address?

That question was asked of Lieutenant Revill by Allen Dulles when the policeman appeared before the commission, and he replied that he had gotten it from one of two detectives.[13] Dulles asked him to find out where they got it, but, as Meagher points out, there is no record in the twenty-six volumes that the commissioner ever received an answer.[14]

The mystery is deepened by another memorandum written by the

Dallas police on November 22. It was addressed to Captain Gannaway and signed by Detectives Westphal and Parks.[15] The memo is
headed, "Subject: Texas School Book Depository, 411 Elm," and
begins, "The following is a list of the names and addresses of the
employees of SUBJECT location." There follows a list of fifty-six
names, most with an accompanying address, and twelve with the
handwritten notation, "not home." The first name on the list is
"Harvey Lee Oswald," and his address is listed as 605 Elsbeth.

The Revill memorandum and the Westphal and Parks memorandum both contain an eight-month-old address, and both have the
same error in the street number. Both had to have come from the
same source, but what was it?

The source was not the records at the Texas School Book Depository. The depository manager, Roy Truly, who had first called Oswald's absence to the attention of the police, testified that he had
given them the address Oswald had listed on his employment application, the Irving, Texas, home of Mrs. Ruth Paine, with whom Marina
Oswald was staying at the time.[16] Possibly, the 605 Elsbeth address
originated through a misreading by the police of a library card Oswald
is alleged to have had in his wallet when he was arrested, issued when
he lived on Elsbeth Street. But there were other identification cards
reportedly found in that wallet and at least one other address. More
importantly, one of the FBI agents who attended Oswald's interrogation reported that Oswald freely revealed his correct current address,
the rooming house in Oak Cliff.[17] Why then would Revill, Westphal, and Parks refer to a library card for their information?

If I could believe Hill's story about the call from the Texas Department of Public Safety, then this would provide a plausible explanation for the mystery. If the state intelligence agency had been keeping a dossier on Oswald, they might have had an out-of-date and
slightly erroneous address which they gave to the Dallas police intelligence at about the time the two memoranda were written. On the
other hand, the story could have been contrived precisely for the
purpose of tying up both this loose end and possibly others that I was
unaware of. I felt that I had to ask Hill about it again under better
circumstances for PSE analysis.

I called Lieutenant Hill at home in the evening at the end of a long weekend. The telephone is ideally suited for PSE work, since the quality of sound transmission in a normal connection will carry a clear reading of stress, if it is present, and background noises are of a much lower volume and can be easily separated from the speaker's voice. By calling Hill at home, I avoided the pressure-cooker atmosphere of the police station, which might produce extraneous stress.

Hill was again friendly and cordial. I said that I wanted to check with him on a couple of points and that I was especially interested in any psychological data that anyone may have compiled on Oswald:

O'TOOLE: You got some information on Oswald the night of the assassination from the Texas Public Safety Department?

HILL: Texas Department of Public Safety. That was late the afternoon after we got back to the station with him.

O'TOOLE: Uh huh. And this was the first that you'd had any information on him at all, right?

HILL: Right, uh huh.

O'TOOLE: Now did they have anthing in there suggesting he might be pathological?

HILL: No, they said he was capable of it, you know, that, ah, they had a dossier on him in Austin. And that he was certainly capable, and he should have been one of the ones we had under surveillance, anyway.

The story was becoming increasingly implausible. A subversive is one thing, but a potential presidential assassin is an entirely different matter. Special Agent James Hosty, the FBI man who had been handling Oswald's case, told the commission that when he heard that Oswald was charged with the assassination, he felt "shock, complete surprise," because, "I had no reason prior to this time to believe that he was capable or potentially an assassin of the President of the United States."[18] While there seem to have been no precise criteria for identifying a potential assassin, it is clear from Hosty's testimony that such a person would have to have a record of violent acts or, at least, threats of such acts. Apart from the alleged attack on General Walker of which the Texas Department of Public Safety presumably knew nothing, there was nothing in Oswald's background to meet those criteria.

PSE analysis of my telephone conversation with Lieutenant Hill did nothing to add credence to his story. Hill showed moderate-to-good stress during the introductory portion of our chat, but the stress went right up to hard and remained there during all of his statements regarding the Texas Department of Public Safety's dossier on Lee Harvey Oswald.

Still, the fabrication of such a story out of whole cloth seemed such a brazen act that I couldn't believe someone would attempt it, even if I had given mighty encouragement through my fumbling facade. It was, at the same time, both flattering and humiliating to think that I had succeeded in appearing so stupid. But, of course, the contents of an intelligence agency's files can be a difficult matter to verify. I drove to Austin to see what I could do.

By means which are rather too sensitive to be recounted here, I was able to obtain an informal indication that no such Oswald dossier had existed in the files of the Department of Public Safety before November 22, 1963. In hope of obtaining a more formal statement, I wrote to Col. Wilson E. Speir, director of the Texas Department of Public Safety, and put the question to him. Colonel Speir replied (to the pseudonym I used) and informed me that the matter "was within the jurisdiction of the Dallas authorities and the Federal Bureau of Investigation. It may be that you would want to correspond with those agencies."

I thought it wiser to defer the matter for a while. After I returned from Dallas, I wrote to Mr. Clarence M. Kelley, the director of the Federal Bureau of Investigation, and asked him about it. Director Kelley wrote back and said, "We are not in a position to comment whether the Texas Department of Public Safety did or did not have a file on Lee Harvey Oswald." Mr. Kelley explained that while the assassination had been within the Bureau's jurisdiction, the investigation was closed and the results had been turned over to the Warren Commission. He suggested I try the National Archives.

This was excellent advice. A telephone call to the National Archives set one of its diligent researchers in motion, and within twenty-four hours I was provided with a copy of an FBI report that I'm sure hadn't seen the light of day in ten years. The report settled the matter.

On November 30, 1963, Special Agent H.T. Burk of the FBI went to Austin to check on precisely this question, because there had been newspaper reports that the state agency had a large Oswald dossier. Burk reported that he interviewed Mr. O. Newt Humphreys, Jr., agent-in-charge, intelligence section, Texas Department of Public Safety and was "advised the only information in their file relative to LEE HARVEY OSWALD are four newspaper clippings."

Burk listed the four clippings. Three of the stories concerned Oswald's defection to the Soviet Union and were written while he was abroad. The fourth, headlined "Mate of Turncoat is Unknown to Mother," was apparently written after his return. All were from Fort Worth newspapers. In the interest of thoroughness, I tried to obtain copies of the clippings to see if they contained anything that might suggest Oswald was capable of a presidential assassination. I managed to get three of them, and they contained no reports of violence or threats of violence on the part of Oswald. I was unable to get the last item from the newspaper because, apparently, the publication date recorded in the FBI report, November 2, 1963, was in error. However, I managed to track down the reporter, Mr. Kent Biffle, who I found had moved to Houston and was on the southwestern bureau of *Newsweek*. He told me that he recalled the story, and there was nothing in it to suggest that Oswald was a violent person.

According to the FBI report, the Texas authorities had been emphatic:

> HUMPHREYS advised no actual investigation whatsoever was conducted relative to life of LEE HARVEY OSWALD prior to assassination of President JOHN F. KENNEDY November 22, 1963, and none has been conducted since that time by Texas Department of Public Safety.
>
> The above [four clippings] constitutes the only information in Texas Department of Public Safety files relative to OSWALD and HUMPHREYS pointed out that Colonel HOMER GARRISON, Director, Texas Department of Public Safety, Austin, Texas, has instructed him to furnish any pertinent information coming to the attention of Texas Department of Public Safety to the FBI immediately which he will do.

GARRISON endeavored to determine the origin of the newspaper stories that Texas Department of Public Safety "had an extensive file on Oswald," but was unable to trace the source of such a story.[19]

Eleven years have passed, and Colonel Garrison, wherever he is, probably no longer wonders about "the source of such a story." But if he does, I can offer him a very likely suggestion.

9 THE MYSTERIOUS MR. HIDELL

> I cannot tell what the dickens his name is.
> —*The Merry Wives of Windsor*, Act
> III, Scene 2.

Approximately seventy-five minutes after a president of the United States was assassinated in downtown Dallas, a force of at least fifteen law-enforcement officers burst into a motion-picture theater in another part of the city to make an arrest. The small army of policemen included several uniformed officers, several plainclothes detectives, two police captains—including the chief of police personnel—and an FBI agent. With service revolvers drawn and shotguns at the ready, the officers stopped the film, turned on the house lights, and began to search the theater. By their own account—those of the fifteen who testified before the Warren Commission—they were not looking for a presidential assassin; they had converged on the Texas Theater because a clerk in a nearby shoestore had reported a suspicious character entering the theater, and they believed that this person might be the killer of Officer J.D. Tippit.[1]

Several of the policemen reportedly struggled with Lee Harvey Oswald, wrested a thirty-eight caliber revolver from his grasp, and subdued him. Oswald was led from the theater in handcuffs past a surging mob that seemed ready to lynch him and put into a police car. There were five police officers in the car with Oswald as he was brought back to police headquarters—Bob Carroll, C.T. Walker, K.E. Lyons, Paul Bentley, and the ubiquitous Gerald L. Hill. Hill told me about the ride to the police station:

As I say, in the car on the way downtown, he was belligerent, he was surly, he wouldn't tell us who he was. We took his billfold out of his pocket, and we found the ID in both names, Oswald and Hidell, that he later was proved to have ordered the gun under. He had library cards and draft cards in one name, and he had identification cards from various organizations in the other name.

Hill told me, as he told the commission, that during the ride neither he nor any of the other four officers were able to identify their captive, because he was carrying identification as both Lee Oswald and Alek Hidell, and he wouldn't tell them which of the two he was. Hill's account of removing Oswald's billfold and finding the identification occurred during a relative lull in the background noise during my interview with him in the police station. I was able to chart it on the PSE.

"We took his billfold out of his pocket" begins with virtually no stress, but reaches good stress on the word "pocket." Stress reaches the good-to-hard level during, "we found the ID in both names, Oswald and Hidell," and remains there during, "He had library cards and draft cards in one name, and he had identification cards from various organizations in the other name."

This was interesting. I replayed the tape of the radio interview with Hill recorded on the afternoon of the assassination. He had given the newsman a long and fairly detailed account of the arrest, including the following remarks about Oswald:

The boy that we apprehended for shooting Officer J. D. Tippit is an employee of the book factory where the shots that killed the president were fired from. He was seen on the floor below the window where the shots were fired some fifteen minutes prior to the shooting. He was a former U.S. Marine marksman who defected to Russia in 1957 and returned to the United States approximately a year ago with a Russian bride, I understand . . . he won't admit anything other than he was a Communist. He started screaming "brutality" as soon as we got the handcuffs on him, and when he got down here and was talking to Fritz, the only thing he said is, "When I told you I was a Communist I told you everything I'm going to tell you," or words to that effect, and, "I want a lawyer, I demand my rights."

Hill went on to describe the trip to the police station, saying that Oswald had been arrogant, had refused to admit anything, had refused the officer's suggestion that he hide his face from the photographers, did not appear nervous, and made threats against the officers. It was during this interview that Hill made the reference to "a thirty-eight snub nose" revolver that the police had taken from their captive.

Hill's radio interview sounded like a preliminary brief for the prosecution. He related all kinds of incriminating details about Lee Harvey Oswald, but he left out something that he might be expected to emphasize: the discovery of forged credentials in Oswald's possession. Hill made absolutely no mention of finding the "Alek Hidell" identification on Oswald. It seems very strange that in such a detailed account of the arrest, made less than a few hours after the incident, Hill would omit such a significant point.

In the supplementary volumes of the Warren Report, I found the transcript of another broadcast interview with Gerald Hill on November 22, 1963. In this one, the subject of the contents of Oswald's wallet is raised by Hill, who tells the newsmen, "The only way we found out what his name was was to remove his billfold and check it ourselves; he wouldn't even tell us what his name was."

Later in the interview a reporter asks, "What was the name on the billfold?" Hill replies, "Lee H. Oswald, O-S-W-A-L-D."

And that was all. Hill didn't refer even obliquely to finding any false identification.[2]

I decided to talk to one of the other four police officers who were in the car on the trip to the police station. I asked Hill if he happened to know where I could find them. I was surprised to learn that three of them—Carroll, Lyons, and Walker—were working out of the same South Dallas station. "Through the years we've been in various parts of the police department," said Hill, "and yet now four of us are working out of the same station—four out of the five."

It was all a bit too clubby for my peace of mind. If I interviewed one of the other three, I was sure he would soon compare notes with

Hill, and my real interests might become apparent. I decided to call on Paul Bentley instead. Fortunately, Bentley was one of the people Jesse Curry had suggested I talk to.

Seated behind a large desk in his spacious office at the First National Bank of Dallas, Bentley told me that he had taken early retirement from the police department five years before and had joined the bank as director of security. Some of the local assassination researchers had expressed their suspicions to me about Bentley's sudden step up in the world. On meeting him, however, I found him very plausible in the role of senior banking executive, and I would not have been surprised if he had been introduced as the bank's president. If there is anything remarkable about Bentley's career, it is that he was occupying so junior a position on the police force only a few years ago.

Bentley is a trim man, perhaps in his early fifties. Like Gerald Hill, he was pleasant and articulate. Unlike Hill, he seemed somewhat aristocratic. I knew that Bentley had been the senior polygraph operator on the Dallas police force and that he was well known in Texas polygraph circles. I had heard that he had a reputation as a very astute interrogator, and I had been warned to be careful.

At the time of the assassination, Bentley worked in the police identification bureau, which was directed by Capt. George M. Doughty.[3] He was assigned to the bureau's crime scene search section under Lt. J.C. Day. Bentley told me how he happened to be at the Texas Theatre that day:

> It so happened that Captain Doughty, who was my captain at the time, was going to the scene of the Tippit shooting and asked me to accompany him out there. He was going out to dust the police car for fingerprints. And we were at the scene of the Tippit shooting when we got the radio message that this particular person fitting the description of Oswald entered the Texas Theatre.

He continued to recount his trip to the theater, participation in the struggle with Oswald, and the trip back to police headquarters.

BENTLEY: Gerry Hill, I think, was driving, and another officer or two in the front seat. We proceeded to bring him back to the

City Hall. Bear in mind that at the time we made our arrest, the only thing we knew as far as this individual was concerned was the fact that he had shot Tippit. We had no information that he was the man who actually committed the assassination of the president until we radioed in that we had a prisoner and gave the names. And I say names, this was taken from his wallet. He used several different names, as you know. But we gave the names. This was when they told us that he was a suspect in the assassination of the president. So we were instructed to bring him directly to Captain Fritz, who was in the homicide and robbery bureau.

O'TOOLE: He had the names of both Oswald and Hidell?

BENTLEY: Right, right.

O'TOOLE: Both of those identifications?

BENTLEY: Seems to me like he was using another name, also. I can't remember. I've got all this stuff at home. I'm not sure. There were several names that he was using on various types of cards, and then we gave the names to the dispatcher who was instructed to bring them to Captain Fritz.

Bentley also described taking the wallet from Oswald: "When I asked for his identification—of course he was handcuffed—he said, "If you want it, take it yourself." He leaned over and I took his wallet from his hip pocket. This was the end of his conversation. He did not say another word all the way to City Hall."

When I ran the tape of this interview on the PSE, I observed that Paul Bentley showed no stress in most of his statements. However, maximum hard stress developed on the words "Bear in mind" and continued throughout his statement that he and the other officers had known nothing beyond Oswald's alleged involvement in the Tippit shooting. There was hard stress both in his statement that Oswald used several names and in his repeated confirmation of this point in answer to my questions.

Bentley's statements, "we radioed in and gave the names," and, "This was when they told us that he was a suspect in the assassination of the president," showed hard stress. According to the Warren Report, Captain Fritz returned to police headquarters at 2:15 P.M. and told a detective to go to Oswald's Irving address and arrest him, and Gerald Hill, who was standing nearby, approached Fritz and informed him that Oswald was already in custody.[4] In other words, the official account claims that the arresting officers did not know that Oswald was the suspected assassin until after they got him back to headquarters. This is also what Hill told the commission and what he told me. But the Bentley revision, which is fairly elaborate, has the officers in the police car transmitting the Oswald and Hidell names to Captain Fritz by radio and then receiving a message telling them that Oswald was the suspected assassin and that he should be brought directly to Fritz.

Bentley added yet another revision to the official story while describing the behavior of the angry mob outside the Texas Theatre: "So the people apparently connected it and, I guess, due to the excitement and tension, we never even thought about whether this would be connected with the assassination. We had no knowledge as to why Tippit was shot, at the time, but we do know that his fingerprints were taken off the passenger side of Tippit's car."

Bentley's knowledge of whether Oswald's fingerprints were found on Officer Tippit's police car can only be hearsay, since he does not claim to have dusted the car himself. But Bentley's information should be extremely good hearsay: by his own account he went to the Tippit shooting scene with Captain Doughty to dust the car for fingerprints, although he continued on to the theater to assist in arresting Oswald. There were only seven other officers in the crime scene search section,[5] and we might expect Bentley to know whether Oswald's prints were found on Tippit's car.

The patrol car was dusted for prints by Sgt. W.E. Barnes, who told the commission, "There were several smear prints. None of value,"[6] and again, "No legible prints were found."[7] I don't know why Paul Bentley told me that Oswald's fingerprints were found on the car, but when I analyzed the statement with the PSE, I found good stress. It may be that once more I had given the impression I was someone who didn't do his homework.

But my principal reason for talking to Paul Bentley was the question of the Hidell identification, so several days after our face-to-face interview, I decided to telephone him and ask about the matter a second time.

O'TOOLE: I wonder if I might take a few more moments of youl time on the telephone just to go over a couple of points with you.

BENTLEY: Surely.

O'TOOLE: At the time of the arrest of Oswald, you were in the back seat of the automobile with him——

BENTLEY: When we brought him to the City Hall, yes.

O'TOOLE: Right. Now you were sitting to his left?

BENTLEY: Right.

O'TOOLE: OK. And you asked about his identification, and he invited you to take his wallet from his pocket, and he leaned over and let you do so?

BENTLEY: Right.

O'TOOLE: Now, which pocket was his wallet in?

BENTLEY: Left rear pocket.

I tried to set this up as closely as possible to a structured examination. That Bentley was sitting to Oswald's left in the back seat of the police car is fairly well-established, and when I charted this interview on the PSE, his confirmation of this point showed only moderate stress. However, when Bentley replied to my question about Oswald inviting him to take the wallet, the word "Right" took on good stress. When he said the words "left rear pocket," the stress went all the way to hard. I wondered if Oswald had even been carrying a wallet.

I knew that the details I was asking Bentley about were out of character, so I decided to do a little work on my cover story.

O'TOOLE: It was in his left rear pocket. This is very interesting. I've been looking into the background of Oswald, and he came into this world left-handed——

BENTLEY: I see.

O'TOOLE:——But his teachers and his mother trained him to be right-handed, and this was a source of conflict.

BENTLEY: Well, he of course was handcuffed at the time, and he certainly would have a hard time getting it out with either hand.

O'TOOLE: With either hand, of course. But what's interesting to me is the fact that he carried his wallet in his left-hand pocket.

BENTLEY: Left rear pocket.

Once again the stress on the words "Left rear pocket" was maximum hard.

> O'TOOLE: Left rear pocket. Well that is interesting, because, as I say, it has something to do with the psychological makeup. He had been trained to be right-handed, and I would expect that——
> BENTLEY: The gun was in his right hand.

Bentley had interrupted, but I stopped speaking and his words, "was in his right hand" could be charted. They contained good-to-hard stress. I continued with my story.

> O'TOOLE: In a normal frame of mind I would have expected it to be in his right-hand pocket, and this kind of supports my idea that there was a kind of dual personality here.

> BENTLEY: I see, yes.

As a cover for inquiring so persistently about the Oswald-Hidell identification, I had concocted a bit of pseudopsychological rubbish in the form of a theory that Oswald might have been suffering from schizophrenia. The stess in Bentley's "I see, yes" dropped to moderate.

> O'TOOLE: Now the identification that he had, though, he had both Hidell and Lee Harvey Oswald?
> BENTLEY: Yes, and if I'm not mistaken, he had some identification by the other names on him, but I can't remember offhand what the names were. Seems to me like there was three or four different names that he had in there.

Bentley's voice showed hard stress once again.

Bentley's reference to Oswald's having identification in names, besides Hidell is another surprising revision of the official account, which reports only the Oswald and Hidell identifications as being found in Oswald's wallet.[8] The Warren Report states that Oswald had rented his room in Oak Cliff under the name O.H. Lee, but there is no reference to finding identification in that name. Perhaps the Lee alias confused Bentley's recollection, and he believed that such identification had been in the wallet. But Bentley was the policeman who confiscated the wallet and examined its contents, and it is surprising that he would be confused about a major detail of the most important police case he ever worked on. And then there is the matter of the hard stress in his account.

O'TOOLE: OK, well, that's one point. Here's another point: as I recall, you first heard that he might be the assassin over the police radio——
BENTLEY: Right, as we were bringing him in.

This showed good-to-hard stress.

I had half-expected that Bentley would equivocate on this matter, but he did not. Apparently he was unaware of how sharply his report conflicted with the official account. If what he said were true, if he or the other officers in the car had transmitted the Hidell alias to headquarters by radio, and if the dispatcher called them back and said that Oswald was the suspected assassin, then Oswald's possession of the Hidell identification could definitely be established. All of the dispatcher and squad-car transmissions were routinely recorded, and the FBI's transcript of the recordings from November 22, 1963 was published as commission exhibit 1974 in the supplementary volumes of the Warren Report. I checked it. According to the FBI log, the first transmission from the car en route to headquarters occurs just after 1:51 P.M.

550/2 (SERGEANT G. HILL): Suspect on shooting of police officer is apprehended and en route to the station.
DISPATCHER (HULSE AND McDANIEL): 10–4. At the Texas Theatre?
550/2 (SERGEANT G. HILL): Caught him in the lower floor of the Texas Theatre after a fight.[9]

The next transmission from the car occurs a few moments later.

550/2 (SERGEANT G. HILL): 223 [Patrolman C.T. Walker] is in the car with us. Have someone pick his car up at the rear of the Texas Theatre and take it to the station. It's got the keys in it.
DISPATCHER (HULSE AND McDANIEL): 10–4.[10]

A short time later Hill called in again to report that they were in a special service unit car and to give their location. Then,

15 (CAPTAIN C. E. TALBERT): You do have the suspect arrested in the Texas Theatre?

550/2 (SERGEANT G. HILL): Yes, sir, him and the gun.[11]

These are the only transmissions between the car and the dispatcher recorded in the FBI log. If the exchange Bentley described to me actually took place, then either it wasn't recorded or it wasn't transcribed.

If Bentley really found the Hidell identification when he examined Oswald's wallet, then he should have reported this fact in his official account of the arrest. The supplementary volumes of the Warren Report contain a copy of a memorandum from Bentley to Chief Curry dated December 3, 1963. Bentley makes only one reference to the wallet: "On the way to the City Hall I removed the suspect's wallet and obtained his name."[12]

That's it. There is nothing about Alek Hidell or any other alias identification; there is nothing about calling any alias information in to the dispatcher. Bentley's report seems to imply very clearly that he found only one name on the cards in the wallet, and that name was Lee Harvey Oswald.

If Oswald was not, in fact, carrying false identification when he was arrested, did he ever use the Alek Hidell alias at any other time? I believe that he did, and I base that conclusion on the fact that the Mannlicher-Carcano rifle found in the book depository was a cheap piece of junk.

If Oswald did not kill the president, then he must have been framed; and either the Mannlicher-Carcano rifle was not his and had been planted on him, or else the rifle was his but had been brought to the book depository that day by someone else. I am inclined to believe the latter alternative.

If Oswald did not own a rifle and someone wished to create the impression that he did for the purpose of linking him to the assassination, then whoever did so would have selected a weapon that could actually be used in the crime. In 1963 a rifle and scope adequate for the job could have been purchased for less than $150, an amount that Oswald could plausibly have amassed. Why, then, purchase a $12.78 weapon that could not be relied upon and plant it on Oswald?

But if Oswald really owned the Mannlicher-Carcano and if this was known by those who selected him to be the patsy, then there would have been a compelling reason to steal the rifle, to leave it in the book depository, and to plant the ballistic evidence that would link the weapon to the assassination: Oswald's ownership of the rifle would already be a matter of record somewhere.

According to the Warren Report, the record of the mail-order sale of the rifle was discovered in the early morning hours of November 23 by a Chicago sporting-goods dealer, and it showed that the weapon had been sent to A. Hidell at a Dallas post-office box on March 20, 1963.[13] Could this record have been forged by a conspiracy? Perhaps it could, but to what purpose? Why introduce an element of doubt into the chain of evidence linking Oswald to the rifle?

The disclosure on November 23 that the rifle had been sold to someone called A. Hidell probably disconcerted the people who had framed Oswald. The use of an alias in the gun purchase could muddy the water. It would be ironic if the manufactured case against Oswald failed because of this. People could reach the right conclusion for the wrong reason.

By the time the purchase record was discovered, Oswald's room in Oak Cliff had been searched and the personal effects he stored at the home of Mrs. Ruth Paine in Irving had been confiscated. The forged Hidell identification may have been found among those things, but there was still room to argue that the cards belonged to someone other than Oswald.* The only way to tie things up securely would be to claim that Oswald had the Hidell identification in his possession at the time of his arrest. Then Oswald would be positively linked to the rifle, and he would also be established as a sinister character who used forged credentials and purchased a rifle under an assumed name. The setback of the Hidell sales record could be turned to the conspirators' advantage. But all this, of course, is only speculation.

Recalling the hard stress I found in Bentley's statement that Oswald's wallet was in his left rear pocket, I analyzed his earlier account of taking the wallet from Oswald's pocket. Here again there was hard

*Meagher presents a plausible argument that Alek Hidell was, in fact, a real person. (*Accessories After the Fact,* pp. 181–199).

stress. Perhaps Oswald had no wallet with him when he was arrested
in the theater. Or perhaps the police officers already knew who he
was, so no examination of his wallet was necessary. I had not asked
Bentley if he had known Lee Harvey Oswald before encountering
him in the theater, but I ran across a television interview with him
recorded on November 23, 1963.[14]

> REPORTER: Did he ever talk in a foreign language?
> BENTLEY: No, he did not.
> REPORTER: Do you think he had an accomplice?
> BENTLEY: I don't know, I didn't (unintelligible because of other
> reporter's voices).
> REPORTER: Mr. Bentley, are you familiar with this subject?
> BENTLEY: No, I'd never seen him before.
> REPORTER: Mr. Bentley, what is your first name?
> BENTLEY: Paul. Paul Bentley.

There was a good level of stress, sometimes reaching hard stress,
during the entire interview. However, some of the hardest stress was
in the phrase, "No, I'd never seen him before."

Did Paul Bentley or any of the other arresting officers know the
name of the man they dragged from the Texas Theatre? Did they
know that he would be charged with the assassination? In an unpublished FBI report I obtained from the National Archives, Mrs. Julia
Postal, the box-office cashier at the Texas Theatre described the
arrest to the agents who questioned her:

> She reported that as the police took this man from the theatre,
> an officer remarked, "We have our man on both the counts." She
> asked what he meant and he said "Officer TIPPIT as well." She
> presumed from this that the man who was then identified as LEE
> HARVEY OSWALD was a suspect in the assassination of the
> President and in the murder of Patrolman TIPPIT of the Dallas
> Police Department. She said this was the first time that she had
> heard of TIPPIT's death, and the officers arresting OSWALD had
> identified him, OSWALD, to her by calling his name.[15]

10 THE PHANTOM POLYGRAPH TEST

He who hath not a good and ready memory should
never meddle with telling lies.
—Montaigne: *Essays*

During the last few weeks of his life, Lee Harvey Oswald lived apart
from his wife. Oswald lived in a furnished room in Dallas, and Marina
and the Oswald children stayed with Mrs. Ruth Paine in Irving, a
Dallas suburb. Oswald applied for a job at the Texas School Book
Depository at the suggestion of Mrs. Linnie Mae Randle, a neighbor
of Mrs. Paine. Mrs. Randle's brother, nineteen-year-old Buell Wesley
Frazier was living with the Randles. Frazier worked in the book
depository and drove his car the fifteen miles between Dallas and
Irving twice each day.

Oswald spent the weekends with his wife at the Paine home in
Irving. On Friday afternoons he would ride to Irving with Buell
Wesley Frazier; on Monday mornings he would return with him to
the book depository. But Oswald broke from his established pattern
on Thursday, November 21. He rode out to Irving on Thursday with
Frazier and returned to Dallas with him on the morning of November 22, reportedly carrying the long paper parcel the commission said
contained the Mannlicher-Carcano.

In the early evening of November 22, Buell Wesley Frazier was
arrested in Irving and taken to the Dallas police headquarters. Thus
began one of the strangest and least-known episodes in the events of
that day. Exactly why Frazier was arrested remains a mystery; according to Dallas police reports, the police began to take an interest in
him when they learned from his sister that he had driven Oswald to
work that morning.[1] They located Frazier at a hospital in Irving,
where he was visiting his stepfather, then took him to the Randle

home and conducted a search. The police confiscated a .303 caliber rifle, an ammunition clip, and a box of ammunition, all belonging to Frazier. They returned to police headquarters with Frazier and his weapon.[2]

The police questioned Frazier and took affidavits from him, his sister, and a clergyman who had accompanied Frazier and Mrs. Randle to police headquarters. Shortly after 9:00 P.M., the police released Frazier and sent him, his sister, and the minister back to Irving in a police car. The car had covered half the distance when the driver received a radio message to bring Frazier back to headquarters.[3]

On returning to the station, Frazier was asked by Captain Fritz to submit to a polygraph examination. The young man consented. Detective R.D. Lewis was called at home and asked to come to headquarters to administer the test. Detective Lewis arrived on the fourth floor of police headquarters at 11:20 P.M. and began to conduct the polygraph examination of Buell Wesley Frazier. It was completed at 12:10 A.M. and, according to the police report, "showed conclusively that Wesley Frazier was truthful, and that the facts stated by Frazier in his affidavit were true."[4] Frazier was released once again and taken back to Irving.

In his affidavit[5] Frazier told of knowing Oswald, of driving him back and forth to Irving on weekends, and of the change that took place in this pattern on Thursday, November 21. He said that Oswald had approached him and asked to ride out to Irving with him that afternoon to get some curtain rods. Frazier said that he had driven Oswald to Irving that afternoon and brought him back to the book depository on Friday morning. He said that Oswald had brought a long paper package to the book depository and told Frazier the parcel contained the curtain rods. Frazier said that Oswald told him he would not be returning to Irving Friday afternoon.

Frazier told essentially the same story, but at greater length, when he testified before the commission on March 11, 1964. Frazier's testimony provided one of the most valuable pieces of evidence in support of the commission's version of events, but it has also been cited by nearly every critic of the Warren Report as a fatal flaw in the official account.

The commission concluded that Oswald went to Irving on Thursday night not for curtain rods, but for his rifle, which was stored in the garage of the Paine home. It concluded that the paper parcel Frazier said Oswald brought to work that morning contained not curtain rods, but the disassembled Mannlicher-Carcano. The inference that Oswald decided to kill President Kennedy on the day before the presidential visit to Dallas is one of the firmest buttresses of the commission's "one lone nut" theory.

But when Frazier testified before the commission, he described the paper parcel in terms that would preclude it from having contained the Mannlicher-Carcano, even in a disassembled state. Frazier said that he had seen Oswald carrying the package with one end cupped in his hand and the other end wedged in his armpit.[6] The barrel of the Mannlicher-Carcano is simply too long to have been carried in this fashion. The only other person who claims to have seen the package was Frazier's sister, Mrs. Linnie Mae Randle. Her description, too, indicates that the package was too short to have contained the rifle.[7] The commission concluded that Frazier and Randle were mistaken about the length of the package.[8]

Critics of the Warren Report have concluded otherwise and have offered Frazier's testimony as evidence that Oswald's package did not contain a rifle. Perhaps because his description of the package has proved so useful to them, the skeptics have accepted the rest of Frazier's story, even though Oswald's sudden trip to Irving on Thursday afternoon raises questions they cannot answer. Meagher writes, "This visit [to Irving] on the night before the assassination was unexpected and is, at first glance, an embarrassment to those who question his guilt."[9]

She also maintains, "There is no reason to doubt Wesley Frazier's story that Oswald asked him for a ride to Irving on Thursday night, saying that he wanted to pick up some curtain rods."[10]

But Oswald's Dallas landlady told the commission that his room was already equipped with curtain rods.[11] And according to Capt. Will Fritz, who interrogated Oswald, "I asked him [Oswald] if he had told Buell Wesley Frazier why he had gone home a different night, and if he told him anything about bringing back some curtain rods. He denied it."[12]

In all probability, Oswald denied it vehemently. Frazier's affidavit had been taken and Frazier was on his way home to Irving when Fritz called the police car and told the driver to bring him back for a polygraph examination. Why, after releasing Frazier, did Fritz suddenly decide that Frazier should be questioned again immediately, preferably with the aid of a polygraph? The most obvious answer is that Fritz confronted Oswald with the affidavit while Frazier was being driven home and that Oswald denied it in terms so emphatic that Fritz felt a lie-detector examination would be required to settle the question.

This minor detail became the focus of the investigation during the evening of November 22. Oswald and Frazier directly contradicted each other. If Oswald had gone to Irving with Frazier on the curtain rod pretext, then his denial of the story was almost conclusive proof of his guilt. Fritz probably realized that if Oswald was lying about this and Frazier was telling the truth, then he could go home to bed secure in the knowledge that the one and only assassin was in custody. But how was the question to be settled?

Oswald wisely refused to submit to a polygraph test until he was represented by an attorney.[13] But since either Oswald or Frazier had to be lying, Fritz must have realized he could establish the truth by testing Frazier. This explains the radio call to the squad car and the sudden u-turn on the outskirts of Irving.

After the PSE results I obtained in analyzing the archive tapes, I, too, was extremely curious about the testimony of Buell Wesley Frazier. Shortly before my trip to Dallas, I obtained a CBS recording of Frazier relating his curtain rod story:

FRAZIER: Well, he come to me on the Thursday, November the twenty-first, and asked me could he ride home with me that afternoon. And I said, "Why, yes," and I said, "Why are you going home this afternoon?" And he replied that he wanted to pick up some curtain rods so he could put some curtains up in his apartment. And I said, "Oh, very well," and then I said, "Well will you be going home with me tomorrow, also?" And he said, "No." He said he wouldn't be going home with me on the twenty-second."

REPORTER: So he told you that he wanted to come out there and pick up some curtain rods, and this was on Thursday morning?

FRAZIER: Yes, sir.

REPORTER: And at that time he told you that he would not ride home with you Friday night?

FRAZIER: Right.

PSE analysis of this recording revealed a remarkable degree of stress throughout. It was such a classic example of the smooth, maximum hard stress waveform, maintained through almost the entire statement, that a PSE specialist to whom I showed it remarked, "On a scale of ten, this stress is somewhere near eleven."

In fact, I wondered if such stress could be the result of mere deception. Judging from the PSE charts, when Buell Wesley Frazier made that statement, he was in a condition of sheer terror.

As with so many other statements on the archive tapes, there were no irrelevant or control statements I could use for stress comparison. No firm conclusion could be drawn merely from the stress in the statement on the tape. I decided that while in Dallas, I would try to meet Buell Wesley Frazier in person.

After I arrived in Dallas, I tried to find Frazier in the local telephone and city directories. I had no success, but through inquiries I managed to get the address of Frazier's sister, Mrs. Linnie Mae Randle. She had an unlisted telephone number, so I went unannounced to her home in Irving. I found the house in a pleasant, middle-class, suburban section of town. I rang the bell, and Linnie Mae Randle came to the door.

Mrs. Randle is a small, dark-haired woman who appears to be in her middle thirties. I stood on her doorstep with my camera and recording paraphernalia and explained why I was there. She seemed to become increasingly tense as I spoke and interrupted to ask how I had gotten her address. She was not angry or unpleasant, but the color drained from her face as she learned of the reason for my visit. She declined to be interviewed, saying that she would have to consult her husband, who was not home. I asked if she would direct me to her brother. She said that he was in the army and that she would not give out his address. She did agree, however, to convey a message to him from me requesting an interview. I returned to Dallas with the impression that my visit had upset her considerably.

Mrs. Randle had given me her telephone number so that I could call her about her husband's decision on my request for an interview. I called several days later, and she told me that she and her husband had decided against it. I wrote a letter to Buell Wesley Frazier requesting an interview and offering an unspecified sum of money as a consideration. I sent the letter to Mrs. Randle to be forwarded to her brother. I never received a reply.

I raised the subject of the Frazier polygraph test in one of my follow-up conversations on the telephone with Paul Bentley. Since Bentley had been the senior polygraph examiner on the police force at the time, I thought he might know something about it.

O'TOOLE: There's one other area that I didn't get into, that I didn't really know about—this guy Frazier who knew Oswald before the assassination. I haven't had an awful lot of success trying to hunt him down. Apparently he is in the army now.
BENTLEY: I see.

There was good-to-hard stress in "I see."

O'TOOLE: But I did discover something of interest: that he was arrested by Captain Fritz the night of the assassination and given a polygraph examination. I was wondering, I know that you had a problem with your ankle, so I assume you were not the one——
BENTLEY: I don't recall that even occurring.

There was maximum hard stress in the words.

BENTLEY: I think, had he been given an examination, I would have known about it. But this may be 100 percent true and I can't recall——
O'TOOLE: This is in the Warren Report.
BENTLEY: I can't recall. Frazier may have been and if this was the night of the assassination, I would not have been on duty.

Whether or not Bentley recalled the incident, there was hard stress in his voice while we were discussing it. I decided to talk to the man who had tested Frazier, Detective R.D. Lewis, who I learned was still on the police force. Recalling my problems with recording Gerald Hill in a police station, I chose to conduct this interview on the telephone. I called the main police number and reached Detective Lewis.

I explained that I was a writer and told Lewis my cover story. Then, to obtain a valid control, I asked him if he knew whether Lee Harvey Oswald had been given a polygraph test after his arrest.

> LEWIS: Well, I didn't give him one. He wasn't given a polygraph examination.
> O'TOOLE: He was not?
> LEWIS: Uh uh.

I was fairly confident that this was true, and when I later charted the interview, I found only moderate stress in Lewis's statement.

> O'TOOLE: I understand that there was a polygraph examination given to this gentleman who was an associate of Oswald's—a man named Buell Wesley Frazier—on the night of November 22. Would you have been the officer who gave that examination?
> LEWIS: I'm not familiar with it. I don't remember conducting any examination whatsoever on Oswald or anyone connected with Oswald.

Suddenly there was good-to-hard stress in Lewis's words.

> O'TOOLE: In other words, you did not give anybody a polygraph examination that night?
> LEWIS: No, uh uh. Not connected with Oswald.

The stress was hard. I thanked Detective Lewis for his time and hung up.

Could R.D. Lewis have forgotten the incident? He was a detective, called from his home at night to come to the police station and give a polygraph examination as part of the investigation of a presidential assassination. It was ten years ago, but who cannot vividly recall where he was and what he did on November 22, 1963?

The subject of the Frazier polygraph test seemed to produce hard stress in Paul Bentley. Now it caused both hard stress and amnesia in R.D. Lewis. I decided to try it out on Gerald Hill. I telephoned Hill at home:

O'TOOLE: I've been trying to get hold of a guy named Buell Wesley Frazier. This is the guy, I guess, who was his car pool out to Irving.

HILL: Right.

This showed moderate-to-good stress.

O'TOOLE: Did you know him?

HILL: No, I never did even see him.

A *frisson* of hard stress appeared on one syllable, but Hill's voice still stayed generally at the moderate-to-good level.

O'TOOLE: Frazier is an interesting character. My researcher sent me a copy from one of the twenty-six volumes that said he had been given a polygraph examination——

HILL: Um hmmm.

Good-to-hard stress appeared.

O'TOOLE:——on the night of the assassination. Apparently he seemed pretty suspicious to Captain Fritz. But I haven't——

HILL: Well, now, he had to be suspicious to somebody else other than Fritz, 'cause Fritz didn't believe in polygraphs. He wouldn't use 'em.

Wham! Near-maximum stress appeared.

O'TOOLE: Is that right?

HILL: This is right.

O'TOOLE: Well——

HILL: He'd lose a case before he'd put anybody on the polygraph.

O'TOOLE: Well, now this is interesting, because, according to the Warren Report, a polygraph examination was administered by a gentleman named Lewis, R.D. Lewis.

HILL: Yeah, uh huh.

O'TOOLE: But I spoke to Mr. Lewis, and he said he didn't recall giving him a polygraph examination or anybody else that night.

HILL: Yeah, like I say, if it was Fritz's show, probably no. Now this may be a situation where he was arrested by either the sheriff's

office or arrested by the Irving P.D., and they utilized our polygraph section to give the test. But if the guy was Fritz's prisoner,
he did not get a polygraph, 'cause, ah, Fritz's own men, as long as
he was there, if they wanted to put somebody on a polygraph, they
had to do it behind his back.

O'TOOLE: Is that right?

HILL: Yeah.

O'TOOLE: Well, that's interesting.

HILL: He was, ah, he didn't believe in it.

There was, of course, hard stress throughout most of this, but that
was of secondary importance. My investigation appeared to be entering a new phase. The psychological stress evaluator had functioned
like a mine detector, showing me where to dig. I was digging, and
I was beginning to find pay dirt.

I did not for a moment believe that the chief of the Dallas homicide and robbery bureau would categorically forbid the use of the
polygraph. Even if he didn't believe in the polygraph's accuracy, he
had to realize the instrument was strong encouragement for suspects
to be truthful. It isn't a crystal ball, but it's a handy investigative aid,
and I couldn't imagine any captain of detectives proscribing it.

Could Hill have been misinformed? It was not very likely. Hill has
served on the force since 1958,[14] and Fritz had retired around 1970.
During the twelve years they both were on the force, Hill must have
gotten to know Fritz well enough to learn whether or not he ruled
out the polygraph. I decided to call Fritz.

Fritz lives in retirement in a downtown Dallas hotel. The switchboard put me through to him. Captain Fritz was polite but firm: he
said he had never given an interview on the subject of the assassination, and he didn't want to start now. I considered saying I just
wanted to know what he thought of the polygraph, but it sounded
crazy, so I decided not to.

But there was at least one other person who could be expected to
know with absolute certainty whether Fritz used the polygraph—the
former chief polygraph examiner for the Dallas police, the prominent
Texas polygraph examiner, Paul Bentley. I called Bentley.

O'TOOLE: I'm sorry to bother you again. I just had one or two
details I wanted to check with you.

BENTLEY: All right.

O'TOOLE: I heard that Captain Fritz had absolutely no faith in the polygraph and he never used it. Can you confirm that?

BENTLEY: I cannot confirm that. It was used constantly in the homicide and robbery bureau.

Bentley showed a lot of stress when I first identified myself to him, but he dropped to almost none on "I cannot confirm that."

O'TOOLE: The individual who told me this said that Fritz just didn't believe in the polygraph and——

BENTLEY: I've run many, many examinations for Captain Fritz personally.

Why did Lewis and Hill risk making such serious and implausible misstatements to deny that the Frazier polygraph test took place when it was, after all, a matter of record? Perhaps Lewis didn't wish to discuss it (or any other aspect of the assassination) with me, but why did he choose this means of refusal. After all, I had no subpoena power; no one had to talk to me. Lewis could have simply declined to do so, as Captain Fritz did when I called him. And Lewis had an excellent excuse: as a member of the Dallas Police Department, he had no business discussing Frazier's polygraph test with me or any other outsider. Why did Lewis claim it didn't happen, and why did Hill make the unlikely and demonstrably untrue claim that Fritz wouldn't use the polygraph? The answer may be that neither of them knew it was a matter of public record, and when I sprang it on them, they said the first thing that came to mind to turn me away from a potentially dangerous subject.

There is no mention of the Frazier examination in the Warren Report. There are only a few brief, passing references to it buried in the twenty-six supplementary volumes, and even these are difficult to locate. To my knowledge, the only other mention of the incident in print appears in Jim Bishop's book, *The Day Kennedy Was Shot.*[15]

One of the few official references to the Frazier test is in the testimony of Detective Richard Stovall, who was one of the policemen in the car that returned Buell Wesley Frazier to police headquarters for the examination. Stovall is still on the force, and I telephoned him.

O'TOOLE: Are you the Detective Stovall who was involved in investigating Wesley Frazier about the time of the assassination?

STOVALL: Um hmm.

O'TOOLE: I wonder if you'd mind chatting with me for a few moments?

STOVALL: [long pause]

O'TOOLE: Ah, would that be all right?

STOVALL: [pause] Well, of course it just depends. Ah, I don't know you, and——

I recounted my cover story to him and told him that I had become interested in the Frazier matter because, based on R.D. Lewis's statement to me, I thought I had discovered a minor error in the Warren Report. I asked Stovall if he remembered whether or not Frazier was given a polygraph examination.

STOVALL: Without looking back at my notes or anything, I couldn't tell you for sure.

O'TOOLE: Uh huh, you don't recall——

STOVALL: But I do feel like that he did have one.

O'TOOLE: Do you remember the details of it?

STOVALL: No, because, see, when they gave those examinations, we weren't up there. Just the polygraph examiner was.

O'TOOLE: Just the polygraph examiner and the subject?

STOVALL: Well, as far as I know.

Hard stress appeared. Stovall returned several times in our conversation to the theme that he had not been present during the Frazier polygraph examination and, therefore, wouldn't know anything about it.

STOVALL: But like I say, usually when a man is given a polygraph test, just him and the, the suspect, you know, the person being given the test and the operator, is usually the only one in there. Of course, sometimes they'll have somebody else in there. Sometimes they'll have someone else observing. But on his, I don't know.

There was hard stress in this and in the following statement:

STOVALL: I believe that he did have a polygraph examination, but I couldn't swear to it because, like I say, you know, once they took them up there. . . .

But here is what Detective Richard Stovall swore to for the Warren Commission, ten years earlier, when, presumably, his memory was fresher:

MR. BALL: When you took the polygraph, you were present during the polygraph examination of Frazier, were you?

MR. STOVALL: Yes, sir.

MR. BALL: And during this examination, did you have before you the affidavit which Frazier had made?

MR. STOVALL: No, sir; I didn't.

MR. BALL: You didn't at that time?

MR. STOVALL: No, sir.

MR. BALL: Who did the questioning?

MR. STOVALL: R.D. Lewis, he's the polygraph operator.

I might explain that to you—in our polygraph room we've got a two-way mirror there and in another room behind it, so that the officer that is investigating the case, if he wants to, can watch the examination being given, and you can hear the questions and the answers.

MR. BALL: Did you go home then after that?

MR. STOVALL: Yes, sir; after we took them back to Irving we went home.[16]

Stovall was, in fact, present during the Frazier examination, although three times he suggested to me that he was not, possibly because of the defective memory of the assassination from which so many Dallas police officers appear to suffer. I never specifically asked Stovall if he had been present during the examination; he kept bringing the matter up himself. But it was a subject that did interest me because of the detailed account of the examination written by Jim Bishop.

Bishop's hour-by-hour chronology of the events of November 22, 1963, contains a brief but very detailed description of the Frazier polygraph examination. Bishop's account of the incident goes beyond anything in the official record.

> It took time to get the control questions and the placidity of the victim juxtaposed so that, on simple interrogations such as: "Do you live with your sister?" the needle would not jump. "Ever fire a gun?" induced a spasm peak. There was nothing incriminating in either question or answer ("Yes"), but Frazier, judging by the needle, bordered on controlled hysteria.[17]

There is nothing like this anywhere in the Warren Report or the twenty-six supplementary volumes. Jim Bishop either made it up (an unlikely thing for a respected journalist to do), or else he was told it by someone present during the examination. Bishop's book is a highly readable, third-person narrative equivalent of the Warren Report. He wrote it in Dallas in 1967, and it must have been obvious to the local officials that he was not there as an investigative reporter. In an epilogue Bishop tells of the cooperation he received from Judge Joe B. Brown, the judge who presided at the trial of Jack Ruby. Bishop says that Judge Brown arranged to have "a host of anonymous men" visit Bishop in his hotel room and describe their personal recollections of November 22. "The people he sent," writes Bishop, "remained 'anonymous' because many of them—for example, police department employees—had been ordered not to discuss the assassination with anyone."[18] (Apparently Bishop didn't ask why, four years after the assassination, people were ordered not to discuss it. If he had, he might have uncovered a story worth writing instead of the cosmetic job he actually produced.)

If Bishop's account of the Frazier examination came from policemen who were there, then one paragraph is extremely interesting:

> Lewis realized that it would be a lengthy test, but he was a patient man. He expected a jump on the needle when he asked a control question such as: "Ever do anything you're ashamed of?" or "When you were little, did you ever lie to your mother?" There were five police officers in the room and the doorway, and there wasn't one who expected to learn anything from Wesley Buell Frazier (sic). All they had managed to do was to scare the wits out of him.[19]

This seems to imply that the results of the examination were inconclusive, which is precisely what all the polygraph examiners to whom I have recounted the details say they would expect. An examination conducted with "five police officers in the room and in the doorway" could hardly produce any other result. And the duration of the examination—from 11:20 P.M. to 12:10 A.M.—is, I am told, far too short a time to examine a subject in a criminal case, least of all a frightened subject.

There was an even more fundamental departure from standard polygraph practice in the Frazier examination, however: that the test was given at all. Polygraph examiners insist on testing subjects when they are fresh and well-rested, so that their physiological responses will be distinct. And they refuse to examine a subject immediately after he has been interrogated, as Frazier was because, if he has been lying, the polygraph effect may be washed out. Why did R. D. Lewis agree to test Frazier in the middle of the night, when the young man had been up since early that morning, was in a state of extreme nervousness, and had been interrogated extensively only a short time before? And why did he permit four other police officers to be in the room during the examination? The conclusion seems almost inescapable that Lewis wanted to come up with an inconclusive result.

Captain Fritz wanted Buell Wesley Frazier given a polygraph test. There were two polygraph examiners on the Dallas police force in November 1963: Paul Bentley—the senior examiner—and R. D. Lewis. On the night of November 22, Paul Bentley was home with his sprained ankle in a cast. When Lewis received the telephone call at his home, he had no choice: he had to come in and give the test.

R. D. Lewis did not testify for the Warren Commission. The Dallas police report of the Frazier examination, published in the twenty-six volumes, is signed by Detectives Rose, Stovall, and Adamcik, but not by Lewis.[20] Lewis had not gone on record anywhere to the effect that Frazier passed the test. If Lewis was the "anonymous man" who told Jim Bishop about the test, he apparently said no more than "all they had managed to do was scare the wits out of him." And when I asked Lewis about the examination, he told me it never happened.

Suppose an honest cop were told to falsify a polygraph examination, to say that someone was telling the truth even though the instrument indicated otherwise. Suppose he were threatened with death if he reported "deception indicated." Short of lying himself, what could he do? He could arrange an examination that would surely result in an inconclusive result and report that result truthfully. It would be a compromise with his conscience, but it would keep him alive.

The actual investigation of Buell Wesley Frazier was conducted by Detectives Richard Stovall and John Adamcik under the direction of Detective Guy Rose. The three detectives were also the officers who searched Mrs. Paine's home in Irving and confiscated Oswald's possessions, and Stovall and Rose were the two policemen who testified that the photograph of the auto parked behind General Walker's home was already mutilated when it was found (see Chapter 6). One of the Dallas police reports submitted to the commission said that Detective Adamcik "understands a little Russian,"[21] although in his testimony to the commission, Adamcik implied that he understood no Russian.[22] In the Dallas police roster and organization chart for November 1963, Adamcik is shown, not as a detective in the homicide and robbery bureau, but as a patrolman under Sgt. Gerald Hill.[23] I wanted to talk to Detective Adamcik about these and other details, but I never reached him. Either he is no longer with the Dallas police, or else the police switchboard operator didn't recognize the name (which I very well may have mispronounced). I did, however, reach Detective Rose.

Rose was much less guarded than Stovall, and his memory seemed to be working better. I told him my cover story and then said I was interested in the details of the Frazier matter. He went through a fairly detailed account of it, omitting only the mention of finding a rifle among Frazier's posessions and the fact that Frazier was brought to Dallas under arrest. I told him about the description of the polygraph examination in Jim Bishop's book and asked whether there had been five officers in the room.

ROSE: No. Actually there was only one officer in the room. He was the polygraph examiner. My partner and I—there was just two of us—we waited till the test was over. But there was only one officer in the room with him.

Hard stress appeared.

O'TOOLE: I see, uh huh. And the results of the polygraph indicated that he was telling the truth?

ROSE: Yes, he got a very good chart, and it showed that he was telling the com——, he was telling just exactly the truth.

Hard stress appeared again.

O'TOOLE: Did Captain Fritz have a lot of confidence in the polygraph?

ROSE: He had confidence in it as an investigative tool. You know, with a polygraph there's about three ways you can go: you can tell a guy is completely lying or that he's completely telling the truth or that the examiner just can't give you—— it's an inconclusive. I find that where an examiner very confidently tells you that a man is telling the truth—and you can see the charts yourself—you can be pretty sure he is telling the truth. Now, if you get an inconclusive, why then you don't know, you're right back where you started. But on this case we did get a good solid chart, he was completely truthful.

The stress dropped off during Rose's explanation of the polygraph, but resumed good-to-hard on "But on this case we did get a good solid chart, he was completely truthful."

When Rose testified for the commission, he was asked about a variety of matters—searching the Paine home, bringing Marina Oswald and Ruth Paine to the police station, sitting in on some of the interrogations of Oswald, and other subjects. As he had been with me, Rose was cooperative and informative with the commission lawyers. As he concluded the examination, Assistant Counsel Joseph Ball asked Rose if he would sign the transcript of his testimony after it was typed—a standard commission procedure—and Rose readily agreed. One can almost visualize Ball turning away as the following colloquy took place:

MR. ROSE: Well, if she [the typist] will just call me, I will drop by anytime.

MR. BALL: Okay, that will be fine. We will do this. Thanks very much.

MR. ROSE: Let's see, there was something else I was going to tell you now, I wanted to mention—we did run Wesley Frazier on the polygraph, did you know that?

MR. BALL: I know you did—we know about that.

MR. ROSE: Yes.

MR. BALL: Thanks.[24]

The only reference to Frazier in Rose's testimony concerned "locating" him at the hospital in Irving and taking an affidavit from him. The commission lawyer showed no special interest in Frazier and didn't follow up on the subject or question whether Frazier had been telling the truth. Instead, he turned to another topic and, a short time later, brought the interview to a close. It was late afternoon, Rose had been the final witness of the day, and presumably everyone was putting away his papers and getting ready to go home. But Rose didn't want to step down until he was sure that everyone knew they had run Wesley Frazier on the polygraph. Why did he feel that this was an especially important point to make?

Armed with Rose's confirmation that Lewis had conducted the Frazier polygraph examination, I decided to have another go at Lewis.

O'TOOLE: I hate to bother you again and make a nuisance of myself, but there's something that I'm trying to check on. It's a small detail, and I'd like to try to jog your memory a little bit. We were talking about polygraph examinations that you gave on the evening of the twenty-second of November, and, as I recall, you did not recollect giving one to Buell Wesley Frazier at that time.

LEWIS: Offhand, no, I don't remember giving anybody one.

Hard stress appeared.

O'TOOLE: Well, I spoke to Gus Rose, and he recollects that you did. And I also found a reference to it in the Warren Report that said you gave this man Buell Wesley Frazier a polygraph. And it's also in Jim Bishop's book, not that that's an authority—*The Day Kennedy Was Shot.* You have absolutely no recollection of this?

LEWIS: I don't remember it, no. I may have, but I don't remember running the guy. Of course I've only run about fifteen thousand——

O'TOOLE: Yeah, I know, and it's ten years ago, but, in the book, it says that—and also in the Warren Report—it says that you were called at home that evening to come in and give the polygraph examination.

LEWIS: What day was Kennedy shot on?

O'TOOLE: He was shot on a Friday.

LEWIS: What, what was the date?

O'TOOLE: The twenty-second of November.

LEWIS: Twenty-second, and ah [pause] I worked that evening.

Mr. Lewis has a remarkable memory. He cannot remember the date of the assassination of President Kennedy; he cannot remember his own work in investigating the case, certainly the most important case of his police career; but give him a date ten years ago, and he can tell you whether or not he was on duty that evening.

O'TOOLE: You worked that evening. So, what time would you have gotten off?

LEWIS: Eleven o'clock that night.

O'TOOLE: Eleven o'clock?

LEWIS: I remember, because my son, I had my son down here. I remember when Kennedy got shot, I was on my way to work, and I stopped at a pawn shop to look for a radio or something. I don't remember what it was I was looking for, but I stopped at a pawn shop somewhere on South Haskell. And just before I got out of the car, around one or something like that, I don't remember what time it was, I got out of my car to go in the store—might have been later than that—and it came out over the news that he had been shot. And I came on downtown and went to work. I went to work at three that day and got off at eleven. So there wouldn't be any reason for them to call me from home.

O'TOOLE: Well this was—according to the report they called you about eleven, I think it was after eleven o'clock.

LEWIS: Oh, well, that may have been so then.

O'TOOLE: Do you recollect giving anybody a polygraph test that day? That evening?

LEWIS: [long pause] Well now that you bring that up, it seems like I did get off that night and went home, and then they called me back. But I don't remember any of the details about it or anything.

O'TOOLE: You don't remember who it was that you gave the test——

LEWIS: No. I couldn't. If my life depended on it I couldn't remember.

Lewis's choice of words is interesting.

LEWIS: If I read a report, you know, I might recollect, I might remember. But just to say I run anybody [Pause]. I do remember running a case or two regarding the Kennedy deal—not people who were accused of shooting him or something, but, I don't remember the details or the circumstances.

At least Lewis's memory had improved since our earlier conversation when he told me he hadn't run any examinations in connection with the case.

O'TOOLE: I see, I see. Well, that would have been——

LEWIS: I don't remember it being that day, you know.

O'TOOLE: Uh huh.

LEWIS: Matter of fact, I think I run several people, but it seems to me, about the best I can remember, it was days after, and not the same day. But there again, I could be mistaken about that part of it.

O'TOOLE: Well, it was a long time ago, and I guess you do run a lot of cases. Ok, well, I'm sorry to bother you again——

LEWIS: If I had some, you know, what was the details supposed to have been regarding it, do you know?

O'TOOLE: Well, ah, according to the Warren Report, this is the sequence of events: Frazier, who was Oswald's associate—he drove back and forth with him to Irving on weekends—Frazier was questioned by the police and he told them that Oswald had come in that morning with a package that Oswald claimed contained curtain rods. And he also said that Oswald declared he wouldn't be going back to Irving that weekend. Now they released Frazier and they put him in a police car. I think Officer Stovall was driving him home. And halfway out to Irving, he got a radio message to bring him back. And they brought him back, and they asked him if he'd take a polygraph test. Now according to the report I've got, they called you at home and asked you to come in. It took you about an hour to get in. You got in about midnight, I guess. And he was given the test. Now I don't know precisely what they asked him, but I presume it was to verify his story that Oswald had this package of curtain rods—what he claimed to be curtain rods——

LEWIS: Yeah, now I do remember running some guy regarding a package and knowing Oswald and curtain rods and so forth. I do remember that, but I didn't remember it being the same day or even the same twenty-four-hour period that the killing happened——

O'TOOLE: I see.

LEWIS: But I do remember running somebody regarding some curtain rods and riding back and forth with Oswald, and did the guy see any gun and so forth.

O'TOOLE: I see. That's the guy. Now, I know this is asking a lot, but do you remember offhand the results of that polygraph examination? Did you get a clear indication that the man was telling the truth?

LEWIS: I don't offhand remember, but I would say that he did, otherwise it would have stuck with me.

This was the point that I was struggling to reach: R. D. Lewis's own statement about the results of the Frazier polygraph examination. There was hard stress in it. But perhaps the PSE results are less significant than Lewis's own unlikely story. His statement that Frazier passed the test can be no more credible than his strangely uneven memory. Summoned from his home in the middle of the night to investigate a presidential assassination, Detective Lewis does his duty and promptly forgets all about it. What to many of us would be a tale for our grandchildren is, to Detective Lewis, just one of fifteen thousand cases.

After my telephone conversation with Lewis, I went to the front desk in my motel, arranged for a late check-out the next day, settled my bill, and returned to my room. I put the DO NOT DISTURB sign on the knob, tossed the key onto the bed, and crossed to the sliding glass door that opened onto the parking lot. My luggage, my equipment, and the tapes were all packed in the trunk. I pulled out of the lot quietly, made a few random u-turns, then got onto the Stemmons Freeway and headed out of town. I had raised a lot of dust, and I didn't want to be around when it settled. My first order of business was to put many miles between myself and Dallas. My second was to find Frazier.

11 FINDING FRAZIER

As well look for a needle in a bottle of hay.
—Cervantes: *Don Quixote*

The man in the car parked across the street was taking my picture with a small movie camera. I didn't notice him until I drove out of the parking lot in front of my apartment house. As I turned onto the street, I glanced up and found myself staring into the lens. I made a mental note of the license plate and drove around the block. When I got back, he was gone.

I went back up to my apartment and made a phone call. Within half an hour I was called back. The car was registered to a man who lived in a town some miles away. It was jointly owned by him and his daughter, who lived with her husband in the apartment house next to mine. I realized with some relief that the mystery cameraman had been making home movies (" . . . and here's where my daughter and son-in-law live . . ."). I had driven into his viewfinder by accident; he probably stopped filming until I was out of frame. End of mystery.

The phone call that saved my peace of mind was to a private citizen with very good police connections, who could routinely ask for a license-plate check. He is part of a vast, loosely organized "old boy network" of former intelligence officers, FBI agents, and policemen. When a person spends a lifetime in security work for some government agency, he doesn't break off all contact with his former associates after he retires. Many alumni go into private practice as investigators or security specialists. Friends still on the inside help because they know and like the graduate, and, in some cases, because he may present an employment opportunity when their own time comes to be put out to pasture. And of course, sometimes the favor is done by the person on the outside, when, for example, the police or federal investigators need a look at a credit file or a long-distance telephone toll record, and they don't have the time (or, perhaps, a good enough reason) to get a court order. Much more of this mutual back scratching goes on than is generally realized, and it works to the detriment of personal privacy and civil liberties. But when one is trying to find a missing person who may not consider himself missing, the old boy network can be a very worthwhile institution.

Frazier's sister said he was in the army. I had his name and his date and place of birth. And an army contact. That seemed like enough, so I called my friend. He called back the following day: there was nobody in the United States Army named Buell Wesley Frazier, he said.

Next I visited a Washington businessman, a friend who had retired from government intelligence work to start his own security company. I explained my problem, and he told me he had a source with very good FBI connections. He said he'd do what he could. About a week later he called me to say that Buell Wesley Frazier was employed by the Boeing Aircraft Corporation in Renton, Washington.

I went to the Library of Congress and checked all the city and telephone directories for Renton, Washington, and all surrounding counties. There were, of course, many Fraziers, but not the one I was looking for. I called Boeing in Renton. The switchboard operator didn't have an extension listed for a Buell Wesley Frazier, but she said employees working in the assembly plant wouldn't be listed unless they were supervisory personnel. She connected me with the personnel department. The woman who answered the phone told me she couldn't give out any information, not even whether or not someone named Buell Wesley Frazier worked there.

It began to seem as though I wasn't going to find my man simply by asking favors of friends. I decided to hire a private investigator for the job. One was recommended to me—a young man who owned his own private-detective firm in a large Midwestern city. For the purpose of this narrative, I shall call him "Stevens," although that is not his name.

From the outset Stevens made me nervous. I told him whom I wanted to find and gave him some of the background. He immediately proposed to mount a full-scale operation, planting bugs in Fra-

zier's home, tapping his telephone, and placing him under surveillance with one of his special vans equipped with telephoto cameras
and videotape equipment. When I explained that I only wanted to
find Frazier so I could talk to him, he seemed a little disappointed.
I told him that under no circumstances did I want him to bug, tap,
or videotape anyone for me.

After a few days, Stevens called me and reported that he had a
contact in Boeing—the director of security (subsequent developments caused me to doubt this and almost everything else Stevens
said). He said that the man had checked the corporate personnel
records and no one named Buell Wesley Frazier worked there now,
or had ever worked for any division of Boeing Aircraft Company.

Stevens proposed going to Dallas and conducting other assassina-
tion-related investigations for me there. He said he had some good
contacts in Dallas and that one of his clients was the First National
Bank of Dallas. I asked him if he knew the director of security there.
He replied that he knew Paul Bentley very well.

By now, I thoroughly regretted bringing Stevens into the case and
especially, telling him so much about the background of my investigation. But it was too late to change things, so I simply told him I'd
think about his proposal, and in the meantime he should do what he
could to find Frazier.

A few days later Stevens called to report his progress. This was the
first of a series of calls from Stevens in which he gradually drew a
bizarre and improbable picture of the mysterious obstacles he was
encountering in finding Frazier. There was a clerk in the Social
Security Administration, who, said Stevens, served as his informant.
She had "gotten burned" when she tried to get a look at Frazier's
file. Next, the clerk had managed a peek at the dossier, and it contained a slip of paper with a list of names—five Dallas cops and my
own. What, asked Stevens, did I make of it?

I made of it that Stevens was trying to plant a wildly improbable
story on me, but I didn't know why. I checked out everything he said.
The woman in the Social Security Administration never heard of
Stevens and didn't work for him; Social Security files are stored on
magnetic computer tape and therefore don't contain "slips of paper."
The names of the Dallas policemen had all appeared in an article I

had written presenting my early findings with the archives tapes and published in the July 1973 *Penthouse* Magazine, and the five names appeared in exactly the same order as they did in the magazine piece. I knew that it was a completely phony tale, but I couldn't understand why Stevens was trying to plant it on me.

About a week later Stevens sent a member of his staff—a "psychic" —to visit me and confirm his story through a "reading." I managed to disguise my mirth as I sat through the seance. Stevens seemed determined to introduce an element of the ridiculous into my investigation, but, again, I could not understand his motive.

Stevens was being paid for his services, and I had explained to him that, if he found Frazier, he could expect more money. He knew that I had a budget from my publisher for investigations. Why did he risk losing my business by handing me such an obviously false story? Several months after I broke off contact with Stevens, I learned that he was running a political dirty tricks operation against a Midwestern public official who had hired him to guard against that very threat. Apparently the double-cross is Stevens's specialty. If I had bought his tale and used it to suggest there was a federal government conspiracy to cover up the assassination, it could have been detonated like a land mine at any time to destroy the overall credibility of my case. In his dealings with me Stevens seems really to have been working for someone else.

I think that Stevens knew I didn't buy his tale, and I believe he suspected I was recording our telephone conversations and testing them with the PSE (he was right). After the affair of the Social Security file, he called me and gave me one item of information which happened to be true, perhaps in the hope of keeping me as a client. He said he had learned that Buell Wesley Frazier was in the army.

The PSE showed that Stevens was, for once, telling the truth. I called my army contact in Washington and asked him to check again. When he called me back he sounded puzzled. Yes, Frazier was in the army; his name was added to the army locator sometime between the first and second inquiries. But there was something unusual about the entry: no location was given. Instead, Frazier was listed only as being in "CONUS," military jargon for "continental United States."

I went back to my Washington businessman friend, the one with the source who had good FBI connections. I told him what I had found and asked for his advice. He thought about it for a few moments then suggested I hire the individual who was his source. I replied that I was a little reluctant to hire another investigator, having been burned already by Stevens. My friend said that he didn't think that would happen this time. He identified the man he had in mind, and for the purpose of this narrative, I shall call him "Big Otto," although that is not his name.

Big Otto was not working as a private investigator; he was president of a security firm in a large Eastern city that sold electronic surveillance equipment. The business wasn't doing very well, and Big Otto was courting my friend's company for a merger. Under the circumstances, my friend said, there wasn't much chance for a double-cross because Big Otto had a lot to lose if he blew his chances for the merger.

"Otto is about 30 percent bullshit," said my friend, "but the rest is real."

Otto had served in both the FBI and the CIA before going out on his own. He still did an occasional freelance job for the government. For example, Otto worked as a double agent, selling ersatz "classified equipment" to Soviet intelligence. He collected a fee from the government for carrying out the deception operation, and he could keep whatever he milked from the Russian agents in the deal.

Otto was an old-timer in the business, and his government contacts were other old-timers, usually senior officials. My friend told me several anecdotes that illustrated Big Otto's well-placed connections. Otto sounded like the man who could find Frazier for me.

My friend sent one of his vice-presidents with me to visit Otto. Otto's company headquarters was in an old, downtown office building. As we stepped off the elevator and approached the door bearing the name of Big Otto's company, I noticed a small television camera mounted above it. Otto greeted us on an intercom as we approached and unlocked his door with an electric relay. We pushed it open and went inside.

Big Otto has to be seen to be believed. He is a white-haired giant of a man in his mid-sixties, with a flowing mustache and a flamboyant manner. While it was not in evidence, I knew there was a pearl-handled, nickle-plated .45 automatic nearby. There had to be.

Otto was sitting behind a massive desk as we walked into his office. There were a pair of television screens on the other side of the room. A black-and-white set showed the corridor outside Otto's office; the color set was carrying the Watergate hearings—the picture, but no sound. Otto gestured for us to sit down and pointed at the color screen, where the the face of a deputy attorney-general was speaking soundlessly.

"That son-of-a-bitch is the biggest bullshit artist in the Justice Department," declared Big Otto in a booming voice.

We exchanged amenities and made a little preliminary small talk. My friend in Washington had already filled in Otto on the background of my project and told him I was looking for Frazier. I discreetly turned the conversation to the subject of my visit. Big Otto fixed me with a stare from beneath a pair of bushy, white eyebrows.

"I'm tired of all this spying crap," he suddenly roared. "I've been doing it all my life, and now I want to make some MONEY!" He punctuated this announcement by slamming a ham-sized fist onto his desk blotter, causing an ashtray and paperweight to spring into the air. I told him that I'd be happy to pay him for his services in locating Frazier.

"That's not what I mean," he snorted. "I've got a contact on the *Daily News*. We can sell him your story and make a million dollars."

I told Big Otto that I already had both a literary agent and a publisher, and what I wanted from him was some investigative work.

"Look, O'Toole," said Otto, "the Bureau investigated this case; it was the biggest investigation in FBI history. I could find this kid for you, but it's not going to do any good because he won't be able to tell you anything that everyone doesn't already know. I don't want to talk about finding people, I want to talk about making some MONEY!" The objects on his desk top leaped into the air again.

"Let me get this straight," I said. "You're saying my investigation is a lot of nonsense, but you think you know how to make some money out of it. Is that about right?"

"That's exactly right," exclaimed Otto. "Let's cut out all this bullshit and make some MONEY!"

In replying to this, I took into consideration the fact that I was there as a guest, and I didn't ignore Big Otto's size or the probability of that nearby, pearl-handled, nickle-plated .45 automatic.

"I think that we are wasting each other's time," I said and stood up. My companion had listened to the exchange in silence, squirming uncomfortably. As I left, he said he'd stick around because he had some other business to talk over with Otto. Big Otto didn't see me to the door, but he bade me farewell over his intercom as I stepped into the corridor. I resisted the impulse to make a fitting gesture of salute at the closed-circuit television camera.

When I got back to Washington, I called my friend.

"Well, you got part of your answer," he said.

I asked him to explain. He told me that after I left, Big Otto had apologized to my companion, the vice-president of my friend's company, and told him there was nothing he could do to help me. Big Otto had tried to run a check on Frazier through his FBI contacts before we arrived, but he was refused the information and told in the most emphatic terms to drop the subject and to have absolutely nothing to do with me.

I had put Big Otto in an uncomfortable position. He wanted very much to help me and do a favor for my friend so he could pursue his merger plans. Based on past performance, Otto should have been able to locate Frazier in a matter of hours. But when he went to the Bureau, his wrist was slapped. And no low-level employee in the FBI's local office could slap the wrist of Big Otto; *that* had to come from Washington.

My friend pointed out that if Frazier had simply been a material witness in the case, there would be no reason for the FBI to have red tagged his file as, apparently, it had. The Bureau had a continuing interest in Frazier, and they didn't want any nosey journalists talking to him.

My friend said that I had gotten part of my answer. He was wrong. What I had gotten was an answer to a question I never thought to ask: Did the Federal Bureau of Investigation discover more about the assassination than it ever reported to the Warren Commission?

Now more than ever, I was determined to find Frazier. Slowly I accumulated a few more bits and pieces. I knew that Frazier had served in the army once before, from 1965 to 1967. He had been trained as a cook at Fort Polk, Louisiana, had earned a marksman's rating with the M–14 rifle, and had been overseas for about five months. He was honorably discharged at Fort Lewis, Washington. He had reenlisted for a four-year hitch on March 26, 1973. Sometime in the last ten years he had gotten married. I knew his Social Security number, his religion, and his blood type. In fact, the only thing I couldn't learn was where to find him.

I got close to him twice. The first time I heard a report that he had been sent to Fort Polk, Louisiana, for some training. I called the Fort Polk base locator. Frazier had been there, but now he was somewhere else. Where? the enlisted man on the phone didn't know. A month later I heard Frazier was at Fort Sill, Oklahoma. My source told me she had gotten a telephone number for him, had called it, and the person who answered said Frazier was away at the moment. When I tried the same number a few days later, no one had heard of Buell Wesley Frazier.

To be objective, I must point out that the United States Army is a big place, and the people who answer the telephone are not always well-informed. Frazier had just reenlisted, and it is entirely plausible that he was being moved around for various kinds of special training and not for the purpose of eluding me. But I cannot explain the absence of forwarding addresses or of any address listed in the Pentagon worldwide locator other than "CONUS." Nor can I easily account for the fact that I was able to learn so much basic information about Frazier, but not a telephone number or mailing address that I could use to reach him.

After several months of fruitless search, I happened to visit Dektor to discuss a technical problem with some of Allen Bell's people. Bell introduced me to a young man named Tony Pellicano, a Chicago-based private investigator who specializes in missing persons. Pellicano is yet in his early thirties, but he has already become something of a legend; he has a distinctive personal style which captivates newspaper and magazine writers. There are, for example, Pellicano's twin Lincoln Continentals, each equipped with a telephone; his karate school (Pellicano holds a black belt and also specializes in kung fu and other oriental martial arts); and the Samuri swords which adorn the walls of his office. But beneath these flamboyant trappings

there is the hunter who always gets his man. Under the rubric of
Fortune Enterprises, Ltd. Tony Pellicano has tracked down more
than three thousand missing persons.

Pellicano started out in his profession as a very young man tracing
deadbeats for a Chicago mail-order house. He learned the tricks of
the trade and discovered that he had an uncanny talent for finding
people. Soon he went into business for himself. Pellicano's cases
range from tracing husbands or wives who desert to finding children
kidnapped in custody battles. He has reunited families separated for
decades and tracked down skid-row derelicts who have inherited
fortunes. I asked him if he could find Buell Wesley Frazier, and he
shrugged and replied that he could find anyone.

I wanted to believe him. Pellicano was not a full-fledged member
of the old boy network—he didn't have close ties with the FBI or
police—and under the circumstances this began to look like a distinct
advantage. Like all magicians, Pellicano won't tell how he performs
his feats, but I was reasonably sure he didn't rely on friends in the
FBI for help.

I have heard that Tony Pellicano sometimes works for free out of
humanitarian motives. However, I cannot testify to this from personal experience. Within a few days of our first meeting, I introduced
him to my publisher in New York. I don't know the exact terms of
the agreement they reached, but I was later told that Pellicano's firm,
Fortune Enterprises, was aptly named.

Whatever Tony Pellicano's fee, he earned every cent of it. Within
forty-eight hours after taking the case, he found Frazier.

Because I didn't expect to hear anything from him for a while, I
was caught off guard by Pellicano's telephone call on a Saturday
morning at the beginning of December.

"I found your guy," he said. It took me a moment to realize what
he was talking about.

"Where?"

"Back where it all began," said Tony Pellicano. "In Irving, Texas."

Frazier was stationed at Fort Hood, an army base about a hundred
miles south of Dallas. He had a home in Irving, and he commuted
there on weekends (another weekend commuter to Irving; history is
full of patterns.)

I didn't care for the idea of going back to the Dallas area, but I had resolved to follow the trail no matter where it led. I told Pellicano I would leave immediately and asked him for the address.

"Forget it," he replied. "I doubt that you can get near him. I know you won't be able to do it at Fort Hood; he lives on base and seems pretty well insulated."

I asked Pellicano what he would suggest.

"Right at this very moment," said Pellicano, "Frazier is getting a haircut. In about an hour he'll be home. I don't know where he's going to be after that, and if we don't move now, I may have to find him all over again. I recommend a telephone contact this afternoon, and I think *I* ought to do it."

Pellicano had already spoken to Frazier's wife and identified himself as a reporter; he thought a call from a second party might jeopardize things. Pellicano, in addition to his other skills, is thoroughly experienced in conducting clandestine PSE examinations, and I had given him a complete briefing on the points of interest in this case. I wanted to be in at the climax, but I realized Pellicano was right. I told him to go ahead.

After a couple of anxious hours, Pellicano called me back. He told me to get ready to tape record from the phone. I set up my machine, and Pellicano transmitted the tape of his interview with Buell Wesley Frazier. It was solid gold.

Tony Pellicano grew up in Cicero, Illinois, and he sounds like Chicago—except when he chooses to adopt a different personality. In the interview with Frazier, Pellicano was "Tom MacSwade," a freelance Texas newspaperman. With amazing ease and authenticity, he switched to the accents and idiom of Texas-Arkansas.

PELLICANO: I am a freelance reporter, and I have been working on a story about the effect that the death of John F. Kennedy had on certain people in the Dallas area, and I have been talking to some folks—a lot of folks with the Dallas Police Department— and, you know, some of the people around whose lives were definitely affected by the serious thing that happened.

FRAZIER: Yes.

PELLICANO: And I come across your name, and I thought I would give you a call.

FRAZIER: I see.

PELLICANO: Would you mind answering a few questions for me?

FRAZIER: I guess not.

Pellicano was trying to relax Frazier and get a few irrelevant responses. There was moderate-to-good stress in "I guess not." Pellicano asked whether Frazier could remember the details of what happened on the day of the assassination. His reply, "Yes I can," showed moderate-to-good stress.

PELLICANO: Ok, now, you know, some of the police officers that I talked to over at the Dallas Police Department, they said that, oh, on the date, the twenty-second, you know, when you were arrested, you were brought up there to the Dallas Police Department, you know?

FRAZIER: Yes.

PELLICANO: And, I guess you didn't know what was going on, you know, what was happening with Oswald, did you?

FRAZIER: Well, they told me.

Now the stress had become good. Pellicano changed the subject and asked what sort of person Oswald had seemed to be. Frazier said he was a quiet sort of person, and he only knew him as a fellow employee. The stress dropped back to the moderate-to-good level.

PELLICANO: Did you know he was a Communist or anything like that?

FRAZIER: No, not until after all this, you know. After it happened, you know, lots of things came out, you know.

The stress climbed to good-to-hard. Pellicano got to the subject of November 21, the day before the assassination.

PELLICANO: He asked you, he said, "Wes, I want to go home, and I want to bring out some curtain rods for my room?"

FRAZIER: That is true. Because, you know, he had an apartment, you know, over at Dallas, you know.

The stress hit maximum hard on "That is true," but dropped down to moderate-to-good on the rest of the statement.

PELLICANO: He said, "I want to pick up some curtain rods," and what did you do, drive him on home?

FRAZIER: No, what he did, you know, Thursday he came out. His wife lives out there in Irving, you know, and so, you know, he told me he wanted a ride home out to Irving to see his wife.

I said, "Very well."

So, you know, he did, and he said, you know, on the way out, he said the next morning he is going to bring in some curtain rods, you know, for his apartment over at Dallas. I said, "Very well," you know, so I didn't think anything else about it, you know.

The stress was nearly maximum hard during the entire statement.

PELLICANO: What happened then? What did you do? You picked him up the next morning?

FRAZIER: You know, he come down to where I live, you know, and he got out and walked in, you know, sit down in the car, you know, so, you know, when I got in the car, I glanced at the package, and I didn't think anything about it, and I asked him, I said, "What is that?" And he said, you know, "That is some curtain rods I told you I was going to bring," you know, so I just dropped the subject right there, you know, because I didn't think anything more about it, you know.

The statement began at moderate-to-good stress and stayed at that level until "And he said, you know, 'That is some curtain rods . . .'" at which point it hit maximum hard. The stress then dropped to the good-to-hard level and remained there for the rest of the statement.

PELLICANO: Did he tell you they were curtain rods?

FRAZIER: Right.

PELLICANO: I mean, did it look to you like it was a package of curtain rods.

FRAZIER: Yes, it did.

There was good-to-hard stress in "Right" and hard stress in "Yes, it did." Pellicano led the conversation into a discussion of curtain rods by saying his wife had just bought some the other day. The stress dropped to moderate. Then there was more talk of Oswald, and Frazier offered the view that he had been more intelligent than most people thought. This produced moderate stress. Then Pellicano got back to the subject of the package of curtain rods.

PELLICANO: Well, when you went to work, did he take that package up with him into the building?
FRAZIER: Yes, he did.

There was maximum hard stress.

PELLICANO: Did you see where he put it?
FRAZIER: No, because he walked on ahead.

There was good-to-hard stress.

PELLICANO: Did he tell you he was going to go home with you that night?
FRAZIER: What night was that?
PELLICANO: That is the Friday, you know, the day that the president died.
FRAZIER: No, because he come up with some theory about—I asked him about this. He said he had to go get his driving license.

Maximum hard stress appeared.
Pellicano asked Frazier about the polygraph examination he had been given. Showing only moderate stress, Frazier gave a detailed description of being hooked up to the instrument and interrogated by a detective.

PELLICANO: There was nobody else in the room with you?
FRAZIER: That is correct.

Maximum hard stress appeared.

PELLICANO: Well, what did he do, ask you all them questions that he asked you before?
FRAZIER: Right. That is true.

There was moderate stress.

> PELLICANO: And did he tell you that you passed the test?
> FRAZIER: Yes, he did. He said I did very well.

There was maximum hard stress.

Pellicano said he was sure that was so, and they talked further about the polygraph and what it was like to take the examination. Then Pellicano asked another question:

> PELLICANO: Do you know Paul Bentley?
> FRAZIER: Paul Bentley?
> PELLICANO: Yes.
> FRAZIER: No, I don't.

There was maximum hard stress in both of Frazier's replies. The form of his response is also interesting. I have asked the same question of several people who, I am sure, never heard of Paul Bentley. Without exception, their response was, "Who is Paul Bentley?" They didn't recognize the name, but they wanted to know the connection in which I expected they might know him before saying they've never heard of the man. But Frazier's denial was immediate and unhesitating.

Frazier's story differed in one point from the official Dallas police account of the events of November 22: he denied that he had been brought back from Irving to take the polygraph examination. According to Frazier, he was brought back to answer some questions that the police had forgotten to ask. The polygraph test, said Frazier, was given before his first trip to Irving in the police car.

> FRAZIER: I remember they had me come back, and they asked me a couple other questions, and I satisfied them, and they let me go.
> PELLICANO: But, when you came back, you didn't take the lie-detector test? You took the lie-detector test before you went?
> FRAZIER: Right. That is true.

Frazier may simply have become confused in his recollection of the swirl of events surrounding him that night, especially since he was frightened. Or he may have deliberately inverted the true sequence of events to minimize the implication that Captain Fritz had doubted his word. And if the latter explanation is so, it does not necessarily demand a sinister interpretation. But, whatever the reason for Frazier's revision, the statement "Right. That is true," shows good-to-hard stress.

Pellicano asked Frazier if he knew before the assassination that Oswald owned the Mannlicher-Carcano rifle.

FRAZIER: Well, actually, to tell you—I never saw it, you know. They found it in the building, you know, after the president was shot, you know.

PELLICANO: You never knew he had this gun, then?

FRAZIER: That is true.

This produced good-to-hard stress.

PELLICANO: Did the police ever ask you did you ever know if he had a gun or nothing?

FRAZIER: They asked me that, and I told them I didn't know, you know, because I told them I never had been over to the man's——

PELLICANO: I'm talking about way before this thing ever happend. Did any police ever come up to you and ask you to get his gun?

FRAZIER: Oh, no.

PELLICANO: Never happened?

FRAZIER: No, never happened.

This produced hard stress.

Pellicano skillfully led the interview to each of the points of interest without ever adopting an accusatory manner. In his role as "a good old boy," who wanted to "get a lot of things out so all these Yankee dudes that have been writing the other stories can shut up a little bit," he was superb.

Although he obviously did his best in finding Frazier and conducting the interview, I don't think Pellicano really believed there was anything to the case until later that Saturday evening. I had been analyzing my copy of the tape with the PSE, and Pellicano had been doing the same thing with the original in Chicago. He had been jubilant when he called to report on his interview and transmit the tape, but he sounded quite subdued when he called back later that evening.

"Every one of the points you listed; he stressed on every one of them."

I said I had gotten about the same results with my own PSE.

"My God almighty," he said quietly.

What role did Buell Wesley Frazier play in the events of November 22, 1963? He was a nineteen-year-old laborer, placed by fate—or some other influence—in the company of Lee Harvey Oswald. Could Frazier have been a conspirator, given the job of implicating Oswald in the assassination? It seems unlikely. There is nothing in his background to suggest the criminal or the fanatic. Attempting to recruit the teenager into an assassination plot would have been a reckless and foolish act. Safer methods could produce the desired effect.

Consider this hypothetical problem: How could a conspirator, seeking to implicate Oswald, arrange to have him go to Irving on Thursday afternoon and bring his rifle to the book depository on Friday morning?

Suppose that a policeman quietly approached an employee of the book depository and told him that Oswald was a Communist and a dangerous radical. Suppose he said that Oswald owned a rifle and was suspected of using it in some crime, but the police could not obtain the weapon through formal, legal means. Suppose the officer asked the man to get the rifle for the police through some pretext in order to make ballistics tests. And suppose Oswald's co-worker agreed to this. What kind of pretext would work?

Oswald had bought the cheap rifle sight unseen from a mail-order house in Chicago. After it was delivered and he had an opportunity to examine it, he probably realized that the weapon wasn't worth even the $12.78 he paid for it. And so the Mannlicher-Carcano lay in disuse in Mrs. Paine's garage, wrapped in an old blanket. He should have welcomed an opportunity to sell it. Oswald may have recovered his investment on November 22; there was $13.00 in his wallet when he was arrested.[1]

Oswald made a special trip to Irving on Thursday to get the rifle, perhaps because the buyer said he needed it for a weekend hunting trip. The trip to Irving cost Oswald nothing but time, since Frazier demanded no payment for driving Oswald back and forth. [2] Having found a buyer for the weapon, Oswald would naturally want to complete the transaction before the man changed his mind.

If this was in fact how things happened, then Oswald did not invent the "curtain rod story." But what about Frazier?

On the evening of November 22, Buell Wesley Frazier was in a far from enviable position. Rumors and suspicions of conspiracy were rampant throughout Dallas and the nation. Lee Harvey Oswald was presumed to have been the assassin, and the threads of a conspiracy were sought among those who were in any way associated with him. Frazier was Oswald's co-worker in the book depository, a neighbor of Oswald's wife, and the person who had chauffered Oswald on the sinister trip to Irving. The alleged assassin and the purported murder weapon had been brought to the scene of the crime in Frazier's car that very morning.

The Dallas police did not simply bring in Frazier for questioning; they *arrested* him. They searched his automobile and his home, and they confiscated his British 303 rifle, the same type weapon that was first reported by the media to have been found in the book depository. [3]

The Zapruder film and the autopsy evidence suggests that there was more than one assassin. It seems likely, then, that more than one potential fall guy had been selected, and on the evening of November 22, Buell Wesley Frazier appeared to be, after Oswald, the leading candidate. It remained only for someone to find a pristine slug from Frazier's .303 rifle on the floor of Parkland Hospital or buried in the soil in Dealey Plaza,* and Frazier could have been thrown into the

---

*The Dallas *Times-Herald* reported on November 24, 1963, "Dallas Police Lt. J. C. Day of the crime lab estimated the distance from the sixth-floor corner window the slayer used to the spot where *one of the bullets was recovered* (emphasis added) at 100 yards." Since the Warren Report claimed that the only bullets found were the fragments in the presidential limousine and the intact bullet on the floor of Parkland, I hoped to ask Lieutenant Day about this when I spoke to him in June 1973. Unfortunately, Lieutenant Day, who had agreed to be interviewed, broke off the interview and referred me to the Warren Report when I began by asking him if more than one rifle had been found in the Texas School Book Depository. Lieutenant Day was

Dallas city jail beside Oswald. If Frazier had not told Captain Fritz the curtain-rod story, if he reported that the trip to Irving to retrieve the Mannlicher-Carcano had been instigated by a Dallas policeman, if he said that he had been an unwitting dupe in the framing of Oswald, would the trap have been sprung? Would the world have awakened on November 23 to learn that Oswald's "accomplice" had been arrested by the Dallas police?

These are, of course, questions and not answers. And they are hypothetical questions, at that. The PSE is not an infallible instrument, and no matter how striking the stress analysis of the Pellicano-Frazier interview may seem, it does not prove beyond all doubt that this reconstruction of events is correct. But there are other questions, far from hypothetical, and they suggest no obvious, innocent answers:

Why did Detective R. D. Lewis deny any recollection of being called from his home in the middle of the night to give a polygraph examination related to the investigation of a presidential assassination? Why did Detective Richard Stovall deny being present during the test? And why did Lt. Gerald Hill claim that Captain Fritz didn't believe in the polygraph and that, therefore, the examination couldn't have taken place?

The midnight polygraph examination of Buell Wesley Frazier lies at the very heart of the mystery of November 22, 1963. Why does it provoke hard stress, false statements, and curious lapses of memory among the Dallas police officers who should be the most familiar with it? Unless and until the government meets its responsibility to reopen the case of the assassination of President Kennedy, the answer to these questions can only be the darkest speculation.

---

head of the crime scene search section and had custody of all the physical evidence linking Oswald to the shootings of President Kennedy and Officer Tippit.

12 DON'T EMBARRASS THE BUREAU: A THEORY

> "A crime," Father Brown said slowly, "is like any other work of art . . . every work of art, divine or diabolic, has one indispensible mark—I mean, that the centre of it is simple, however much the fulfillment may be complicated.
>
> ". . . Every clever crime is founded ultimately on some one quite simple fact—some fact that is not itself mysterious. The mystification comes in covering it up, in leading men's thoughts away from it."
>
> —G. K. Chesterton: *The Queer Feet*

> When you have eliminated the impossible, whatever remains, however improbable, must be the truth.
>
> —Sherlock Holmes

Every student of mathematics learns that a set of simple equations cannot be solved if there are more unknowns than equations. Give him two equations with three unknowns, and he will find no answer, or he will find an infinite number of different answers, which is the same thing. But add the third equation, and he will be able to eliminate, in turn, the x, the y, and the z and find the unique solution to his problem.

Human puzzles rarely offer the crisp clarity of mathematics, but the mystery of Dallas seems in many ways like a set of 99 equations containing 100 unknowns. President Kennedy was murdered while riding in a motorcade; Oswald was shot by Jack Ruby in the basement of the Dallas City Hall: these things we know for certain, because they happened to be recorded on film and videotape. Beyond them, nearly everything must be assigned some relative degree of credibility or doubt. An infinite variety of mutually exclusive theories can be postulated to explain the same set of facts. Speculation leads nowhere because it leads everywhere.

My own investigation has focused on a single unknown, perhaps the most important one in the Dallas equations: did Lee Harvey Oswald assassinate President Kennedy? Reviewing the official account and the work of many other private assassination researchers, I found that there were serious flaws in the case against Oswald. In analyzing the recorded statements of those witnesses whose testimony was most damaging to Oswald, I found a consistent pattern of the stress normally associated with deception, and several of the witnesses I personally interviewed made serious misstatements of fact. Finally, three prominent lie-detection specialists have confirmed my analysis of Oswald's own statements regarding his innocence. The reader must reach his own conclusion, but mine is that, beyond any possibility of a reasonable doubt, Lee Harvey Oswald did not kill President Kennedy.

But settling the question of Oswald's innocence also solves several other unknowns which follow as a natural consequence. The evidence implicating Oswald did not come about by chance. Oswald could not have been the victim of circumstance; he must have been the victim of people who deliberately implicated him in the assassination. The physical evidence was collected and examined by the Dallas police. The witnesses against him were first located and questioned by the Dallas police. The Warren Commission's case against Oswald was essentially the case that had been built by the Dallas police as of November 23, 1963. The conclusion seems inescapable that at least some of the people who framed Lee Harvey Oswald were members of the Dallas police.

The framing of Lee Harvey Oswald tells us something about the assassination conspiracy. As Justice Warren pointed out, there were two general conspiracy theories—foreign Communists or domestic right-wing radicals. Oswald had very obvious ties to the Soviet Union, Castro's Cuba, and domestic Communist organizations. If he were framed as the assassin, we must look in the opposite political direction for the real murderers. It is an understatement to say that, as a group, American policemen of the 1960s tended more toward the political right than the center or left. This was especially so in the South. While it seems unlikely that the Dallas Police Department employed many members of the American Civil Liberties Union, the Americans for Democratic Action, or the Communist party, the force may well have included members of the John Birch Society, the Minutemen, or the Ku Klux Klan. This proves nothing, but it is consistent with the conclusion that the assassination was a right-wing parapolitical action.

But if the conspiracy involved a few right-wing extremists who happened to be in the Dallas Police Department, does it stop there or extend further? Was the operation ordered by the Klan, Texas oil interests, or elements of the FBI or the CIA? Unfortunately, the psychological stress evaluator is not a crystal ball: I cannot offer any conclusive answers to these questions. But I can suggest a hypothesis, which, if it does not offer a comprehensive theory of the assassination, at least explains a great many loose ends. The hypothesis is: Lee Harvey Oswald worked as an informer for one or more FBI agents in the Dallas area.

Reports that Oswald worked for the FBI began to be heard only a few weeks after the assassination. President Gerald Ford (then a congressman), who served on the Warren Commission, wrote in his book *Portrait of the Assassin:*

> No sooner had the Commission investigating President Kennedy's assassination assembled its staff and tentatively outlined methods of operation than it was plunged into an astounding problem. On Wednesday, January 22, the members of the Commission were hurriedly called into emergency session by the chairman. Mr. J. Lee Rankin, newly appointed General Counsel for the Commission, had received a telephone call from Texas. The information was that the FBI had an "undercover agent," and that that agent was none other than Lee Harvey Oswald, the alleged assassin of President Kennedy![1]

The incident began when Rankin received a telephone call from Waggoner Carr, the attorney-general of Texas. Carr passed on to Rankin a report that Oswald had been "an undercover agent" for the FBI since September 1962 and had been paid $200 per month from an account designated "No. 179." Carr said that the source of the report was Henry Wade, the Dallas district attorney.[2]

The January 22 commission meeting was hurriedly called to discuss the report. During the meeting Carr was again contacted and asked if he could identify the ultimate source of the story. Carr replied that he had spoken to District Attorney Wade, who "had been unable or unwilling to specify the source of this allegation in more detail."[3]

Two days later, Chief Justice Warren and Lee Rankin met in Washington with Carr, Wade, Dallas Assistant District Attorney William Alexander, and two prominent Texas attorneys, Leon Jaworski* and Robert Storey. The Texans reported that the rumors of Oswald's FBI affiliation were circulating among newspapermen in Texas, and may have originated with Alonzo Hudkins of *The Houston Post.* Wade added that he had also heard a report that Oswald had been a CIA informant and was designated by the Agency as No. 110669.[4] Wade had been an FBI agent from 1939 to 1943, and he said that, based on his own experience, he knew the FBI would pay such an informer in cash and would keep records on him by number, not by name. The Texans offered several bits of circumstantial evidence of Oswald's FBI connection, including his use of post-office boxes and aliases, a two-hour interview of Oswald by the FBI in September 1962 during which, presumably, he was recruited, and the fact that Oswald had in his notebook the name, address, and telephone number of an FBI agent, plus the license-plate number of his automobile. [5]

After the meeting, the lawmen returned to Texas, leaving behind a severely shaken chief justice. Warren scheduled a meeting of the commission for the following Monday to decide how to deal with the problem. During the weekend, the story of Oswald's alleged FBI affiliation began to surface in the Eastern press.[6]

*The same Leon Jaworski became special Watergate prosecutor ten years later, after Nixon removed Archibald Cox from that post. In 1963, Jaworski and Storey had been selected by Carr to conduct a Texas court of inquiry into the assassination. When this was cancelled after President Johnson appointed the Warren Commission, the two were assigned a liaison role between the commission and the Texas state government.

The commission met at 2:30 P.M. on Monday, January 27, 1964. Except for Rep. Gerald Ford, the full commission was present, as well as Counsel Rankin and a stenographer. The words spoken behind those closed conference-room doors became part of the top secret record of the Warren Commission, locked away from public view until its unexplained release ten years later, in June 1974.[7]

The transcript shows that the meeting began with J. Lee Rankin reviewing the situation for the commissioners, starting with the telephone call from Attorney-General Carr on the previous Wednesday. Rankin revealed that he had actually received a report on the FBI-Oswald matter from the Secret Service the day before the Texas official called him. Apparently Rankin hadn't noticed the report buried in a bunch of other Secret Service documents.[8]

The Secret Service report contained essentially the same information the Texans volunteered, but it gave as its source a Dallas deputy sheriff named Allan Sweatt. Noting the date on the report, Rankin expressed some concern that nearly three weeks had passed before it was turned over to the commission. "We wondered whether the Secret Service was withholding something from us, since they had this in their hands clear back on January 3, the date of the report. The explanation since has been that they were trying to check it out." In fact, the Secret Service had gotten the information from Sweatt in mid-December, nearly six weeks earlier. Rankin observed, "it seemed like kind of a long period since they hadn't gotten any further report from Mr. Sweatt at all."[9]

But resolving such minutiae was far from the minds of the commissioners. Even the question of whether or not Oswald had been employed by the FBI seemed of secondary importance. The problem that loomed paramount in the minds of the six commission members and their counsel seemed to be: How is the commission to deal with the rumors of an FBI-Oswald link without displeasing J. Edgar Hoover? The commission apparently tried to toss the hot potato to the Justice Department, but it was quickly tossed back:

MR. McCLOY: Willens [the commission's Justice Department liaison] has indicated that [Deputy Attorney-General] Katzenbach says they will be greatly embarrassed.

MR. RANKIN: Greatly embarrassed.

MR. McCLOY: Greatly embarrassed.

SEN. RUSSELL: If what?

MR. RANKIN: If the Attorney General were asked to check this out and then report to us.

JUSTICE WARREN: But they seem to think there would be no embarrassment for us to check it out ourselves. They think that is all right, they think it is all right for us to do that. Now, my own thought is this—I am not going to be thin-skinned about what Mr. Hoover might think, but I am sure that if we indicated to Mr. Hoover that we were investigating him he would be just as angry at us as he was, or would be at the Attorney General for investigating him.[10]

The attorney-general in question was Robert Kennedy, the murdered president's brother, and there is ample record that Hoover's feelings toward him were far from friendly. Justice Warren was probably wrong; no matter how much the FBI director might resent outsiders probing his agency, he would feel infinitely more bitter if the intruder were Robert Kennedy. Katzenbach told Rankin that such an action by Kennedy would "make very much more difficult for him to carry on the work of the Department for the balance of his term."[11]

The core of the commission's dilemma was this: whether to investigate the rumor or to ask Hoover about it? The commission really had no investigators of its own; it relied on the FBI to locate and interview witnesses. If the commission's staff lawyers tried to conduct their own probe of the alleged FBI-Oswald link, word would surely get back to Hoover that the commission was, in effect, investigating his agency. On the other hand, if the commission approached Hoover directly with the allegation, he would certainly offer his assurances that it was untrue; then any further probing by the commission would be an implicit impeachment of Hoover's word. Faced with the taboo against hurting the feelings of J. Edgar Hoover, there seemed little the Warren Commission could do to explore this aspect of the assassination.

In fact, limited as they were to the investigative services of the

FBI, the commissioners felt that they could not adequately explore any aspect of the assassination. After Commissioner John McCloy referred to some discrepancies in the FBI's version of the assassination, the following exchange took place:

MR. RANKIN: Part of our difficulty in regard to it is that they [the FBI] have no problems. They have decided that it is Oswald who committed the assassination, they have decided no one else was involved, they have decided——

SEN. RUSSELL: They have tried the case and reached a verdict on every aspect.

REP. BOGGS: You have put your finger on it.

MR. McCLOY: They are a little less certain in the supplementals than they were in the rest.

MR. RANKIN: Yes, but they are still there. They have decided the case, and we are going to have maybe a thousand further inquiries that we say the Commission has to know all these things before it can pass on this. And I think their reaction probably will be, "Why do you want all that? It is clear."

SEN. RUSSELL: "You have our statement, what else do you need?"

MR. McCLOY: Yes, "We know who killed cock robin." That is the point. It isn't only who killed cock robin. Under the terms of reference we have to go beyond that.[12]

Defenders of the Warren Commission often point to the months of work that went into its report, the hundreds of witnesses who gave testimony before it, and the exhaustive investigation carried out by the FBI on its behalf. It is disquieting now to learn that as of January 1964, before even a single witness had testified and seven months before the writing of the final report, the FBI had adopted an adversary position toward the Warren Commission and, in the words of Senator Russell, "tried the case and reached a verdict on every aspect."

The commission may have hoped that the FBI-Oswald rumor would just go away, but it was already obvious that it would not. An article raising the question had appeared in *The Nation*, and reports of Oswald's FBI employment had been published in the *New York*

Times. McCloy noted, "This is going to loom up in all probability
to be one of the major issues of the investigation . . . we are going
to have to have a very solid record on it."[13] And Rankin observed,
"I don't see how the country is ever going to be willing to accept it
if we don't satisfy them on this particular issue, not only with them
[the FBI] but with the CIA and every other agency."[14] But the
commissioners could not have been very encouraged by the remarks
of one of their number who happened to be a former director of the
CIA.

> MR. DULLES: There is a terribly hard thing to disprove, you
> know. How do you disprove a fellow was not your agent? How do
> you disprove it?
> REP. BOGGS: You could disprove it, couldn't you?
> MR. DULLES: No.
> REP. BOGGS: I know, ask questions about something——
> MR. DULLES: I never knew how to disprove it.
> REP. BOGGS: So I will ask you. Did you have agents about whom
> you had no record whatsoever?
> MR. DULLES: The record might not be on paper. . . .[15]

Boggs then asked Dulles if the intelligence officer who recruited
an agent wouldn't know of his employment.

> MR. DULLES: Yes, but he wouldn't tell.
> JUSTICE WARREN: Wouldn't tell it under oath?
> MR. DULLES: I wouldn't think he would tell it under oath, no.[16]

It seemed to come as a surprise to the other commissioners to learn
that secret agents sometimes lie, even under oath. As if to remove
any doubt about his implication, Dulles added, "What I was getting
at, I think under any circumstances, I think Mr. Hoover would say
certainly he didn't have anything to do with this fellow."[17]

In other words, the commission couldn't expect to get at the truth
simply by going to Hoover and asking him about it. Hoover would
deny it whether or not it was untrue.

The commissioners spent a good deal of time debating the merits
of summoning Alonzo Hudkins, the Houston reporter said by the
Texas officials to be the source of the rumor, and examining him

under oath to learn his source. They anticipated that Hudkins might claim a journalist's privilege to protect confidential sources, and, although they realized that such a privilege is not guaranteed in the law, they seem to have feared the publicity such a confrontation might have generated. In fact, the commissioners seemed to worry that even raising the question with Hudkins would give him material for a story they wouldn't like to see printed. "Now this man Hudkins published an article in January," said Senator Cooper, referring to a story Hudkins had written about the FBI-Oswald link. "But if he were brought before us and put under oath and testified then he could publish whatever he wanted to about his testimony."[18]

Considering the amount of time the commission members agonized over how to go about learning the source of Hudkins's information that Oswald was an FBI informer, it seems surprising that their counsel, J. Lee Rankin, didn't tell them that he already knew. Sometime after the January 27 meeting Rankin wrote an undated memorandum for the files entitled "Rumors that Oswald was an undercover agent." The memo was released by the National Archives a few years ago, and in it Rankin states that on January 23 he received word of a Secret Service interview with Hudkins in which the reporter said he got the FBI-Oswald story from Allan Sweatt, the Dallas deputy Sheriff mentioned in another Secret Service report as the source of the story.[19]

If Rankin had related his discovery to the commissioners, they would surely have dropped the question of interviewing Hudkins and, instead, thought about summoning Sweatt to ask about his source. And if they had, Rankin could have answered that question as well: according to his memorandum, he received an oral report on the previous Friday from a Secret Service agent who had interviewed Sweatt. The deputy named his source as William Alexander, the assistant district attorney who had accompanied Wade and Carr to Washington.[20]

That this morsel would have fascinated the commissioners can be guessed from the following exchange:

REP. BOGGS: What role did this man Alexander play in this?
MR. RANKIN: Well, it appeared to have started earlier than—

he was as active, but it is possible, I don't know——

JUSTICE WARREN: I think he is the fellow who blew the whistle so far as this Commission is concerned. I think that is where Carr got his information, don't you think?

REP. BOGGS: From Alexander?

JUSTICE WARREN: From Alexander, yes. And Alexander was up here and sat in that chair, and said that it wasn't exactly the way Carr had presented it, that there were two different things. One, that was involved in Carr's story to Lee [Rankin]. One of them had to do with the hearing in chambers on some papers they wanted from the [Jack Ruby] defense, and then after that was over he went out into the corridor and then down to the press room and he said they were all talking about it then, he said all the press were, it is a matter of common knowledge among the press, this rumor, and he just shrugged the whole thing off, and Carr was sitting where the Senator is and he didn't object to anything that Alexander said, although it varied radically from what he told you [Rankin] a day or so before.[21]

All this is very strange. The commission first heard of the FBI-Oswald rumor from Texas Attorney-General Waggoner Carr, and he, in turn, said he heard it from Dallas District Attorney Henry Wade. Then Carr and Wade met with Justice Warren, and they brought along Wade's assistant, William Alexander. Alexander turned out to be the real authority on the matter, and he attributed the story to the press in general and Alonzo Hudkins in particular. But Hudkins got the story from Deputy Sheriff Sweatt, and Sweatt said he got the story from Bill Alexander. All roads lead to the assistant district attorney. The rumor that caused the Warren Commission so much anguish seems to have originated with the same man who "blew the whistle" on it for the commission. Curious.

The evidence suggests that Alexander caused the story to be planted in the press and then, after it surfaced, called it to the Texas attorney-general's notice so that he would report it to the commission. Next, Alexander visited the commission with Carr and Wade to present several circumstantial items in support of the rumor. While these actions seem very strange, they are nothing compared to J. Lee Rankin's failure to call Alexander on the carpet and demand to know just what the hell kind of game he was playing.

Since there is no record of that question being asked, we can only search for a motive by analyzing the effect of the rumor that Oswald was an FBI informer. In theory, such a connection would be completely irrelevant to Oswald's purported role as assassin. The FBI does not claim to select its informers on the basis of character or stability, but rather because they are involved in some group or organization of interest and may be persuaded to provide information about it for pay. By definition, FBI informers are usually the kind of people who do the the very things the FBI investigates. The FBI may use them, but it doesn't vouch for them. In reality, however, revelation that Oswald had been a paid FBI informer would have been disastrous for the Bureau.

The Federal Bureau of Investigation was not only the creation of J. Edgar Hoover, it was an extension of his personality. During the nearly four decades before the assassination, Hoover had devoted himself completely to his organization. A bachelor, Hoover had no family to compete for his attentions. The FBI was his child, it would be the only thing Hoover left behind. Hoover's formula for building the power of his organization was basically simple: first, be very good; second, seem infallible. More than any other public official of his time, Hoover had mastered the art of public relations. The books, magazine articles, radio and television programs that promoted the myth of the FBI were done with the full cooperation of Hoover and his press aides. By 1963, the sixty-eight-year-old Hoover and his FBI had become legend.

But the image of the FBI had already been damaged by the assassination. Hoover was smarting under criticism that the Bureau had failed to make available to the Secret Service and the Dallas police its information on Lee Harvey Oswald. The charge that Oswald had been on the FBI payroll, that he may even have purchased the rifle and ammunition that killed the president with money paid to him by the FBI, could have been fatal to the public image that Hoover had labored so long to create. Hoover himself must have reacted to the rumor with personal outrage; one can envision the wave of terror that swept down through the Bureau when he heard about it. If Oswald had been recruited to work for the FBI, who would have had the courage to tell this to the director?

The visit of Wade and Alexander to the commission and the consequent inquiry to J. Edgar Hoover must have had a disruptive effect on the FBI investigation in Dallas. Suppressing the rumor of an Oswald-FBI connection would have taken priority over the assassination probe.* If the FBI investigation had begun to develop information that Oswald was framed by members of the Dallas Police Department, would the Bureau have been charged with covering up for one of its own? For such a threat to be effective, someone had to have hard evidence to make the charge stick, conclusive proof that Oswald did work for the FBI. Let us examine the facts that suggest this.

The first contact between Oswald and the FBI apparently took place on June 26, 1962, shortly after he returned from the Soviet Union.[22] The Fort Worth office of the Bureau called him in for a two-hour interview, the ostensible purpose of which was to determine why Oswald had gone to Russia and whether he had been asked to work for Soviet intelligence. The official FBI report written after this interview shows that the Bureau had conducted an intensive investigation into Oswald's background and viewed him as a subject of considerable interest.[23] Considering Oswald's history, this does not appear unusual.

Oswald was next contacted by the FBI about two months later on August 15. There is nothing remarkable about such a follow-up interview, but the method used by the agents in approaching Oswald seems somewhat unusual: they set up a stake out in an automobile near his home and approached him as he walked down the street.[24] The agent who was in charge of the case, John Fain, testified that he had chosen this approach to demonstrate to Oswald that the FBI wasn't trying to embarrass him, and "we felt if we talked to him there

*Some readers may find this statement excessively cynical; however, those familiar with the workings of bureaucracies in general and intelligence agencies in particular will recognize its truth. Many intelligence officers and agents who risk life and limb in their country's service would not similarly jeopardize their careers or pensions.

in the car informally, he would better cooperate with us."[25]

This doesn't seem to make sense. Fain didn't explain why he thought Oswald would be less embarrassed by being accosted on the street near his home than by being visited at his apartment. In fact, Fain said that Oswald invited the agents into his apartment:

> FAIN: Actually he invited us in when we stopped him. He said, "Won't you come in the house?" And I said, "Well, we will just talk here. We will be alone to ourselves and we will be informal, and just fine." So he got in the car with Agent Brown.[26]

In this statement Fain seems to have presented a more plausible reason for sitting in a car with another FBI agent and waiting for an indefinite period until Oswald appeared on the street: the agents had something to discuss with Oswald that they did not want overheard. Talking to him in the automobile insured their own privacy.

Assuming that the FBI agents approached Oswald to recruit him as an informer, how would they have gone about it? Based on their reports, Oswald's attitude toward them was neither completely hostile nor fully cooperative. In the first interview he was "a little insolent" and would not discuss his reasons for going to Russia, [27] but during the second interview he agreed to notify the FBI if he were ever contacted by Soviet intelligence.[28] Oswald had become disillusioned with the Soviet Union, but he continued to espouse marxism after his return to the United States, so he probably would have resisted any suggestion that he inform on domestic leftist groups.

However, Oswald had at least one vulnerable point, and this came across loud and clear in FBI Agent Fain's report of the second interview:

> . . . OSWALD stated the American Embassy [in Moscow] tried to persuade him to return to the United States alone, and without his wife, MARINA. He told the Embassy he could not do that. The Embassy reportedly pointed out to OSWALD it would be a difficult matter to obtain a passport for OSWALD's wife, who was a Russian. The Embassy tried to influence him to come back alone, find a job, get established, and later send for his wife. OSWALD stated he refused to follow this course. He told the American

Embassy he feared he would never see his wife again if he left her in Russia.[29]

A recent study of FBI informers groups such people into several categories and discusses one in particular: "Another equally unreliable group [of informers] lives under the shadow of some prior cloud: fear of being charged as an accomplice, of deportation, of perjury charges."[30]

Marina Oswald was not a United States citizen. She was admitted to the United States at the pleasure of the government. She could be ejected at its displeasure. And she meant enough to Oswald that he refused to leave the Soviet Union without her. Whether or not they used it against him, the agents must have realized they found a nerve.

Did the FBI threaten Oswald with Marina's deportation? According to Oswald, they threatened Marina herself. After his arrest, Oswald was first interrogated by Captain Fritz, who was shortly joined by an FBI agent, James Hosty. Hosty had been assigned Oswald's case when Oswald returned to Dallas and had visited Mrs. Ruth Paine and Marina some weeks before the assassination. According to Fritz, Oswald became enraged when Hosty identified himself, and "he beat on the desk and went into a kind of tantrum."[31]

> BALL: Was there anything said about Oswald's wife?
> FRITZ: Yes, sir. He said, he told Hosty, he said, "I know you." He said, "You accosted my wife on two occasions," and he was getting pretty irritable. . . . I asked him what he meant by accosting, I thought maybe he meant some physical abuse or something and he said, "Well, he threatened her." And he said, "He practically told her she would have to go back to Russia."[32]

Given that the FBI had the motive and means to recruit Oswald as an informer, what other evidence exists to suggest that it actually did? One of the strongest supports for this thesis is an incident that occurred several months before the assassination in August 1963.

Oswald was arrested for disturbing the peace while distributing pro-Castro leaflets in New Orleans. While in custody, Oswald asked to speak to an FBI agent. Special Agent John Quigley of the New

Orleans office visited Oswald in jail and interviewed him. When Quigley testified before the commission, he said that he had never heard of Oswald before that meeting, he did not know why Oswald had asked to see an FBI agent, and Oswald did not explain this during the interview.[33] Quigley interviewed Oswald for an hour and a half,[34] during which time Oswald discussed his activities in the Fair Play for Cuba Committee and his dealings with a local member of that committee named A. J. Hidell.[35]

If Quigley's story is accepted at face value, Oswald's actions are incomprehensible. A pro-Castro activist is arrested while leafletting, and he immediately asks to talk to an FBI agent, to tell him about the Fair Play for Cuba Committee and A. J. Hidell. Yet this could have been exactly what happened if Oswald was working as an informer for the FBI's Dallas office.

Oswald was arrested after an altercation with some anti-Castro Cubans who objected to his leafletting. The charge was disturbing the peace, and Oswald may have been afraid that he was going to spend a few weeks in jail as a result. Declaring his informer status to the local FBI might have seemed a possible breach of security, but requesting an interview with an agent was a discreet way of letting the Bureau in Dallas know where he was. Quigley would have been the unwitting messenger.

Since "A. J. Hidell" was the only name Oswald mentioned to Quigley in his discussion of the New Orleans Fair Play for Cuba Committee, it may have had some special significance. Specifically, Hidell may have been the pseudonym Oswald used in connection with his informer activities. As J. Edgar Hoover explained in an affidavit to the commission: "An informant is assigned a permanent symbol number and a code name to afford him security. . . . The individual also is given a fictitious or cover name by the field office which he, of course, is made aware of, and he affixes it to his communications with the office."[36]

Quigley's report on the interview with Oswald, including his mention of the Hidell name, would have been routinely put into the FBI's information network. Since Oswald told the agent he had recently moved to New Orleans from Texas, a copy of the report would have been sent to the Fort Worth or Dallas Bureau office. Normally this entire process would require several days, so it cannot explain the fortunate developments that immediately followed Quigley's visit to Oswald: Oswald was released on bail that same day; two days later he went to court and was charged with "creating a scene."[37] He pleaded guilty and was given a ten-dollar fine.[38] But in view of the minor charges against Oswald, such leniency is not too unusual. The remarkable feature of the New Orleans arrest episode is Oswald's request to see an FBI agent and the substance of the consequent interview.

The next link between Oswald and the FBI is the presence in Oswald's address book of the name, office address, telephone number, and automobile license-plate number of Special Agent James Hosty. According to the Warren Report, Hosty left his name, address, and phone number with Mrs. Ruth Paine so she could contact him, but she passed this information along to Oswald.[39] The license-plate number was allegedly noted down by Marina while Hosty was visiting her and Mrs. Paine. The Report said she had been instructed to do this by Oswald.[40]

There are several problems with this explanation, however. Hosty visited the Paine home twice, on November 1 and November 5, 1963. During the first visit, according to Mrs. Paine, Hosty parked down the street from her house to avoid drawing attention to his visit, and the license plate of his car was not visible from the house.[41] During the second visit Marina was in her room, joining Hosty and Mrs. Paine only just before the FBI agent departed.[42] The commission's investigators established that it would have been impossible for Marina to have read the plate on Hosty's car from her room; they went to the Paine house and unsuccessfully attempted to read the plate on a car parked in front of the house from the window of Marina's room.[43] Marina testified that she copied the plate number for Oswald, but she never explained how she managed to do it.[44]

The fact that Hosty's name and identifying data were in Oswald's address book was not immediately reported to the commission by the FBI. In a December 23 FBI report listing the names in Oswald's address book, the Hosty entry was omitted. The FBI submitted a later report to the commission on February 11, 1964, correcting the omission, but the commission staff already knew of the Hosty entry by then. Meagher points out that the means by which the commission learned of the item is unknown, but it seems not to have been the FBI.[45] The recently declassified documents disclose that the subject of the Hosty entry in Oswald's address book came up in the general discussion on January 24 between Rankin, Warren, and the Texas delegation. While they do not specifically say so, the documents indicate that Wade and Alexander may have been the commission's source for this item.

In his testimony before the commission, J. Edgar Hoover explained that the December 23 FBI report had been prepared for the Bureau's own investigative purposes—implicitly, to check on the individuals listed in the address book—and the Bureau already knew why Hosty's name was in the book, hence the omission.[46] This seems plausible, but not persuasive. This explanation was probably the same one given to Hoover by the Bureau office in Dallas. He may not have been happy with it, but in view of the burgeoning rumors of an FBI-Oswald link, he had no choice but to offer it to the commission.

The theory that Oswald was a Bureau informer explains why the Dallas FBI office did not pass its file on Oswald to the intelligence bureau of the Dallas Police Department. And it also explains why the head of the Dallas FBI office, Gordon Shanklin, blew his stack after Oswald's arrest.

Immediately after hearing of the arrest. Shanklin sent Hosty to police headquarters to sit in on the interrogation.[47] When Hosty arrived at the police station, Shanklin was on the phone to another FBI agent, James Bookhout, who was already at the station.[48] Captain Fritz, who had summoned Bookhout to the phone, listened to the conversation on an extension. Fritz described the conversation for the commission:

> FRITZ: He said is Hosty in that investigation, Bookhout said no. He said, "I want him in that investigation right now because he knows those people he has been talking to," and he said some other things that I don't want to repeat, about what to do if he didn't do it right quick. So I didn't tell them that I even knew what Mr. Shanklin said. I walked out there and called them in.[49]

Fritz did not explain why he chose to eavesdrop on a conversation between the head of the FBI's Dallas office and one of his agents or why this was at the moment more important than interrogating the suspected presidential assassin sitting across from him. Fritz had a reputation as an extremely astute detective, and he may have already begun to suspect a connection between the Bureau and his prisoner. Fritz had been alone with Oswald for ten or fifteen minutes before the call, and Oswald may have asked to see an FBI agent, just as he did in New Orleans.

The evidence that Oswald was a Bureau informer does not prove that, in fact, he was, so this must remain a theory. But it is a useful theory that explains several minor mysteries about Lee Harvey Oswald. And the theory explains a great deal more with the addition of another hypothesis: That one or more Dallas FBI agents, acting as individuals, helped to frame Lee Harvey Oswald.

There is a hazard inherent in the use of informers or subagents: they are not really members of the agency they work for, and the agents or case officers controlling them become their only channel to the agency. The agent who controls an informer is in an excellent position to use him for his own private purposes.

The Cubans who were caught breaking into the Democratic party headquarters in the Watergate seem to have believed sincerely that the burglary was an authorized CIA operation. They believed this because they were recruited for the job and led by E. Howard Hunt, with whom they had worked before in his capacity as a CIA intelligence officer. They were given cash for their expenses, just as in the authorized operations, and there were no written orders. There never are.

An FBI agent in control of Lee Harvey Oswald could have made Oswald an unwitting accessory to his own frame-up. Specifically, he could have insured that Oswald was alone in some corner of the book depository when the shots were fired so no witness could confirm his alibi. And he could have caused Oswald's suspicious departure from the book depository after the shooting and his visit to the Texas Theatre. It could have been done with the utmost ease and simplicity, and I offer the following scenario as an example of how it might have been arranged.

Oswald had neither a driver's license nor an automobile. In the sprawling urban complex of Dallas-Fort Worth, this would severely limit his mobility. It would be natural, then, to require Oswald to obtain a license and furnish him with a car in order to broaden the range of his informer activities. In mid-October Oswald began taking driving lessons from Mrs. Ruth Paine.[50] Buell Wesley Frazier testified that Oswald told him he planned to buy a car.[51] Albert Bogard, a Dallas auto salesman, testified that Oswald entered his showroom on November 9 and took a car out for a test drive.

> BOGARD: . . . he told me that he wasn't ready to buy, that he would be in a couple or 3 weeks, that he had some money coming in. And when he finally started to leave I got his name and wrote it on the back of one of my business cards, and never heard from the man any more.[52]

Bogard said he recognized Lee Harvey Oswald's picture in the newspapers as the same man who had visited the showroom[53] and reiterated that Oswald had said he expected some money in two or three weeks:

> BALL: Now, when you got back to the showroom, you said you did some figuring. What kind of figuring?
> BOGARD: Just took out some papers and going to write up how much the car would cost and, just like with anybody else, just trying to close the deal, and he said he would have the money in 2 or 3 weeks and would come in and——
> BALL: Did you tell him you needed a down payment?
> BOGARD: He said he would have it.
> BALL: Did you tell him how much?
> BOGARD: Yes.
> BELL: How much?
> BOGARD: Three hundred dollars, I think. And he said he didn't have the money then and would just pay cash for it at a later date.[54]

It should be noted that the date of this incident was one day less than two weeks before November 22.

Thus, according to the scenario, Oswald's FBI control notified him that he would receive funds for the purchase of an automobile sometime during the latter part of November. Arrangements for actual delivery of the money would be determined later. Meanwhile Oswald learned to drive and selected a car.

As an FBI informer, Oswald would have been assigned a reporting procedure for contacting his control. This could have been a telephone number he was instructed to call at preestablished times on specified days. Since Oswald had no telephone in his furnished room in Oak Cliff, and use of his landlady's telephone would have brought unwelcome attention to his contacts, the most practical arrangement would have been to use a telephone in the book depository. The book depository manager, Roy Truly, happened to be asked about this point by the commission:

> McCLOY: Did [Oswald] have the use of a telephone when he was in the building?
> TRULY: Yes, sir. We have a telephone on the first floor that he was free to use during his lunch hour for a minute. He was supposed to ask permission to use the phone. But he could have used the phone.
> DULLES: Pay telephone or office telephone?
> TRULY: No, sir; it is a regular office telephone. It is a pushbutton type.[55]

Truly's reference to a "pushbutton type" phone indicates that there were several lines on the book depository's office phone, a common feature of business phone services even in small establishments. There were undoubtedly other extensions than the one on the first floor. There was surely an extension in the second-floor offices near the lunchroom where Oswald was seen less than ninety seconds after the shooting. With the presidential motorcade due to pass by on the street outside the book depository during the lunch hour, those second-floor offices would almost certainly have been vacant at 12:30 P.M. on November 22.

By instructing him to be at the phone in the second-floor office to receive a call at about 12:30, the control would be sure that Oswald was effectively removed from public view while the assassination shots were being fired.

But there would still have been a margin for misadventure: the motorcade might have passed a few minutes early or late, and one of the second-floor office employees could have wandered back into the building and gone upstairs. To control these variables, it would have been necessary to post someone on the first or second floors to delay, through some pretext, anyone who came into the building and headed for the second floor. It would also have been advisable to place the call to Oswald from a phone in or near the book depository, so that the call could be timed to coincide with the motorcade's passage. There is evidence that this was exactly the method used.

An unpublished FBI report now available in the National Archives recounts an interview with NBC newsman Robert MacNeil, who was riding in the press bus several cars behind the presidential limousine. After the shots, MacNeil got off the bus and followed some police officers up the grassy knoll.

> We climbed a fence and I followed the police who appeared to be chasing someone, or under the impression they were chasing someone, across the railroad tracks. Wanting to phone news of the shooting, I left there and went to the nearest place that looked like an office. It was the Texas School Book Depository. I believe I entered the front door about four minutes after the shooting. I went immediately into the clear space on the ground floor and asked where there was a phone. There were, as I recall, three men there, all I think in shirt sleeves. What, on recollection, strikes me as possibly significant is that all three seemed to be exceedingly calm and relaxed, compared to the pandemonium which existed right outside their front door. I did not pay attention to this at the time. I asked the first man I saw—a man who was telephoning from a phone by a pillar in the middle of the room—where I could call from. He directed me to another man nearer the door, who pointed to an office. When I got to the phone, two of the lines were already lit up. I made my call and left. I do not believe any police officers entered the building before me or until I left. I was in too much of a hurry to remember what the three men there looked like. But their manner was very relaxed. My New York news desk has since placed the time of my call at 12.36 Dallas time.[56]

Except for the timing, MacNeil's report fits the scenario perfectly. Three men were waiting calmly on the first floor of the book depository, and one of them was on the phone. One of the trio directed MacNeil to another phone in an office (presumably on the first floor, since MacNeil makes no mention of going upstairs). MacNeil found that two lines were already in use. The man on the first floor had picked up the telephone, busying the first line, dialed the same number he was calling from, and the call came in on the next available line, ringing the extension in the second-floor office. Oswald picked it up, lighting up the second line, and heard the voice of his Bureau contact. Then MacNeil entered, saw the man on the telephone, was directed to another phone, found two lines in use, and made his call out on a third line.

If MacNeil was right about the timing of this episode, then it happened a couple of minutes too late to fit the scenario; Officer Baker confronted Oswald in the second-floor lunchroom less than ninety seconds after the shooting. Of course, the conspiracy clockwork could have slipped, delaying the call to Oswald. Oswald might have gone to the lunchroom for his Coke while he was waiting, there to be met by Officer Baker. Then, a moment later, he could have returned to the office and received the call. Oswald was seen going into the office after the Baker incident,[57] although there was no report that he used the telephone. But the witness who saw Oswald there considered it unusual: "I thought it was a little strange that one of the warehouse boys would be up in the office at that time. . . ."[58]

In any case the presence of MacNeil's three calm men on the first floor and Oswald's presence on the second floor, support the hypothesis that a prearranged telephone contact was the means by which Oswald was kept out of sight during the shooting. Given that assumption, we might wonder what Oswald was told by his contact during that telephone conversation. The obvious answer is that he was instructed to proceed to the Texas Theatre to meet his contact and receive the money to purchase an automobile.

In almost all countries of the Western world, a motion picture theater is the perfect scene for a "live drop." A Soviet intelligence training manual puts it this way:

> Intelligence officers can make extensive use of movie theatres when organizing agent communications by spending a certain amount of time in them before a meeting. The fact is that there are few people in most movie theatres, especially on weekdays during working hours. Movie theatres located away from the cen-

ter of the city are often practically empty. Thus, by arriving at a designated time at a previously determined movie theatre and taking advantage of the many empty seats, the intelligence officer and agent can hold a meeting right in the theatre.[59]

But the Soviets didn't invent the idea, and they don't hold a patent on it. The FBI certainly uses the same technique when documents, money, or other material must be passed between agent and informer. The Texas Theatre was near Oswald's Oak Cliff furnished room, and it is likely that he had met his control there several times before November 22.

The Warren Report states that Oswald left $170 with his wife on the morning of the assassination[60] and implies that this was a valedictory gesture by a man who did not expect to return home ever again. It seems less melodramatic, but more plausible, to conclude that Oswald's generosity was prompted by his expectation of receiving a large amount of cash that afternoon. Oswald may have been told he'd be given enough to buy a car and have something left over.

Obviously there was no actual intention of meeting Oswald and giving him any money; the pretext served to get him to the Texas Theatre. His sudden afternoon moviegoing seemed furtive and served to characterize Oswald as a suspicious person, but there was probably a more important reason for luring him to the theater. As the Soviet manual points out, a theater away from the center of town is practically empty during working hours. The semidarkness of the Texas Theatre would have been an excellent place to kill Oswald while he was "resisting arrest." But something went wrong. There may have been more patrons in the theater than expected, the house lights may have been turned up too soon, or perhaps some of the police officers who responded to the report of a suspect at the theater were not in on the game. In any case chance bought Lee Harvey Oswald forty-eight more hours of life.

We might consider the circumstances under which the police were called to the Texas Theatre. Johnny Brewer, the manager of a shoe store near the theater, testified that he noticed a man standing in the doorway of his store.[61] Brewer said the man attracted his attention because, "He just looked funny to me."[62] After the man left the doorway, Brewer went out onto the sidewalk to look at him, and he testified that he saw the man go into the Texas Theatre without buying a ticket. Brewer called this to the attention of the box-office cashier, who telephoned for the police.[63]

Both the cashier, Mrs. Julia Postal, and the ticket taker, Warren Burroughs, testified that they did not see anyone sneaking into the theater, although they did not challenge Brewer's testimony.[64] Brewer told his story on the CBS tapes,[65] and PSE analysis could not confirm it: there was hard stress throughout most of his statements. Yet Brewer may well have been telling the truth; arranging to have a decoy sneak into the theater without paying seems like an effective means of causing the police to be summoned. The remarkable thing is the number and rank of the law-enforcement officers who responded to the call.

There were, for example, two police captains among the fifteen men who stormed into the Texas Theatre, and one of them was the chief of personnel, Capt. W. R. Westbrook.[66] Westbrook's presence at the theater seems not only incongruous with his normal duties, but also interesting because it was in the company of Captain Westbrook in the personnel office that Sgt. Gerald Hill first heard news of the assassination.[67] Hill and Westbrook then separated, and each followed his own odyssey, both arriving at the Texas Theatre at approximately the same time. Westbrook rode to the scene of the Tippit shooting with William Alexander.*[68] Before arriving at the theater, he stopped to help discover Oswald's jacket beneath a car in a parking lot.[69] Westbrook appears to have taken charge of things in the theater immediately after the arrest.[70] After turning Oswald over to Captain Fritz, the arresting officers, including Paul Bentley and Gerald Hill, met with Captain Westbrook in the personnel office.[71]

But the most interesting member of the small army of lawmen who

*It is not clear from the Warren Commission's testimony whether or not Alexander was present at the arrest in the Texas Theatre. His presence at the scene of the Tippit shooting seems unusual in view of the statement by his superior, Henry Wade: ". . . it has never been my policy to make any investigations out of my office of murders or anything else for that matter. We leave that entirely to the police agency. . . . The only time we investigate is after they are filed on, indicted. . . ." (*Hearings*, Vol. 5, p. 215.)

went to the Texas Theatre was an FBI agent. Gerald Hill mentioned the agent in his testimony before the commission:

> HILL: At about this time Captain Westbrook and a man who was later identified to me as, I believe his name was Barnett, an FBI agent——
> BELIN: Would it be Barrett?
> HILL: Yes.
> BELIN: Do you remember his first name?
> HILL: Bob was identified to me later in the day by Captain Westbrook. Came in from, I presume they came in from the north fire exit, which would have actually been coming in from outside, and came over to us, and Captain Westbrook instructed us to get the man [Oswald] out of there as soon as possible.[72]

By all accounts, the police went to the Texas Theatre to arrest a suspect in the Tippit shooting. Why, little more than an hour after the assassination, was an FBI agent assisting in a local police matter?

Hill testified that Barrett entered the theater with Captain Westbrook after Oswald was subdued, but in his radio interview on November 22, Hill told a completely different story:

> . . . then when we got to the library and found out that was another false alarm, the third call came in that he had been seen entering the Texas Theatre. Bob Barnett from the FBI and I went into the theater and everybody else covered off outside.

Hill's statement on the afternoon of the assassination indicates that Barrett took part in the actual apprehension and arrest of Oswald, but in his testimony to the commission several months later, Barrett's role has been reduced to showing up with Captain Westbrook after the excitement was over. Why did Hill change his story? Perhaps because some people were beginning to wonder why an FBI agent was there at all.

But someone in the Dallas police—apparently Captain Westbrook —wanted to make certain that the FBI's involvement was a matter of record. Gerald Hill told the commission about writing up the arrest report and waiting for it to be typed:

When we got it back ready to sign, Carroll and I were sitting there, and it had Captain Westbrook's name for signature, and added a paragraph about he and the FBI agent being there, and not seeing that it made any difference, I went ahead and signed the report.

Actually, they were there, but I didn't make any corrections.

And as far as the report, didn't allege what they did, but had added a paragraph to our report to include the fact that he was there, and also that the FBI agent was there.

Now as to why this was done, your guess is as good as mine.[73]

But apparently the commission didn't even guess about the matter. The staff never asked Captain Westbrook about it when he testified, and FBI Agent Robert Barrett was never called to testify. Barrett's name is mentioned a few times in the Warren Commission testimony, usually in connection with his role in the Bureau's investigation into the possibility of conspiracy.

In fact, the Warren Commission seems to have lost interest quickly in the subject of Oswald and the FBI. The day after it met to consider the matter, it sent J. Lee Rankin to visit J. Edgar Hoover and ask him about it. Hoover denied the story and stated that the name of every FBI informant was known at FBI headquarters.[74] A few weeks later he said the same thing in an affidavit, and, shortly thereafter, similar affidavits were submitted by ten FBI agents who had some contact with the Oswald case.[75]

Gordon Shanklin, the head of the FBI's Dallas office, signed one of the affidavits. He stated only that he had never made or authorized any payment to Lee Harvey Oswald and that he could find no record of any such payment. He omitted the denial, contained in most of the other ten affidavits from FBI officials, that Oswald had been an FBI informer.[76] Apparently the commission was satisfied with that and did not explore the possibility that Oswald's cooperation had been procured through threats to deport Marina, rather than through payment of money.

The FBI investigated itself and assured the Warren Commission there was no truth to the rumors of an FBI-Oswald link. The commission let it go at that. The FBI turned its attention once again to investigating the assassination. It named Oswald as the killer and found no conspiracy.

If the FBI's investigation was hamstrung by evidence that Oswald was a Bureau informer and indications that some of its own personnel may have been involved in the conspiracy, the Bureau could have become the reluctant accessory to a cover-up. Since the testimony of Marina Oswald, who repeatedly changed her story and contradicted herself, was essential to much of the Warren Commission's case against Lee Harvey Oswald, it is interesting to note that the FBI put considerable pressure on her. Again the lever was the threat of deportation.

> MARINA OSWALD: Sometimes the FBI agents asked me questions that had no bearing or relationship, and if I didn't want to answer they told me that if I wanted to live in this country, I would have to help in this matter, even though they were often irrelevant. That is the FBI . . . I think that the FBI agents knew that I was afraid that after everything that happened I could not remain to live in this country, and they somehow exploited that for their own purposes, in a very polite form, so that you could not say anything after that. They cannot be accused of anything. They approached it in a very clever, contrived way.[77]

Marina's charge is confirmed by Oswald's brother, Robert, who reported the following:

> ROBERT OSWALD: . . . Marina did not want to speak to the FBI at that time. And she was refusing to. And they were insisting, sir. And they implied in so many words, as I sat there—if I might state —with Secret Service Agent Gary Seals of Mobile, Ala.—we were opening the first batch of mail that had come to Marina and Lee's attention, and we were perhaps just four or five feet away from where they were attempting this interview, and it came to my ears that they were implying that if she did not cooperate with the FBI agent there, that this would perhaps—I say, again, I am implying —in so many words, that they would perhaps deport her from the United States and back to Russia.[78]

Marina Oswald has been severely criticized by some skeptics for the way she incriminated her late husband in her testimony before the commission; for example, much of the case that Oswald attempted to kill Gen. Edwin Walker rests on her statements. However, in view of the situation in which she found herself, her actions are understandable. Oswald was beyond help when she gave her testimony, but the very real prospect of deportation still existed. Apart from her presumed preference for living in the United States rather than Russia, there was the probability that the Soviet government would not have offered her a warm welcome if she returned. Oswald had involved the USSR in an extremely delicate and embarrassing situation, and the Kremlin leaders would not be expected to show any gratitude towards his widow.

In an interview published in March 1974, Marina expressed her fears about returning to the Soviet Union when she was asked if she would ever return there: "Oh, no, they might put me in jail or something. Once you have a taste of freedom you aren't willing to risk it. I never even think about going back."[79]

But considering this, it seems remarkable that she hasn't taken the simplest and easiest step to insure that she will never have to go back: after twelve years in the United States, Marina Oswald still has not become a citizen. Her reason? "I haven't had time to memorize all those questions about the Constitution."[80]

If Marina Oswald ever becomes an American citizen she will be beyond the threat of government intimidation. And that may be precisely the reason why she cannot. Efforts in Congress to pass legislation that would reopen the case of President Kennedy's assassination have met with failure, but a simple avenue lies open to our lawmakers that could bring at least some of the facts to light: Congress could pass a special bill conferring United States citizenship on Marina Oswald. That one small seed might yield an abundant harvest of truth.

One question remains: if Oswald was an FBI informer lured into a frame-up by the agents controlling him, why didn't he say something during those twelve hours of interrogation at Dallas police headquarters? The answer to this puzzle may also solve another mystery: even though Oswald was innocent, why did he show almost no stress when he uttered the words, "No, I didn't shoot anybody, no sir"? Oswald didn't know what was happening, but, whatever it was, he was certain his FBI contact would get him out of it.

Was the New Orleans arrest in August a dry run to see if Oswald could be relied on to keep his mouth shut in that situation? If it was, his discretion may have been his own death warrant.

I really don't know what this situation is about. Nobody has told me anything, except that I'm accused of murdering a policeman. I know nothing more than that. I do request someone to come forward to give me legal assistance.

Someone.

13 THE CREDIBILITY GAP

> If we owe regard to the memory of the dead, there is yet more respect to be paid to knowledge, to virtue and to truth.
>
> —Samuel Johnson: *The Rambler, No.* 60

Was Jack the Ripper a member of the royal family? What is the secret of the Great Pyramid? Is this a photo of the Loch Ness monster? Who killed JFK?

The murders in Dallas have been relegated to the funny papers of history. They share the pages of national tabloids with unidentified flying objects and the abominable snowman. The doubts and questions that persist have been recycled into a second-hand sensationalism to divert and titillate the curious. Truth is buried even deeper by an avalanche of yellow newsprint. Seen so often in the company of hoaxes and crackpot fantasies, the charge that President Kennedy was killed by a conspiracy takes on a tinny, carnival sound. The issues dim and a weary public sighs: Well, perhaps the Warren Commission was right, after all.

In more respected media, the official account of the assassination has been granted implicit acceptance—Oswald is no longer "the *alleged* assassin"—and some writers have offered a curious kind of analysis, the psychosociological evasion. This argument begins with the implicit assumption that, since the government neither makes mistakes nor tells lies, the Warren Report must be true. Given that, the apologist asks why so many of us continue to doubt, then he puts us on his unlicensed couch to probe for the roots of our irrational skepticism.

One of the most egregious examples of this pseudopsychological twaddle was published on the opinion-editorial page of *The New York Times* on the tenth anniversary of the assassination. The writer began

by describing the Warren Report as "the most completely docu-
mented story of a crime ever put together."* She noted that it "has
been challenged, but its mountain of positive evidence has yet to be
refuted." She observed that there had been "a host of outlandish
conspiracy theories" and that "many rational people continue not
only to believe but passionately to defend them." Why, she asked,
and then proceeded to tell us: "The answer of course is in the
emotions, in the deeper, the still unsettled feelings most Americans
have about that traumatic event in Dallas."

In psychological terms, she explained, the whole thing was related
to parricide, the murder of the father by the son. There followed a
short disquisition on Freudian psychology and the Oedipus complex
as background; then she stated:

> The assassination of President Kennedy was a parricide, an
> enactment in the political arena of the ancient drama. Oswald, it
> is true, lacked a father. His mother was father and mother both.
> Yet in spite of the incompleteness of the family circle, Oswald had
> the Oedipal emotions. Like most people, and all neurotics, he
> failed to resolve them. But, unlike most, he chose to enact the
> unresolved part of the drama—violently. Feelings that were origi-
> nally confined within his family were displaced outward into poli-
> tics, against the father of the country. To Oswald, and to the rest
> of us, the emotional significance of the deed was that of parricide.
>
> Twisted though they were, the feelings that were in Oswald are
> in us all. Because he is so relentlessly visible, the President is alive
> in our emotions. He awakens the keenest memories and feelings.
> President Kennedy's attractiveness, his charm spread over us like
> a mantle, made the feelings he evoked more poignant still. We
> hold onto conspiracy theories because they are a defense, a screen,
> a barrier, against having to accept those feelings in ourselves.*

Arguments of this type will inevitably achieve a certain degree of
acceptance; problems of ballistics, forensic medicine, and conflicting
testimony can be tiresome and difficult to follow, but the glib plati-

*Priscilla McMillan, "That Time We Huddled Together in Disbelief,"
New York Times, November 22, 1973, p. 39.

tudes of paperback psychology demand little intellectual effort. Don't
let those nagging doubts bother you, they're all in your mind.

If there is any element of truth in the psychosociological evasion,
it is that in the minds of many Americans, not only the president,
but the whole federal establishment is a kind of father-king-god that
does no wrong and makes no errors. Every moviegoer and television
viewer knows that the FBI is staffed by infallible and benevolent
Eagle Scouts. These are the same sleuths who solved the mystery of
Dallas for us. The Warren Report is U.S. Government Inspected
Grade A Truth.

But in the spring and summer of 1973, many who thought this way
were rudely summoned back from fantasyland by the unfolding story
of Watergate. The FBI investigation into the circumstances surrounding the burglary was repeatedly touted as the most exhaustive
probe since the investigation of President Kennedy's assassination.
The official truth promulgated by the Justice Department was that
the Watergate burglary was the unauthorized act of a handful of
misguided zealots, a "seven lone nuts" theory. But then one of the
zealots decided to talk, and eventually the world was given an unhur-
ried view of the crawling colony that lives beneath the rocklike edifice
of the federal government.

One of the staunchest defenders of the Warren Report was CBS
newsman Dan Rather. Rather was in Dallas when Kennedy was
killed, and he followed the Warren Commission's investigation
closely. It was Rather who conducted CBS News's independent
investigation which resulted in the documentary that is frequently
mentioned in this book. Rather is unique: unlike most proponents of
the Warren Report, he has studied the evidence; and unlike most
who have studied the evidence, he accepts the Report.

But in the wake of the Watergate revelations in August 1973,
Rather expressed some doubts. In a CBS News "First Line Report,"
he asked whether Lee Harvey Oswald ever knew or had contact with
E. Howard Hunt or Gordon Liddy "or any of the others in that
mysterious and dangerous crew convicted in the Watergate crime.
. . ." Rather said that he was moved to raise the question by the
Cuban connections of Hunt and Liddy, and he recalled Oswald's
association with both pro- and anti-Castro Cubans. Rather's interest

may also have been aroused by reports circulating among the Washington press corps that E. Howard Hunt had been in Mexico City at the time of Oswald's alleged visit there in September 1963.

While there are some tenuous links between Watergate and Dallas, a firm connection remains to be established. Yet the Watergate revelations demonstrate many home truths that serve to put the Warren Commission's investigation into perspective. We learned, for example, that L. Patrick Gray, the acting director of the FBI, on the instructions of two presidential advisers, burned politically explosive files in his fireplace, files that were evidence in the FBI's Watergate investigation. We learned that Assistant Attorney-General Henry Peterson, who was in charge of the Watergate investigation for the Justice Department, kept the White House fully informed on his progress. We learned that E. Howard Hunt, after he was arrested, successfully blackmailed the president of the United States to obtain funds for his legal defense and nearly succeeded in extorting a promise of executive clemency. These were some of the facts that were not turned up in the FBI's "most exhaustive investigation since the JFK assassination."

We have seen that blackmail is a frequently used instrument of persuasion in Washington. We know now, for example, that the late J. Edgar Hoover used derogatory information uncovered by the FBI against those who opposed him and to further the political aims of those who supported the Bureau. Is it incredible, then, to think that blackmail may have been turned against the FBI to hamstring its investigation in Dallas? Or that the Bureau, in turn, threatened Marina Oswald with deportation to Russia unless her testimony supported the official assassination story?

There is little evidence to connect E. Howard Hunt to the assassination, but the fact that a man capable of acting out his own bizarre fantasies once worked for the Central Intelligence Agency is disquieting. Even more troubling is the knowledge that G. Gordon Liddy was an FBI agent. While neither man is typical of those organizations, the two demonstrate that we should use the word "impossible" sparingly.

Watergate was a massive conspiracy that permeated the White House, the Justice Department, the FBI, and the Committee to

Reelect the President. Yet, despite the sheer numbers of people involved, it eluded the official investigation. The truth emerged only after one of the conspirators decided to talk.

How big was the Dallas conspiracy? It was certainly much smaller. Our political tradition requires frequent personal contact between national leaders and the public, so killing the president of the United States is not especially difficult; the hard part is getting away with it. And yet even this can be done with relatively few people.

The key to getting away with murder—especially a famous murder —is the availability of a convenient scapegoat. The enormous pressures felt by law-enforcement officials in the wake of a celebrated crime are immediately relieved by the announcement, "The police have arrested a suspect." There is a brief glimpse of the wretch on television as he is hustled into the police station, and we know that he is the one. An unsolved murder is a frightening thing, particularly when the victim is the president of the United States, but we regain our peace of mind when the killer is in custody. We need to believe that the person in handcuffs is the murderer.

The frame-up formula is much simpler than might be imagined. First, select a close-knit community such as Dallas where a clear distinction exists between the local citizens and "outsiders." Next, select a scapegoat who can find little or no sympathy in that community or anywhere else in the country: a self-avowed Marxist who once renounced his citizenship and defected to the Soviet Union will do very nicely. Then recruit some police, not the entire department, just a few key officers who are in a position to fabricate a chain of evidence linking the scapegoat to the crime, officers in the crime scene search unit, the crime lab, and perhaps a polygraph examiner to confirm the truthfulness of witnesses against the fall guy and impugn the word of those who might exonerate him. And finally, because the fabricated case will not withstand the adversary proceedings of a murder trial, kill the scapegoat. It could be done as simply as that.

The assassination of President Kennedy must have involved two interlocking conspiracies. The first would have been very small, consisting only of the gunmen and those individuals who hired and paid them. The second would have been somewhat larger, involving all those who took part in the framing of Lee Harvey Oswald. Undoubtedly, the second conspiracy grew to include more people after the shots were fired in Dealey Plaza, people who would not have agreed to the murder of a president, but who would risk neither their own position nor safety by defending a Communist. Kennedy was not a popular president in Dallas, and, in any case, there was nothing anyone could do to bring him back. Lee Harvey Oswald was a man who had turned on his country, renounced his citizenship, and gone to live in Russia. Then he turned on Russia, came back to America, and espoused the cause of Fidel Castro. Certainly, in the view of many, Oswald was already guilty of crimes far worse than the one of which he stood accused. And after the shot fired in the basement of the Dallas City Hall, Oswald's guilt became a theoretical matter. Would any Dallas policeman then accuse his fellow officers of murder and come to the defense of a dead Communist?

The inevitable federal investigation into the assassination would have posed a threat, but not one that couldn't be countered. The federal authorities were caught off balance by the assassination and placed on the defensive. The Secret Service had failed to protect the president; if the assassination were the work of a conspiracy, then the FBI had also failed in its duty and let the plot go undetected. It was in the Bureau's interest to support the belief that the crime was the work of one twisted man with a gun.

But failure to penetrate the conspiracy was not the worst charge that the FBI might have had to bear if it pursued the unanswered questions of Dallas too ardently. There was the evidence that the accused assassin had been paid by the FBI, and, infinitely more damaging, there was the possibility that the conspiracy included one or more FBI agents. If the Bureau's investigation ever got near the truth, it must have been during those first few weeks after the assassination. And it was precisely then that a corner of the cloak was lifted by the Dallas authorities to reveal fragments of evidence linking Oswald to the Bureau. These were "plausibly deniable," but if the men in Washington had proved intractable, a much more persuasive case might have been revealed to demonstrate that Oswald was a Bureau informer.

With the FBI in check, the Warren Commission would have been neutralized. The commission could not recruit and establish its own investigative agency to probe the assassination; it had to rely on existing investigative organizations, mainly the FBI. If Chief Justice Warren or the other commissioners had been dissatisfied with the job done by the FBI, there was, in the last analysis, nothing to be done about it. They were placed in such a position that in the interest of national stability, they would have to go along with the case that was thrust upon them by the Dallas police and the FBI. Like so many others in Dallas and Washington, they found that "going along" was the lesser of two evils.

This is, admittedly, a theory, a reconstruction of events to explain available evidence. That evidence includes the PSE analysis of the recorded testimony of more than forty persons having direct knowledge of the assassination, eyewitnesses to both the Kennedy and Tippit shootings, Dallas police officers, medical and ballistics experts, two members of the Warren Commission staff, one commissioner, Chief Justice Warren, and Lee Harvey Oswald. In any one case, perhaps in several cases, the instrument may have erroneously indicated deception. But in other instances, I was able to establish positively through parallel means that what the individual said was not true. And in the case of Lee Harvey Oswald's denial of guilt, there seems little room to doubt that he was telling the truth. The full mosaic of PSE results and other evidence reveals a clear, unshadowed picture of events, and that is the one I have presented here. President Kennedy was killed by a conspiracy. Lee Harvey Oswald was innocent. The conspirators included policemen, and, perhaps, federal agents.

Inevitably, those who delight in specious leaps from the specific to the general will interpret this as an indictment of right-wing politics, policemen, the FBI, the city of Dallas, the state of Texas, and, perhaps, the South. That is not my intention.

Some of the famous murders of our time have been done by doctors, yet we do not hold the medical profession to blame for their crimes; the fact that some lawmen break the law proves only that they too are recruited from among the human race. To say that the assassination was motivated by right-wing politics is not to condemn political conservatism; every day people murder for love or money, but we do not view their sins as arguments for poverty or chastity.

Ideology is an abstraction, and Texas is a state of mind. The murders of November 1963 were done by individuals.

If John Kennedy had lived to serve out his presidency, would the nation have suffered the same sorrows it has known during the eleven years since his death? There seems to be no answer to that question. But the events in Dallas caused a special kind of sickness in our land: the covering up of the assassination brought the big lie to America. The Warren Report was not the first instance in which the United States government lied to the American people, but it was the first case of massive public lying in our times, and it marks the point at which we stopped believing what we were told. The credibility gap has become an American idiom.

Bad times have come to our country, and one is moved to look backward and ask where we went wrong. There can be no single answer to that question: there are too many different currents in the flow of human history. But the assassination of President Kennedy marks the point at which we took leave of the truth. Unless we find and fix this thing, we will never put ourselves right. We must reopen the case.

During the ten years since they dissolved the Warren Commission, most of its members, like the crime they probed, have faded into history. The chairman and three of the members are now dead; two others have retired from public life. The seventh member has become president of the United States. He alone can rescue our history for us.

When Gerald Ford took his presidential oath on August 9, 1974, he told us why this must be done. "Truth," said President Ford, "is the glue that holds government together. . . ."

THE KUBIS STUDY:
DOES THE PSE WORK?

On February 13, 1974, the *Washington Post* carried a story head-lined "Army Criticizes Voice Analyzers As Lie Detectors," reporting that "the Army Land Warfare Laboratory has flunked a new lie-detecting device that is supposed to measure tiny, giveaway modula-tions in the human voice when a lie is told." The story went on to say that an army study of the PSE had been released by Republican Congressman Harold V. Froehlich of Wisconsin. The study, said the *Post,* revealed that the PSE was clearly inferior to the polygraph and virtually worthless as a lie-detection instrument. A similar story was carried by the Scripps-Howard News Service and published in news-papers across the country. The item was picked up by several syn-dicated columnists and, within a day or so, thousands of people had read that the new voice lie detector they'd been hearing about didn't work.

The army study bore the name of one of the most respected polygraph researchers in the country, Dr. Joseph Kubis of Fordham University. In a field almost completely dominated by practical, down-to-earth law-enforcement officers, Kubis is one of the few aca-demic investigators who have worked to bring a measure of scientific respectability to the polygraph. It would be hard to name an individ-ual who would appear more qualified to test a new lie-detection instrument. His signature on the army study made it an especially damning judgment of the PSE.

The Kubis study was a victory for the American Polygraph Association in its ongoing war against the psychological stress evaluator, and the polygraph purists lost no time in publicizing the report. The APA's journal, *Polygraph*, reprinted the lengthy document in its entirety, devoting almost half of its March 1974 issue to it. The lie-detector traditionalists were delighted to have finally a scientific endorsement of their charge that the new voice instrument won't work.

As might be expected, the creators of the PSE did not suffer all this silently. Col. Allen Bell, Jr. told the *Washington Post* that he was challenging Dr. Kubis to a "one-on-one showdown, with the polygraph versus the PSE." Bell had offered the same challenge to the orthodox several times before, never finding any takers. Kubis was no exception.

Bell and his associates distributed a seven-page press release presenting a detailed attack on the accuracy and methodology of the Kubis study, but the rebuttal was more complex and less newsworthy than Congressman Froehlich's announcement and was never carried in any news medium. The Dektor staff worked up a more extensive rebuttal of the Kubis study and submitted it, together with six separate studies that found the PSE an effective instrument for lie detection and behavioral research, to a congressional committee investigating the use of lie detectors in the federal government.*

The Dektor rebuttal focused on the design of Kubis's experiments, which involved using college students in extremely artificial "simulated crimes." Dektor pointed out that Kubis not only obtained poor results with the PSE, but also did badly with the polygraph. The PSE inventors questioned the relevance of Kubis's experiments to real lie-detection situations.

Actually, Dr. Kubis claimed only to have shown that voice lie-detection instruments "may [not] be accepted as valid 'lie detectors' within the constraints of an experimental paradigm." Or, in other words, the PSE won't work in the lab. When I spoke to Dr. Kubis,

---

Use of Lie Detectors by The Federal Government: An Informational Report Prepared For The Foreign Operations and Government Subcommittee of the Committee on Government Operations, the Congress of the United States (Springfield, Va.: DEKTOR Counterintelligence and Security, Inc., 1974).

I asked him if he felt his study also proved that the PSE won't work in actual criminal investigations. He replied that he did not believe he had proved this, but "it raises the question of checking it out in such situations."

But the PSE *has* been tested in such situations in studies conducted at the University of Utah, by police departments, and by other users of the instrument. And it has also been found to work in low-stress laboratory situations in a study carried out at Washington and Lee University in Virginia.* I was surprised by Dr. Kubis's poor PSE results, so I looked into the circumstances of the Kubis study.

The first thing I discovered was that Kubis didn't really perform the study himself. It was carried out by a younger assistant, Dr. William J. Krossner.

"Dr. Kubis is a very busy person," Krossner told me. "He runs about a quarter of a million dollars in grants at any one time, and he's doing a lot for NASA in Houston, so I was the chief polygraph examiner and really ran the project."

Did Krossner also run the PSE in the Kubis study? Not exactly, that was farmed out elsewhere. In fact, neither Dr. Kubis nor his assistant ever actually operated a PSE during their study at Fordham. They tape recorded polygraph examinations, then shipped the tapes elsewhere for PSE processing. The Kubis study of the PSE was done by mail!

But even more startling was the identity of the PSE examiner who actually ran the Kubis tapes: Dr. Gordon Barland of the University of Utah, the same Dr. Barland who had tested the PSE with criminal suspects and found it effective and the same man who had reviewed my PSE analysis of the Oswald tapes. I called Barland and asked him if he had suddenly changed his mind about the PSE.

"Not at all," Barland replied. "In fact, I've been getting even better PSE results recently. There's no question about it, the PSE is an effective lie-detection device."

What about the Kubis study?

"Dr. Kubis is a very good scientist," Barland answered. "He's a pioneer in lie detection, and he's done a number of very reputable

---

*James W. Worth and Bernard J. Lewis, *An Early Validation Study with the Psychological Stress Evaluator* (unpublished).

studies. But he's not an electrical engineer, and the recordings that were made under his supervision by various people involved in the study were of very poor quality."

Barland said that the Kubis tapes were made at a low recording level, with the microphone placed too far from the subject. He had to send some of the tapes back to Kubis, and even the ones he kept were of marginal quality and not really suited for PSE processing.

From his own experiments with both "simulated lies" and actual criminal investigations, Barland felt that much better results are obtained with the PSE in high-stress situations than in low-stress experiments. But, he added, Dr. Kubis should have gotten better results than he did. "I think," said Barland, "that if we had better quality recordings, there would have been no problem at all."

Later I called Dr. Kubis and asked him to comment on Dr. Barland's remarks. "Well, the instructions were to return the tapes that he couldn't work with," he said. "The instructions were very clear on that."

Perhaps they were, but that is not the point. Dr. Kubis delegated his study of the PSE to an assistant. Neither Kubis nor his assistant troubled to learn how to operate the PSE, so they subcontracted the actual PSE work to someone several thousand miles away. The tapes they made were defective, as was the communication between the experimenters. The Kubis study was invalid. *That* is the point.

The United States Army does not endorse the Kubis study. In fact, the army resisted Congressman Froehlich's efforts to have the "For Official Use Only" designation removed from the document. When, after four months, it finally agreed to release the study, the army's Investigations and Legislative Division wrote to Froehlich:

> As noted previously in our letter of 26 October 1973 forwarding copies of the report to you, the Army is not in a position to either validate or refute the evaluations or conclusions reached by the report's author, and thus release of the report does not indicate Army acceptance or endorsement of the findings and conclusions of the study.

I tried to reach Congressman Froehlich and ask for his comments on all of the above points, but I was unable to do so. Even after several conversations with his administrative aide, I was unable to find out what the congressman really had in mind when he unloaded the Kubis study on the public. The aide said that while he had not specifically discussed these issues with the congressman, he doubted that Froehlich would support legislation limiting the use of lie detectors for personnel screening or prohibiting the clandestine recording of conversations. Froehlich doesn't seem to be an ardent civil libertarian, so there must be some other motive for his action.

In distributing his press release regarding the PSE, Congressman Froehlich inadvertently misled a great many people. However, his record for this sort of thing was established a few months earlier and, fortunately, still stands. In mid-December 1973, Froehlich told the press, "The United States may face a serious shortage of toilet tissue within a few months."

Froehlich's statement should go down in history as the fastest self-fulfilling prophecy on record. It was repeated by a comedian on network television that night, and the next morning panicky shoppers began pushing shopping carts full of toilet tissue to supermarket checkout counters. Within a week the last roll had disappeared from the shelves. It took the paper manufacturers the best part of a month to catch up. In the meantime, Congressman Froehlich turned his attention to the psychological stress evaluator.

NOTES

Chapter 1   On Doubting the Report

1. Sten Forshufvud, Hamilton Smith, and Anders Wassen, "Arsenic Content of Napoleon I's Hair Probably Taken Immediately after His Death," *Nature*, October 14, 1961, pp. 103–105; *Scientific American*, August 1962, pp. 56–58; Sten Forshufvud, *Who Killed Napoleon?* (London: Hutchinson and Co., 1962).
2. Richard Warren Lewis and Lawrence Schiller, *The Scavengers and Critics of the Warren Report* (New York: Dell Publishing Co., 1967).
3. *New York Times*, January 12, 1967, p. 23; March 7, 1967, p. 21; May 30, 1967, p. 19.
4. *Book Week*, July 24, 1966, p. 1; *New York Times*, November 23, 1966, p. 1.
5. William F. Buckley, Jr., syndicated column, September 9, 1966.
6. *New York Times*, February 14, 1967, p. 24.
7. *Ibid.*, November 23, 1966, p. 1.
8. *Ibid.*, February 21, 1967, p. 20
9. *San Francisco Chronicle*, September 17, 1970, p. 12.
10. *New York Times*, November 28, 1966, p. 29; and December 20, 1966, p. 36.
11. *Ibid.*, April 13, 1967, p. 18.
12. *Ibid.*, October 20, 1967, p. 14.
13. *Ibid.*, January 4, 1965, p. 30.
14. *Ibid.*, March 17, 1967, p. 13.
15. *Los Angeles Times*, October 30, 1966.
16. *New York Times*, March 9, 1967, p. 25
17. *Life*, November 25, 1966, pp. 38–53; *The Saturday Evening Post*, December 2, 1967, p. 88.
18. *New York Times*, September 25, 1966, section 4, p. 10.
19. Dan Rather, "Rethinking the Unthinkable," *CBS News First Line Report*, August 10, 1973.
20. *Washington Evening Star*, November 6, 1969, p. A–2
21. Jesse Curry, *JFK Assassination File* (Dallas, Tex.: American Poster and Printing Co., 1969), p. 61.
22. *Ibid.*, p. 62.
23. *Ibid.*, p. 86.
24. Interview with Jesse Curry in Dallas, Texas, May 16, 1973.
25. *Los Angeles Examiner*, January 20, 1970, p. A–16.
26. *Los Angeles Times*, November 22, 1966.
27. *Washington Post*, April 28, 1970, p. A–1.
28. *Ibid.*
29. Leo Janos, "The Last Days of the President: LBJ in Retirement," *Atlantic Monthly*, July 1973, p. 39.
30. *Report of the President's Commission on the Assassination of President John F. Kennedy* (Washington, D.C.: U.S. Government Printing Office, 1964) (hereafter, *Report*), p. 471.

Chapter 2 Problems with the Report

1. Carl Sandburg, *Abraham Lincoln: The Prairie Years and The War Years*, one volume ed. (New York: Harcourt Brace Jovanovich, Inc., 1954), pp. 203–207.
2. *Report*, pp. 280–283.
3. *Ibid.*, p. 283.
4. *Hearings Before the President's Commission on the Assassination of President Kennedy*, Vol. 5 (Washington, D.C.: U.S. Government Printing Office, 1964) (hereafter *Hearings*) pp. 591–592.
5. *Ibid.*, Vol. 9, p. 179.
6. *Report*, p. 504.
7. *Ibid.*, p. 781.
8. *Ibid.*, p. 804.
9. *New York Times*, November 25, 1964, p. 36.
10. *The Witnesses: Selected and Edited from The Warren Commission's Hearings by The New York Times* (New York: McGraw-Hill, 1964).
11. Sylvia Meagher, *Subject Index to the Warren Report and Hearings and Exhibits* (New York: Scarecrow Press, 1966).
12. Sylvia Meagher, *Accessories After the Fact* (Indianapolis, Ind.: Bobbs-Merrill Company, Inc., 1967).
13. *Ibid.*, p. xxvii.
14. *Ibid.*, p. xxviii.
15. *Ibid.*, pp. 263–264.
16. *Hearings*, Vol. 14, p. 629.
17. *Ibid.*, pp. 640–655.
18. *Ibid.*, p. 631.
19. *Ibid.*, p. 637.
20. *Ibid.*, Vol. 4, pp. 150–202; Vol. 12, pp. 25–42; Vol. 15, pp. 124–133.
21. *New York Times*, October 18, 1964, section 7, p. 8.
22. *Ibid.*, February 18, 1968, section 8, p. 18.
23. *Report*, p. 79.
24. Reported by Tom Webb of WBAP-TV, Fort Worth, Texas; *News Coverage of the Assassination of President*

Kennedy, MR 74–52:1 (tape); The John F. Kennedy Library, Waltham, Massachusetts.
25. *Hearings*, Vol. 7, p. 108.
26. *Ibid.*, Vol. 24, p. 831.
27. *Ibid.*, p. 228.
28. *Ibid.*, Vol. 19, p. 508.
29. *Ibid.*, Vol. 3, p. 295.
30. *Report*, p. 81.
31. Meagher, *Accessories After the Fact*, pp. 99–100.
32. *Hearings*, Vol. 7, p. 108.
33. *Ibid.*, Vol. 1, p. 119.
34. *Report*, pp. 119–121.
35. *Ibid.*, p. 123.
36. *Ibid.*
37. *Ibid.*, p. 124.
38. *Ibid.*, p. 127.
39. *Hearings*, Vol. 4, p. 289.
40. *Report*, p. 181.
41. Meagher, *Accessories After the Fact*, p. 208.
42. *Ibid.*, pp. 207–208
43. Richard E. Sprague, "The Framing of Lee Harvey Oswald," *Computers and Automation*, October 1973, p. 24. Sprague makes extensive reference to the privately published work of Fred Newcomb of Sherman Oaks, California.
44. *Hearings*, Vol. 4, pp. 288–289.
45. *Report*, pp. 569–571.
46. Meagher, *Accessories After the Fact*, pp. 49–54, 104–105, 111–133, 193–199.
47. *Hearings*, Vol. 6, pp. 129–130.
48. *Report*, p. 79.
49. *Ibid.*, p. 85.
50. Josiah Thompson, *Six Seconds in Dallas* (New York: Bernard Geis, 1967), pp. 1–12.
51. *Report*, pp. 97–98.
52. *Ibid.*, pp. 98–105.
53. *Ibid.*, p. 97.
54. *Ibid.*, p. 106.
55. *Ibid.*, p. 112.
56. CBS News, "November 22 and The

Warren Report," broadcast over the CBS television network, September 27, 1964.

57. *Hearings*, Vol. 4, pp. 114, 128.

58. *Life*, November 25, 1966, p. 48.

59. *Report*, pp. 111–117.

60. *Ibid.*, pp. 81, 95.

61. *Ibid.*, pp. 583–584.

62. Melvin A. Eisenberg, Memorandum for the Files (April 22, 1964), Subject: *Conference on April 21, 1964, to determine which frames of the Zapruder movies show the impact of the first and second bullets;* File: MPI, The National Archives, Washington, D.C., p. 2; *Hearings*, Vol. 2, pp. 374–376, 382.

63. *Ibid.*, Vol. 4, pp. 109, 113–114, 121, 127.

64. *Report*, p. 543.

65. *Ibid.*, p. 107.

66. *Ibid.*, p. 19.

67. *Ibid.*, pp. 116–117.

68. Meagher, *Accessories After the Fact*, pp. 5–8.

69. *Hearings*, Vol. 4, p. 29.

70. *Ibid.*, Vol. 3, p. 447.

71. *Ibid.*, pp. 450–451.

72. *Ibid.*, Vol. 11, p. 233.

73. *Ibid.*, Vol. 3, pp. 443–444.

74. *Ibid.*, pp. 446–447.

75. *Ibid.*, Vol. 26, p. 455.

76. *Ibid.*, Vol. 24, p. 2.

77. *Ibid.*, Vol. 26, p. 62.

78. *Report*, pp. 193–194.

79. *Ibid.*, p. 194.

80. *Ibid.*, p. 195.

81. Richard E. Sprague, "The Assassination of President John F. Kennedy: The Application of Computers to the Photographic Evidence," *Computers and Automation*, May 1970, pp. 29–60.

82. *Report*, p. 322.

83. *Ibid.*, pp. 183–187.

84. *Ibid.*, p. 562.

85. Cyril H. Wecht and Robert Smith, "The Medical Evidence in the Assassination of President John F. Kennedy," *The Forensic Science Gazette* Vol. 4, no. 4, p. 19 (September 1973).

86. *Hearings*, Vol. 2, p. 348.

87. *Ibid.*,

88. *Ibid.*, Vol. 2, p. 377.

89. *Ibid.*, p. 378.

90. *Report*, p. 543.

91. *Hearings*, Vol. 2, p. 373.

92. *Commission Document No. 7*, The National Archives, Washington, D.C.

93. *Hearings*, Vol. 2, pp. 361–362.

94. Wecht and Smith, "Medical Evidence in the Assassination," p. 14.

95. Cyril H. Wecht, "A Critique of President Kennedy's Autopsy," Appendix D in Thompson, *Six Seconds in Dallas*, p. 278.

Chapter 3   The Technology of Truth

1. J. Kirk Barefoot, ed., *The Polygraph Technique* (American Polygraph Association, 1972), p. 17.

2. Clarence H. A. Romig, "State Legislation Concerning the Polygraph in June 1973," *Journal of the American Polygraph Association*, June 1973, p. 85.

3. Fred E. Inbau and John E. Reid, *Criminal Interrogation and Confessions* (Baltimore, Md.: Williams and Wilkins, 1967), p. 107.

4. *Frye* v. *United States*, 293 F. 1014 (D.D.C. 1923).

5. Barefoot, *The Polygraph Technique*, p 46.

6. *Washington Post*, November 16, 1972, p. C–1.

7. *United States* v. *Ridling*, 350 F. Supp. 90 (S.D.Mich., 1972). The reference was to Rule 702, Proposed Rules of Evidence for U.S. District Courts.

8. Fred E. Inbau and John E. Reid, *Truth and Deception: The Polygraph ("Lie Detector") Technique* (Baltimore, Md. Williams and Wilkens, 1966) pp. 1–3.

9. *Ibid.*, pp. 3–5, 8–9; Burke M. Smith,

"The Polygraph," *Scientific American* January 1967, pp. 25–31. Smith's article, apart from containing some excellent diagrams and other material showing the electromechanical apparatus used in the polygraph, is also a very balanced and objective discussion of the scientific and ethical questions relating to the use of the instrument in lie detection.

10. Barefoot, *The Polygraph Technique*, pp. 18–19; Inbau and Reid, *Truth and Deception*, pp. 5–6.

11. Barefoot, *The Polygraph Technique*, pp. 21–22.

12. Inbau and Reid, *Truth and Deception*, p. 36.

13. *Ibid.*, pp. 32, 107.

14. *Ibid.*, p. 37.

15. Barefoot, *The Polygraph Technique*, p. 11.

16. *Ibid.* p. 12.

17. Inbau and Reid, *Truth and Deception*, p. 50.

18. *Ibid.*, p. 27.

19. Gordon H. Barland and David C. Raskin, "An Experimental Study of Field Techniques in 'Lie Detection,'" *Journal of the American Polygraph Association*, March 1972, pp. 22–26.

20. Milton A. Berman, "Drugs, Drug Abuse and the Polygraph," *American Polygraph Association Newsletter*, January–February 1971, p. 14; Miltor A. Berman, "Drugs Versus the Polygraph," *The Journal of Polygraph Studies* (published by the National Training Center of Lie Detection, New York New York) January–February 1967.

21. First noted in J.A. Larson, "The Cardio-pneumo-psychogram and Its Use in the Study of Emotions with Practical Applications," *Journal of Experimental Psychology* 5(1922): 323–328.

22. Inbau and Reid, *Truth and Deception*, p. 177.

23. *Ibid.*

24. *Ibid.*, p. 82

25. Irving told this anecdote so convincingly that on March 19, 1972, after the writer had admitted the hoax, "Sixty Minutes" rebroadcast this portion of the Wallace-Irving interview.

26. Clifford Irving, *What Really Happened* (New York: Grove Press, Inc., 1972) p. 284.

27. *Ibid.*, p. 287.

28. *Ibid.*, pp. 289–290.

29. *Ibid.*, p. 290.

30. *Time*, January 24, 1972, p. 13.

Chapter 4   The Psychological Stress Evaluator

1. Interview with Donald McIntosh in Baltimore, Maryland, October 3, 1973.

2. *Psychological Stress Evaluator PSE–1*, a technical brochure published by Dektor Counterintelligence and Security, Inc., Springfield, Virginia.

3. *Ibid.*

4. Michael P. Kradz, *The Psychological Stress Evaluator: A Study*, Howard County Police Department, Ellicott City, Maryland, 1972 (available from Dektor Counterintelligence and Security, Inc., Springfield, Virginia).

5 *Baltimore News American*, Howard County Edition, June 6, 1972.

6. The cases were Jerome Goodman, Circuit Court of Howard County, Ellicott City, Maryland, October 28, 1971; Dolores King, District Court, 10th District, Ellicott City, Maryland, April 9, 1972; Dolores Jackson, District Court, 10th District, Ellicott City, Maryland, May 30, 1972.

7. Olof Lippold, "Physiological Tremor," *Scientific American*, March 1971, p. 65.

8. The physiological basis of the PSE is discussed in greater detail by Gion B. Green in "Truth Verification,"

Security World, October 1973, pp. 38–40.

9. "APA Position on Dektor PSE–1," American Polygraph Association, August 1973.

10. *Ibid.*

11. *Ibid.*

12. "The American Polygraph Association Ethics—Principles and Practice," *APA Newsletter,* May–June 1968, p. 9.

13. "APA Position on Dektor PSE–1."

14. Gordon H. Barland, "Use of Voice Changes in the Detection of Deception," a paper presented at the 86th meeting of the Acoustical Society of America, Los Angeles, California, October 31, 1973.

15. The Bastrop, Louisiana, Police Department; the Camden County, New Jersey, Prosecutor's Office; the Cherry Hill, New Jersey, Police Department; the Clifton Heights, Pennsylvania, Police Department; the Contra Costa County, California, Sheriff's Department; the Florida Department of Public Safety; the East Whitland, Pennsylvania, Police Department; the Endicott, New York, Police Department; the Iberville Parish Sheriff's De-

partment, Palaquemine, Louisiana; the Jefferson Parish Sheriff's Department, Gretna, Louisiana; the Lenoir, North Carolina, Police Department; the Morehouse Parish Sheriff's Department, Bastrop, Louisiana; the Ocean City, Maryland, Police Department; the Ouchita Parish Sheriff's Department, Monroe, Louisiana; the Polk County, Florida, Sheriff's Department; the St. Petersburg, Florida, Police Department; the Stockton, California, Police Department; the Tangiapahoa Parish Sheriff's Department, Amite, Louisiana; and the Vienna, Virginia, Police Department. Larger law-enforcement agencies are also using the PSE but have kept that fact secret for political and tactical reasons.

16. *Burlington Free Press,* Burlington, Vermont, May 29, 1973, p. 21.

17. *Ibid.*

18. Dr. Paul R. Haskins, chief, Alcohol and Drug Rehabilitation Unit, Veteran's Hospital, Danville, Illinois.

19. Thomas E. Reeves, registered psychologist, director, Vermillion County Mental Health Center, Danville, Illinois.

Chapter 5 Tapes from the Archives

1. Interview with Jesse Curry in Dallas, Texas, May 16, 1973.

2. *Report,* p. 199.

3. CBS News, "November 22 and The Warren Report," broadcast over the CBS television network on September 27, 1964.

4. *Report,* p. 145

5. *Ibid.,* p. 146.

6. Curry, *JFK Assassination File,* p. 62.

7. CBS News, "November 22 and The Warren Report."

8. *Hearings,* Vol. 6, p. 452.

9. Meagher, *Accessories After the Fact,* pp. 299–301.

10. CBS News, "CBS News Inquiry: The

Warren Report," broadcast over the CBS television network on June 25–28, 1967, Part 3.

11. *Hearings,* Vol. 3, p. 355.

12. Meagher, *Accessories After the Fact,* p. 257.

13. CBS News, "November 22 and The Warren Report."

14. Meagher, *Accessories After the Fact,* p. 256; Mark Lane, *Rush to Judgement* (New York: Holt, Rinehart and Winston, Inc., 1966), pp. 178–189.

15. *Hearings* Vol. 6, p. 468; *Ibid.,* Vol. 7, pp. 273–274.

16. *Report,* p. 168.

17. CBS News, "November 22 and The

Warren Report."
18. CBS News, "CBS News Inquiry: The Warren Report," Part 1.
19. *Ibid.*
20. *Ibid.*, Part 2.
21. *Ibid.*, Part 1.

22. *Ibid.*
23. *Hearings* Vol. 7, pp. 45–59.
24. *Ibid.*, p. 64.
25. CBS News, "CBS News Inquiry: The Warren Report," Part 2.

Chapter 6   The Commission

1. Edward Jay Epstein, *Inquest* (New York: The Viking Press, 1966).
2. *Ibid.*, p. xviii; Interview with Wesley J. Liebeler in Los Angeles, California, May 31, 1973.
3. *Ibid.*
4. *Ibid.*
5. Epstein, *Inquest*, pp. 153–154.
6. CBS News, "CBS News Inquiry: The Warren Report," Part 4.
7. *Ibid.*

8. Louis Lomax Program, October 16, 1966.
9. *Hearings*, Vol. 11, pp. 294–295.
10. *Ibid.*, p. 411.
11. *Ibid.*, Vol. 5, p. 437.
12. Mark Lane, *Rush to Judgement*, p. 350.
13. *Hearings*, Vol. 22, pp. 582–583.
14. Epstein, *Inquest*, p. 13.
15. CBS News, "CBS News Inquiry: The Warren Report," Part 4.

Chapter 7   The Man Who Did Not Kill the President

1. *Report*, p. 619.
2. *Ibid.* p. 613.
3. *Ibid.* p. 627
4. *Ibid.* p. 623.
5. CBS News, "November 22 and The Warren Report."
6. William W. Turner, *Invisible Witness* (Indianapolis, Ind.: Bobbs-Merrill, 1968), p. 84.
7. *Report*, p. 201.
8. *News Coverage of the Assassination of President Kennedy* MR 68–20:5, side 2, (tape); The John F. Kennedy Library, Waltham, Massachusetts.
9. *Report*, p. 375.
10. *Ibid.* Appendix 13.
11. *Ibid.* pp. 379–382.
12. *Ibid.* p. 380.
13. *Ibid.* pp. 149–152.
14. *Ibid.* p. 152.
15. *Ibid.*

16. *Ibid.*
17. Meagher, *Accessories After the Fact*, p. 74n.
18. *Hearings*, Vol. 3, p. 274.
19. *Ibid.*, Vol. 6, p. 392.
20. *Report*, p. 154.
21. *Ibid.*, pp. 154–155.
22. *Ibid.* p. 613.
23. *Hearings*, Vol. 2, p. 256.
24. *Ibid.*, Vol. 7, p. 439.
25. *Report*, chapter 7.
26. *Ibid.* p. 423.
27. *Ibid.*
28. *Ibid.* p. 607.
29. *Ibid.* p. 623.
30. *Ibid.* p. 627.
31. Telephone interview with Gordon Barland in Salt Lake City, Utah, January 9, 1974.
32. Marguerite Oswald, *Aftermath of An Execution* (Dallas: Challenge Press 1965).

Chapter 8   The Phantom Dossier

1. Meagher, *Accessories After the Fact,*
   p. 298.
2. Curry, *JFK Assassination File.*
3. *Report,* p. 165.
4. *Hearings* Vol. 7, p. 47.
5. *Hearings,* Vol. 24, p. 239.
6. *Ibid.* Vol. 7, p. 55.
7. *Report,* p. 172
8. Thompson, *Six Seconds in Dallas,* pp.
   292–295; Mark Lane, *A Citizen's Dissent,* (New York: Holt, Rinehart and
   Winston, Inc., 1968), pp. 75–120.
9. CBS News, "November 22 and The
   Warren Report."

10. *Ibid.*
11. *Hearings,* Vol. 17, p. 495.
12. *Ibid.* Vol. 4, p. 441.
13. *Ibid.* Vol. 5, p. 42.
14. Meagher, *Accessories After the Fact,*
    p. 92.
15. *Hearings,* Vol. 24, pp. 259–260.
16. *Ibid.* Vol. 3, p. 230.
17. *Ibid.* Vol. 4, p. 467.
18. *Ibid.* pp. 461–462.
19. *Commission Document 21,* The Na-
    tional Archives, Washington, D.C.,
    pp. 44–45.

Chapter 9   The Mysterious Mr. Hidell

1. *Report,* pp. 176–180.
2. *Hearings,* Vol. 24, pp. 804–805
3. *Ibid.* Vol. 19, p. 135.
4. *Report,* pp. 179–180.
5. *Hearings,* Vol. 19, p. 135.
6. *Ibid.,* Vol. 7, p. 272
7. *Ibid.,* p. 274.
8. *Report,* p. 571.
9. *Hearings,* Vol. 23, p. 875
10. *Ibid.,* p. 876.

11. *Ibid.,* p. 877.
12. *Ibid.,* Vol. 24, p. 234.
13. *Report,* pp. 118–119.
14. *News Coverage of the Assassination
    of President Kennedy,* MR 68–20:5,6;
    side 2, (tape) The John F. Kennedy
    Library, Waltham, Massachusetts.
15. *Commission Document No. 735,*
    The National Archives, Washington,
    D.C., p. 266.

Chapter 10   The Phantom Polygraph Test

1. *Hearings,* Vol. 24, p. 292.
2. *Ibid.,* p. 293.
3. *Ibid.*
4. *Ibid.*
5. *Ibid.,* p. 209.
6. *Ibid.,* Vol. 2, p. 243.
7. *Ibid.,* pp. 248–251.
8. *Report,* p. 134.
9. Meagher, *Accessories After the Fact,*
   p. 36.
10. Ibid., p. 46.
11. *Hearings,* Vol. 10, p. 297.
12. *Report,* p. 604.
13. *Ibid.,* p. 623.

14. *Hearings,* Vol. 7, p. 44.
15. Jim Bishop, *The Day Kennedy Was
    Shot* (New York: Funk and Wagnalls,
    1968).
16. *Hearings,* Vol. 7, p. 192.
17. Bishop, *The Day Kennedy Was Shot,*
    p. 472.
18. *Ibid.,* p. 530.
19. *Ibid.,* p. 472.
20. *Hearings,* Vol. 24, p. 293.
21. *Ibid.,* p. 287.
22. *Ibid.,* Vol. 7, pp. 207, 209–210.
23. *Ibid.,* Vol. 19, p. 124.
24. *Ibid.,* Vol. 7, p. 232.

Chapter 11   Finding Frazier

1. *Report,* p. 617.
2. *Hearings,* Vol. 2, p. 219.
3. Reported by Tom Webb of WBAP–TV, Fort Worth, Texas, *News Cover-* *age of the Assassination of Presiaen,* *Kennedy,* MR 74–52:1 (tape), The John F. Kennedy Library, Waltham, Massachusetts.

Chapter 12   Don't Embarrass the Bureau: A Theory

1. Gerald R. Ford and John R. Stiles, *Portrait of the Assassin* (New York: Simon and Schuster, 1965), p. 13.
2. J. Lee Rankin, Memorandum for the Files, Subject: *Rumors that Oswald was an undercover agent,* File: Government Agencies Involved—FBI; Oswald, L. H., Post-Russian Period. The National Archives, Washington, D.C., p. 1.
3. *Ibid.,* p. 2.
4. *Ibid.*
5. *Ibid.*
6. Ford and Stiles, *Portrait of the Assassin,* p. 14.
7. *President's Commission on the Assassination of President Kennedy: Report of Proceedings Held at Washington, D.C., Monday, January 27, 1964;* The National Archives, Washington, D.C.
8. *Ibid.,* p. 131.
9. *Ibid.,* p. 132.
10. *Ibid.,* pp. 160–161.
11. *Ibid.,* p. 137.
12. *Ibid.,* pp. 171–172.
13. *Ibid.,* p. 166.
14. *Ibid.,* p. 149.
15. *Ibid.,* p. 152.
16. *Ibid.,* p. 153.
17. *Ibid.,* p. 154.
18. *Ibid.,* p. 168.
19. Rankin, Memorandum on Oswald-FBI rumors, pp. 2–3.
20. *Ibid.,* pp. 5–6.
21. *Report of Proceedings on January 27, 1964,* pp. 181–182.
22. *Hearings,* Vol. 4, p. 415.
23. *Ibid.,* Vol. 17, pp. 717–731.
24. *Ibid.,* Vol. 4, p. 420.
25. *Ibid.*
26. *Ibid.*
27. *Ibid.,* p. 416.
28. *Ibid.,* p. 429.
29. *Ibid.,* Vol. 17, p. 737.
30. Frank Donner, "Political Informers," *Investigating the FBI,* ed. by Pat Watters and Stephen Gillers (New York: Ballantine Books, 1974), p. 314.
31. *Hearings,* Vol. 4, p. 210.
32. *Ibid.*
33. *Ibid.,* pp. 432, 435.
34. *Ibid.,* p. 437.
35. *Ibid.,* Vol. 17, pp. 758–762.
36. *Ibid.,* p. 815.
37. *Ibid.,* Vol. 10, p. 61.
38. *Report,* p. 729.
39. *Ibid.,* p. 327.
40. *Ibid.*
41. *Hearings,* Vol. 3, p. 100.
42. *Ibid.,* pp. 99–100.
43. *Ibid.,* Vol. 9, p. 398.
44. *Ibid.,* Vol. 1, p. 48.
45. Meagher, *Accessories After the Fact,* p. 212.
46. *Hearings,* Vol. 5, p. 112.
47. *Ibid.,* Vol. 4, p. 462.
48. *Ibid.,* p. 209.
49. *Ibid.,* p. 238.
50. *Ibid.,* Vol. 2, p. 505.
51. *Ibid.,* p. 221.
52. *Ibid.,* Vol. 10, p. 353.
53. *Ibid.,* p. 355.
54. *Ibid.,* p. 354.
55. *Ibid.,* Vol. 3, p. 240
56. *Commission Document No. 206,* The National Archives, Washington, D.C.
57. *Hearings,* Vol. 3, p. 274.
58. *Ibid.*
59. Oleg V. Penkovskiy, *The Penkovskiy*

Papers (New York: Doubleday, 1965), p. 119.

60. *Report,* p. 421
61. *Hearings,* Vol. 7, p. 3.
62. *Ibid.,* p. 4.
63. *Ibid.,* pp. 4–5
64. *Ibid.,* pp. 11, 15.
65. CBS News, "November 22 and The Warren Report."
66. *Hearings,* Vol. 7, p. 111.
67. *Ibid.,* p. 44.
68. *Ibid.,* p. 79.
69. *Ibid.,* p. 115.
70. *Ibid.,* p. 33.

71. *Ibid.,* pp. 22–23; 43; 59–60; and Vol. 24, p. 234.
72. *Ibid.,* Vol. 7, pp. 50–51.
73. *Ibid.,* p. 60.
74. *Hearings,* Vol. 17, p. 814.
75. *Ibid.,* pp. 815–818, 741–752.
76. *Ibid.,* p. 742.
77. *Ibid.,* Vol. 1, pp. 79–80.
78. *Ibid.,* p. 410.
79. Thomas Thompson, "Marina Oswald: A Casualty of History Recovers," *People* Weekly, March 4, 1974, p. 27.
80. *Ibid.,* p 28.

INDEX

ACKNOWLEDGMENTS Public interest in the unanswered questions about the assassination of President Kennedy has undergone a renascence lately, the result of national events and several popular novels and motion pictures inspired in one way or another by the Dallas tragedy. However, the subject was very much out of fashion in publishing circles in January 1973 when I began the work presented in this book. My thanks then to Bob Guccione of *Penthouse* for his vision and fortitude in supporting an undertaking that many others felt lacked popular appeal. I am also grateful to Eric Protter, then articles editor at *Penthouse*, for the essential role he played in launching the project.

I could not have found my way through the maze of material, both published and unpublished, relating to the Dallas assassination, nor would I have known of the ongoing research into the case, without the assistance of the Committee to Investigate Assassinations. I am particularly grateful to the committee's director, Bernard Fensterwald, and to Mary Ferrell and Al Chapman. But I owe a very special debt to Robert Smith of the committee for letting me draw so often upon his encyclopedic knowledge of the assassination of President Kennedy.

Of course, it would have been impossible even to conceive of the project recounted in this book but for that remarkable invention, the psychological stress evaluator. To the remarkable inventors of the PSE, Allen Bell, Jr., Charles McQuiston and Wilson Ford, I owe the most profound thanks. I am especially indebted to Colonel Bell and his associates for the extensive technical and operational assistance they furnished during my investigation. My thanks also to Anthony Pellicano for his invaluable work locating a missing witness.

While no one but myself is responsible for the accuracy and validity of the facts and conclusions presented in this book, I am grateful to the many practitioners of the lie-detection craft for their aid and advice. I am especially thankful to Mike Kradz of Dektor, Gordon Barland of the University of Utah, and L.H. "Rusty" Hitchcock, formerly of United States Army Intelligence.

Finally, my very special thanks to Mary Ann Werntz, not only for the many ways in which she helped make this book possible, but also for pointing out some of the flaws in the Warren Report and convincing me that things just could not have happened that way.

PSE CHARTS

PSE waveforms showing four increasing levels of stress

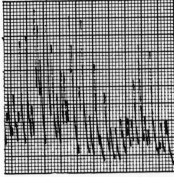

1) *Left* NO STRESS
The irregular shape of the waveform indicates no stress is present.

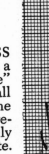

2) *Right* MODERATE STRESS
The presence of stress causes a smooth, "trimmed-hedge" appearance in the overall shape. The dome-like outline of the lower edge of the waveform indicates the stress is only moderate.

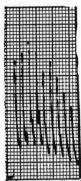
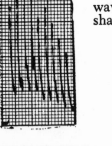

3) *Left* GOOD STRESS
An increased degree of stress straightens the overall shape of the waveform, resulting in a rectangular shape tilted diagonally.

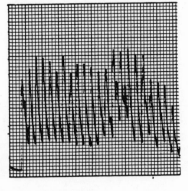

4) *Right* HARD STRESS
Near-maximum stress creates a smooth, horizontal block.

PSE chart of a known lie

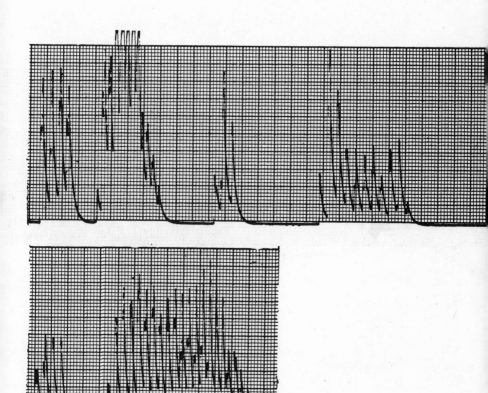

Clifford Irving tells a television interviewer, "I got the transcripts from Howard Hughes." The PSE chart of Irving's statement shows hard stress on the name "Hughes." Irving later admitted he never met Hughes.

Lee Harvey Oswald denies he is

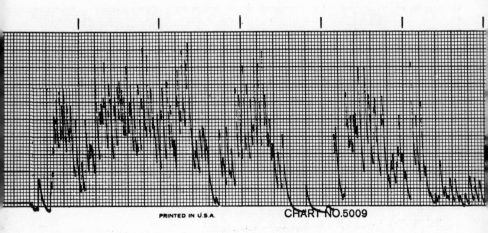

PRINTED IN U.S.A. CHART NO.5009

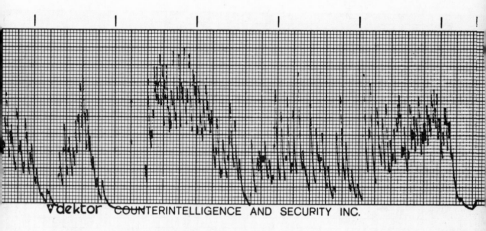

Vdektor COUNTERINTELLIGENCE AND SECURITY INC.

REPORTER: "Did you shoot the President?"
OSWALD: "I didn't shoot anybody, no sir."

The PSE chart of Oswald's statement reveals no stress. Lie detection experts have confirmed that Oswald was telling the truth.

An eyewitness identifies Oswald as the assassin

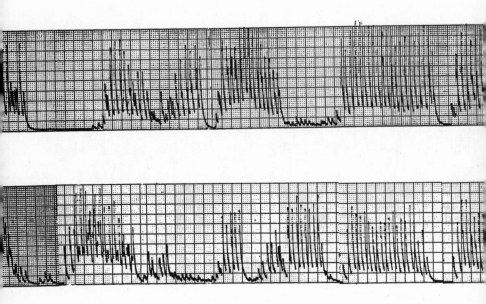

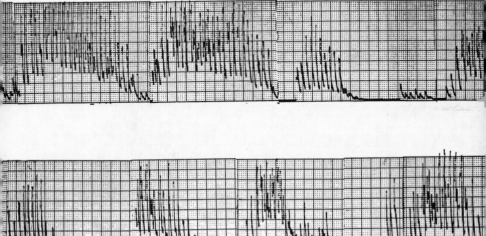

BRENNAN: "This man—the same man I had saw prior to the President's arrival—was in the window and taking aim for his last shot."

Howard L. Brennan was unable to identify Oswald as the assassin in a police line-up on November 22, 1963. However, months later he told the Warren Commission the gunman he saw was Oswald. The PSE chart of Brennan's statement reveals hard stress.

Oswald is implicated by testimony of book depository co-worker, Buell Wesley Frazier

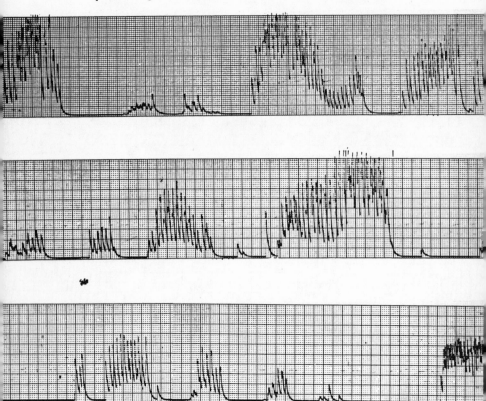

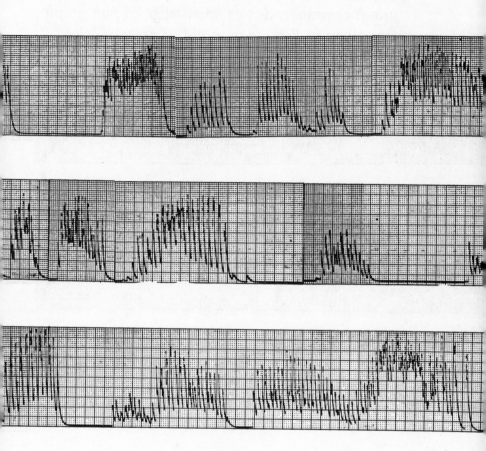

FRAZIER: ". , . and I said, 'Well, why are you going home this afternoon?' And he replied that he wanted to go home and pick up some curtain rods so he could put some curtains up in his apartment. And I said, 'Oh, very well.' "

PSE charts of Frazier's statements contain hard stress.

Paul Bentley, former senior Dallas police polygraph examiner, denies knowledge of polygraph test given to Frazier on night of assassination

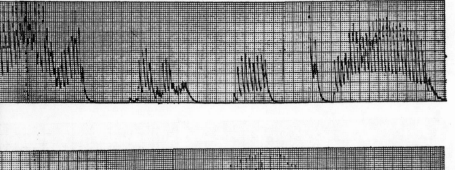

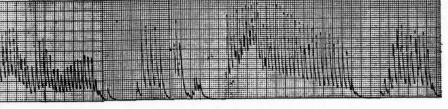

BENTLEY: "I don't recall that ever occurring."

PSE reveals hard stress in Bentley's statements.

R. D. Lewis, Dallas police polygraph examiner, denies giving Frazier polygraph test

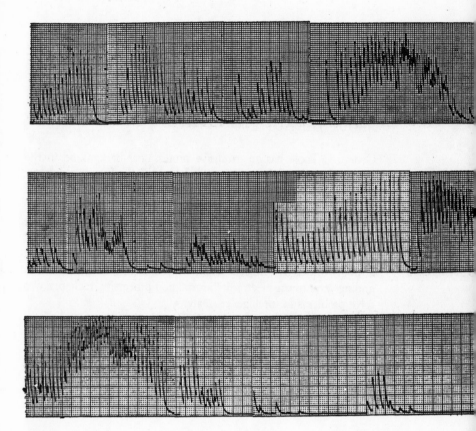

LEWIS: "Offhand, no. I don't remember it ... no, I couldn't. If my life depended on it I couldn't remember it."

The PSE shows good-to-hard stress in Lewis's statements. Lewis later admitted to the author that he remembered giving Frazier a polygraph test.

ABOUT THE AUTHOR

George O'Toole has an extensive professional background in the technical aspects of intelligence work. He is a former computer specialist who served with the Central Intelligence Agency as chief of its Problem Analysis Branch. Born in New York City in 1936, he studied mathematics at Iona College and worked with some of the earliest electronic computers in the mid-1950s. Later he helped found two consulting firms and worked in the space program and on a variety of defense projects. While with the CIA, he specialized in finding ways to use electronic information processing technology to solve problems in intelligence analysis.

Since leaving the government, O'Toole has served as a consultant to several Washington, D.C. "think tanks," but he now spends most of his time writing. His work on espionage and intelligence has appeared in such diverse places as *The New Republic*, *Penthouse* and *Genesis*. His first novel, *An Agent on the Other Side*, was published in 1973 by David McKay.

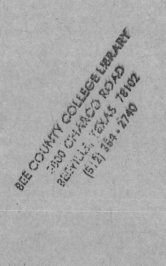